By George

By George

HILARIOUS TALES
FROM ENGLAND'S MOST FANATICAL
FOOTBALL SUPPORTERS

DAVID STANFIELD

JOHN BLAKE

Published by John Blake Publishing Ltd,
3 Bramber Court, 2 Bramber Road,
London W14 9PB, England

www.johnblakepublishing.co.uk

www.facebook.com/Johnblakepub   facebook.

twitter.com/johnblakepub   twitter

First published in paperback in 2012

ISBN: 978-1-84358-813-9

British Library Cataloguing-in-Publication Data:

A catalogue record for this book is available from the British Library.

Design by www.envydesign.co.uk

Printed in Great Britain by CPI Group (UK) Ltd

1 3 5 7 9 10 8 6 4 2

Papers used by John Blake Publishing are natural, recyclable
products made from wood grown in sustainable forests.
The manufacturing processes conform to the
environmental regulations of the country of origin.

Every attempt has been made to contact the relevant copyright-
holders, but some were unobtainable. We would be grateful
if the appropriate people could contact us.

This book is dedicated in loving memory
of my mum, Linda Stanfield

Contents

Introduction

Why write this book? Why tell this story? Well, this is *my* story and one that needs to be told. Ask any football fan and they will tell you endless stories of their team. They can tell you about away trips to Carlisle on a cold December Tuesday night, or an end of season game on the beach in Brighton, but my story isn't about any club team, it's about England. When you follow England or ask anyone who has, you'll know that the things that happen, camaraderie and togetherness can't be beat.

I've read or browsed through loads of different football autobiographies and hooligan books, but I've never read an in-depth story about England fans doing what they do best: following England over land and sea. So after two World Cups and endless home and away trips, it's time for me and my friends to tell our story.

My name's Stan, AKA George the First. You'll have seen me on the telly with my crusader mates and probably thought 'what

By George

a load of idiots in fancy dress', but let me tell you, you can't even begin to imagine what goes on – on and off camera – when those suits go on.

Chapter 1

How I became a cross dresser

My story has to start when everything changed forever – when I went from being an ordinary England fan into one of the Georges, better known as the M.I.G.S (The Men In George Suits).

We'd qualified for the World Cup in Germany, and the draw had been made. What a group! Paraguay, Trinidad & Tobago and Sweden. On paper it was a great draw and off the field it was an even better draw: SWEDEN! Those who went to the Euros with me had experienced what the Swedish girls were about when we'd watched Sweden v Denmark – but hang on, I'm getting ahead of myself. Our story began when a group of lads from Slip End and the neighbouring village, Caddington, had been following England.

We formed our own England supporters group known as S.E.C.E.F (Slip End and Caddington England Fans) – I thought of the name, to the disgust of the boys from Caddington who said Caddington should come first as I was the only one from

1

Slip End. The boys aren't that smart at the best of times, and I told them I'd been online and discovered that '*secef*' was Hungarian for 'fuck off'. When they heard that, they were over the moon at the name and couldn't wait to meet a Hungarian so they could put this new word to good use. Little did they know they would only have to wait a few months.

S.E.C.E.F included me, Ian, Dave, Bruce, Paul, Steve, Jimmy, Lee, Alan and Dale. We elected a committee to take executive decisions on our trip to Germany. Bruce was elected Chairman and Alan Treasurer. We decided to drive to Germany and pick up a camper van, so Bruce sorted out the camper and booking the ferry for the two vehicles taking all those going.

Just before the April meeting, Paul phoned. He'd had an idea – we should all dress up as St George. He'd seen the suits on the internet, apparently. I told him that we'd look like a load of pricks, but he said that he'd mocked up some photos of everyone wearing the suits and that he'd bring them along to the meeting.

The penultimate meeting at S.E.C.E.F's official head-quarters, Caddington Social Club, was headed by Bruce – and as usual he got a barrage of abuse from his lifelong nemesis, Dave. The two had a real love/hate relationship; Bruce loved Dave and Dave hated Bruce. At the start of the meeting Bruce told us Alan and Dale wouldn't be going to the World Cup after all, leaving just eight of us, but then someone I hadn't seen for years turned up – Nick Beeson, AKA Chubb. He wanted to come out with us for the first game against Paraguay, and he was accepted by the group as we thought it politically correct that we had one gay member.

Bruce said the ferry was booked for Ian's motor and Dave's van. He'd booked the camper which we'd pick up in

Düsseldorf, so everything was sorted. At the end of the meeting, Paul told everyone about the George suits and handed round his pictures of St George with all of our faces on them. After a few minutes of laughter and piss-taking, Ian – who is well over six foot, about twenty stone and aptly named 'The Yeti', said, 'Fucking hell, if those suits make me look that slim, I'm having one!'

Dave had sat studying his picture and then blurted out, 'Fuck me, don't this bloke in this photo look like me!' We absolutely pissed ourselves, especially as we knew he was serious.

Four of us decided that we would buy suits just for the craic. Ian and Lee point blank refused, worried that their reputation as hooligans would be ruined. The two lads saw themselves as prominent members of Luton Town crew The MIGs, but in reality the only banning orders they'd had were from 'All you can eat for £15' restaurants.

The night before we left for Germany I went for a few drinks with Paul, Steve and Lee – trouble was, 'a few' turned into many and we ended up drinking Green Monster – my own lethal concoction of snakebite and blue curaçao. At about 10pm I went into the toilet and emerged as St George – the whole club was in uproar and people immediately broke into a chorus of 'Keep St George in my heart, keep me English', which happens quite a bit when we're seen in our suits.

I'd intended to just put the suit on for a laugh, but with such a reaction I kept it on all night. Paul also changed into his suit: 'Fuck me, now there's two of them!' someone shouted. 'That's right – I'm George the First, I announced, holding my arms aloft, 'And this is George the Second!' I added, pointing at Paul.

By the time the club shut, we were hammered – all except Lee who was on antibiotics. Not for a dose; the closest Lee had got to a bird's knickers in recent months was hanging his Mum's washing out. Anyway, Lee drove my van when we left the pub and we all went over to Ian's house, even though Ian didn't know we were coming. Now you've heard about the size of Ian, so waking him up was a risk to our health. But Ian was my oldest and best mate and where other people had to be careful of him, I could get away with murder. The only trouble was that for all his size, Ian's going out with my sister Sharon (who stands a massive five foot three inches) and she was boss. It was her we really had to worry about.

We stood outside my sister's house, and I came up with the clever idea of breaking in. The downstairs window was ajar so I got a screwdriver from the van, slid the screwdriver in, lifted the handle and opened the window. I climbed in and opened the front door to let Paul and Steve in.

Once in we raided Ian's beer supply and I decided Steve needed a haircut, so I got my hair clippers out. We sat Steve in the dining room and proceeded to give him a skinhead, even though he'd only asked for a short back and sides. We hadn't been cutting Steve's hair for long, though, when there was a loud knock at the door. We heard movement from upstairs and started running around the house looking for somewhere to hide, as we knew my sister and Ian would not be best pleased firstly by whoever was knocking at the door and secondly by the fact that there were two St Georges and a half a skinhead in their house.

Ian charged down the stairs — we knew it was him as it sounded like a herd of wildebeest on the move — and he was screaming at the top of his voice 'Who the fuck is that?'. This was quickly followed by my Sister screaming 'I bet it's that fucking stupid brother of mine'. How wrong could she be — they didn't even hear me enter.

How I became a cross dresser

Ian wrenched the door open and came face to face with two old bill. 'Do you know what fucking time it is?' he asked (obviously his Mickey Mouse watch had stopped). The first copper told him that a neighbour had witnessed someone wearing a red cape breaking into their house.

My sister shouted, 'Does it look like there is anyone hear with a fucking red cape on, burglar or not?' At that point I came out of hiding behind the lounge curtains to reveal that the burglar in question was indeed her 'fucking stupid brother'. The two policemen looked stunned when I appeared; my sister on the other hand, who wouldn't put anything past me, said, 'What the fucking hell are you doing here and how did you get in?' Paul then emerged, holding Steve up.

The first copper said, 'Excuse me, Madam, do you know these...?' He wasn't quite sure what to call us. 'Yes, I fucking do know them. It's my brother and his drunken mates.' Ian was laughing as he wandered back up the stairs to leave my sister to it. His parting shot was 'Don't nick any of my lager!'

The police came in and I explained why we broke in and why we were dressed as knights. My sister didn't seem to be listening – she was too busy looking strangely at Steve who looked like he'd got a bad case of alopecia.

The police apologised to my sister for disturbing her, and as they were about to leave the second copper asked, 'Any chance of a photo, mate? The boys down the station are never going to believe this!' So me and Paul stood either side of the copper, while his mate took a picture.

The two old bill left my sister's and I waited for the torrent of abuse which was surely coming. She looked me in the eye, shook her head and started laughing. 'Look, Shaz, sorry about...' I began, but before I could finish she raised her hand

and said, 'Will someone please finish cutting that bloke's hair? He looks fucking ridiculous.' Then she turned and went to bed.

I finished Steve's hair and we called it a night, after having another couple of Ian's beers of course. Ian woke me at about 5.30am, while I was still sprawled out on his sofa. He'd already screamed at Steve and Paul and I knew it was my turn. 'Come on, get up – we're off to the World Cup now and we're not waiting for you,' he said. I walked into the kitchen where Steve looked like he was in a daze. He was in a house he'd never been to before and he couldn't remember how he'd got there. I did have to laugh when he scratched his head only to discover that all his hair had gone. I said nothing, but he knew who'd scalped him.

Bruce, Dave, Jimmy and Lee arrived soon after and Jimmy looked at me and said, 'Told you Stan would be hammered.' The boys would be shocked if I wasn't. We packed the bags into Dave's van, jumped into Ian's motor, and off we went. It only took Ian a matter of seconds to start telling the others of the previous night's events, which they thought were hilarious.

On the way to the motorway, we picked Chubb up, who looked like death warmed up. 'Fuck me, Chubb, what's wrong with you?' I said. 'I've got the shits something terrible and I've been up all night,' Chubb replied. Oh well – with all the S.E.C.E.F members now present and correct (well, sort of) we were off to Germany.

Chapter 2

Are we nearly there yet?

I slept all the way to Dover using Chubb as a pillow. He was quite comfy to lean on with the extra weight he carried – if you looked at him, you'd think he was hiding a beach ball up his jumper.

Once on the ferry we put the George suits on and this time we were joined by Bruce – arise, George the Third. The three of us stood at the back of the ferry, with the great shores of England still in sight, dressed as crusaders. We couldn't believe the reaction – the boat was packed with English fans and they all wanted a photo with us.

Once off the ferry, it was time to pick up the most important thing to a Englishman: BEER and lots of it. We headed to a beer hypermarket and filled Dave's van, and we even got Chubb a couple of bottles of Babycham. Our next stop came at a Belgian service station and Paul, Bruce and I got Georged up again before we crossed the border into Germany, almost invasion-style. When we got to the German border, they were checking passports. We were about forty cars from the check-point when the three of us stood up in Ian's motor, with our heads sticking out of the sunroof, and started up a chorus of the theme from *Dambusters*. Arms raised like aeroplanes, we started belting out 'Der, der, der, der, der der, der, der' and the next thing we knew, all the English fans in the cars around us got out and joined in. The German border control didn't have a clue what was going on and just started waving cars through without checking anyone's passports.

Chubb had previously asked Ian to stop when he got a chance, as he needed the toilet, but had since fallen asleep. We were driving along the Autobahn, and I was thinking to myself how perfect everything was, when suddenly the car was filled with the most stomach churning smell of shit I'd ever smelt. 'Oh my God, what the fuck is that smell?' I desperately asked, trying to hold my nose. Ian slammed the brakes on, almost sending us all through the windscreen. Chubb, in his bad condition, had shit himself in his sleep.

We woke Chubb up as we piled out of the car. Everyone was retching, except Ian who screamed, 'GET OUT YOU DIRTY BASTARD!' Chubb ambled out of the car. The shit was all up his back and the shorts he was wearing were covered in it. 'Chubb, you've got to get those clothes off, mate, and clean yourself up,' Bruce said. Dave, Lee and Jimmy fell out of Dave's van laughing their heads off. I just wanted to throw up – and unfortunately it all got too much for Paul and he was sick at the side of the road.

Chubb began stripping naked – his entire body was covered in shit. Ian threw him a couple of old rags to clean himself with, but all it was doing was spreading the shit rather than removing it. We got Chubb's towel and shower gel out of his bag – now all we needed was a constant flow of water. So we improvised. We shook cans of beer up, opened them, and sprayed Chubb while he washed his body.

With Chubb cleaned up – sort of – and his clothes and towel dumped in the ditch, we set off again for Düsseldorf. We followed the sat nav until we'd reached our destination, but where were we? There wasn't a camper van in sight; we were on a main street with lots of tall buildings. Ian drove down the street to see if we could find the camper hire firm. We'd been driving around for ten minutes when Dave flashed his lights for us to stop, so we pulled over and all got out. 'What's going on?' said Dave. Ian explained that we couldn't find the camper hire place, and we flagged down a police car. Two policemen got out and looked at the address, and they then started laughing and said, 'Sorry, my English friends, but the place you are looking for is in Mulheim.' 'What part of Düsseldorf is that?' I asked. The policeman replied 'It's not even in Düsseldorf – you're in the wrong city. It's about forty miles north from here.'

Bruce had the wrong details. 'The wrong fucking city? I told you – let Bruce sort it out and he'll fuck it up, he does this every fucking time.' Dave wasn't happy and he and Bruce started having a full-blown row. We had to separate the two of them as the police seemed like they were about to intervene and probably nick them both.

Finally we arrived at the correct location, in the correct city! My main concern was the beer getting warm. Luckily the place had several water fountains, so I emptied a crate of lager into one of them. Bruce went to sort the camper out, but there was more bad news. 'Right, boys…we've got a bit of a problem!' 'What the fuck now?' said Dave. 'Because we've arrived later than expected, they've let our camper go. We've got to wait about three hours for one to be ready.'

I thought Dave would go fucking ballistic, but he didn't get a chance as the boys were already tearing into Bruce. Bruce just stood there taking all the abuse the boys could give him. Ian said, 'Fuck this – you've fucked up, Bruce, so you can sort it out. I'm not waiting three fucking hours, I'm going to Frankfurt now. You can stay here on your own and drive the camper to us'.

I went to the toilet before we left and when I got to the building where the toilets were, I found Lee gathering up ham rolls from a table laid out with refreshments. It was all free but it didn't seem up to much – just a few rolls and bottles of drink. I was just about to go into the toilet when I saw two blokes pouring beer from a keg. 'Is the beer free as well?' I asked, to which they answered, 'Yes, Germany are playing Costa Rica so we have invited all the local community to come and have a beer.' A huge smile shot across my face – this guy had just said the magic words. FREE BEER.

I left the building and got to the lads, who were ready to go. 'Look, lads, I know Bruce has fucked up, but I'm not leaving him here on his own. I'm staying,' I announced. 'Fine, but we're not – we've already fucked about too much and we still ain't got anywhere to stay,' Ian shouted.

When the vehicles were out of sight, Bruce turned to me and said, 'Cheers, Stan.' 'That's OK, Bruce, I replied. 'They've got free beer up there and a barbecue later!' 'Well I can't drink. I've got to drive later. I'll sort out the paperwork and see you up there in a bit,' Bruce said.

It was nearing half-time in the opening game by the time Bruce eventually joined me. He looked astonished when he saw me. There I was on the table with a German hat and scarf on and my face painted, singing the 'Ten German Bombers' song, with all my new German friends joining in. Obviously I was pissed as fart.

Bruce grabbed my leg, looked up at me and said, 'What the fucks going on?' 'They needed a song to sing and they asked me to teach them one. They fucking love it, Brucie baby!' I shouted. Bruce turned and went outside to get himself some barbecue food.

Bruce almost had to drag me away from my new friends once the camper was ready to go. We we're just about to pull off, when I realised the beer was still in the fountain. I dived (well fell out of the camper), staggered over to the fountain. Bruce helped me load the fridge of the camper with the lager and we were off to Frankfurt.

Chapter 3

Off the rails

I stayed in the back of the camper the whole journey. Bruce was pissing himself in the front and almost crashed on several occasions, especially when I was doing 'Oops Upside Ya Head' on the floor, which apparently looked more like someone having an epileptic fit on acid.

We arrived in Frankfurt about 10pm and Bruce called Ian. He and Steve arrived twenty minutes later. 'We've had a fucking nightmare finding somewhere to stay – we had to park at the side of the road and all we want to do now is have a beer,' Ian said. 'Talking of beer…where's Stan?' Steve asked. The camper door crashed open and I fell out.

They weren't impressed that I was so pissed, but off we went to the 'campsite'. The lads weren't lying when they said it was at the side of the road – we had to park outside the campsite. At least there were portacabin toilets and showers next to us.

Chubb crawled into the camper and said he just wanted to sleep as he was feeling terrible. We left him and headed down the road until we came across a bar that was playing proper hardcore music. It was all kitted out like a beach party outside, but inside was dark and dingy with a few strobes going off. I started chatting to two German lads and they asked me if I wanted to have a drinking competition. Of course, I said yes. We ordered double Jagermeisters and had six doubles each. One German lad spewed most of shot four and his dinner up, so he was gone. Just one left. The second German was struggling as he downed another double, and then his sister came over screaming at us to leave him alone. Dave – AKA Kofi Annan – stepped in to calm the worried sister, offering to buy her a drink. She definitely fancied Dave. It's strange how some women have a thing for blokes who look like Gollum out of *Lord of the Rings*.

While the sister was with Dave, the brother had wandered off and completely passed out, still standing upright. Cue the English sense of humour. We undid his jeans, pulled them down with his boxers, and placed a beer on his head. Cameras were flashing like there was no tomorrow – until his sister spotted what was going on. She stormed over and went mental. Even Dave couldn't calm her down.

I woke up the next day in the camper and couldn't even remember leaving the club. I was still pissed when I got up, so I opened the door of the camper van, lit a fag and got myself a can of beer. I'd had a couple of cans when one by one the lads started emerging from their tents, all looking a bit worse for wear after their first night in Germany. Steve and Lee went into the campsite and nicked a dozen or so filled rolls to feed the well hungover troops.

We left the camper and all walked towards the river where the fans' festival was being held. Paul, Steve, Jimmy and Chubb (who still looked like shit) were going as they didn't have tickets for the match. The Germans built huge fans' parks in every city, with massive screens for everyone to watch the games on. We stayed with the boys for a bit and then Ian, Dave, Bruce, Lee and I made our way to the square. There must have been four thousand England fans there and the atmosphere was mental. After a few beers had been sunk, we were all back on our game and Bruce and I Georged up.

Once the suits went on everyone, including the police, wanted a photo with the two Georges. After a few hours, Ian rounded us up and we made our way to the underground. The station had a choice of about six tunnels. Ian – standing six foot plus, remember – walked up to this old geezer of about eighty with a walking stick and said, 'OLA! Do you know where the TRAIN is for the FOOTBALL?' The old German guy looked up at Ian and looked terrified. This did not deter Ian who just kept repeating, 'The train for the football? The train?' At this point we were cracking up at the expression of the old boy's face. Ian was exasperated at this point and yelled, 'THE TRAIN? THE TRAIN? CHOO CHOO CHOO CHOO?' He started doing motions like he was a steam train and running around making 'choo choo' noises. In all the lo-commotion, the little old man hurried away as fast as he could and we were still none the wiser as to which train – or 'CHOO CHOO' to get, but we'd had a laugh trying to find out.

We eventually got on the train and I got talking to a Scouse lad who went by the name of Jamie. It turned out that Jamie and his seven mates had been in Germany for three weeks already and had no more than £500 between them. They were now all shacked up with some fat single German birds, who were feeding them and giving them money in exchange for them pretending to be their boyfriends.

As we neared the stadium, Jamie's mate pulled the emergency stop lever and when the train stopped, all eight of them jumped off and ran across the fields. The whole carriage started singing the *Great Escape* tune as we saw them all disappear into the woods. The guard came along, lifted the lever, and we were off again. When we eventually arrived it then took us over two hours to get into the ground, as we had to keep stopping for hundreds of photos. I bumped into Jamie again, who told me they hadn't any tickets so the day before they'd come to the stadium to work out the security situation. To get past checkpoint one, they'd worked out that they needed to go through the woods and over the surrounding perimeter fence – hence jumping off the train. Then, while they were standing around trying to work out what to do next, they'd seen a water truck. They all picked up three crates each and simply followed the delivery guy straight past security. All they needed now was to get into the stadium itself. 'I think I can help you with that, Jamie!' I said. I got Lee to take our photo with the two stewards and as I looked over my shoulder, Jamie and his mates were in. Jamie put his thumb up and said, 'Nice one Stan, we owe you one.' Then they vanished into the crowd like they had into the woods.

After watching England beat Paraguay 1-0, Lee and I made our way back to the square. The other lads were already there, but Chubb had gone back to the camper as he still felt like shit. The whole place was going mental, celebrating England's victory.

An hour later we saw Bruce (still in his George suit) absolutely hammered staggering through the square and heading for the large fountain. He climbed up onto the fountain – a group of Mexicans were already up there and they started singing, which annoyed Bruce, who then started pushing and shoving the Mexicans. After pushing all the Mexicans off the fountain, Bruce was hailed as King by all his new-found followers below. Bruce then conducted a rousing rendition of all the football songs he could think of from his perch atop the fountain, and every drunken wet English fan joined in. Someone then tried to pull him into the fountain, and he turned round and had a go at the guy – which was a big mistake, because while his back was turned, I ran over and shoved Bruce straight into the water.

I went over to Dave, who was pissing himself. Bruce then joined us. He stripped off the wet George suit and stood there in his shorts. Paul went behind him and pulled his shorts down to his ankles. Bruce was that pissed, it took him a while to notice – and the thing was, he had nothing on under his shorts. He soon twigged when everyone started singing, 'You're not very big, you're not very big'! We were crying with laughter, but suddenly Bruce shouted 'OH FUCK!' and opened his bum bag, which was strapped to his body. He pulled out his £300 mobile phone, his passport and all his money, all of which were soaking wet and ruined. He went mental, but we just started wetting ourselves again.

That night we drank by the riverside and had a whip – each of us put in 30 Euros which Dave would hold. At 2am, Dave vanished. 'I bet he's fucked off down the brothel with the fucking whip money, the bastard,' Bruce screamed. We looked for Dave for a bit, but gave up. Ian, Jimmy, Bruce and Lee where all driving back to England in the morning so agreed to call it a night with Ian virtually carrying me back to the camper. I woke the following morning to hear Bruce screaming at Dave, 'Where's the fucking whip?' Dave looked in a right bad way and said, 'Did I hold the whip last night? I can't remember!' He went through his pockets and came up with about 11 Euros. Bruce was not happy, and as the two of them went at it again I just sat in the deckchair on the pavement, opened a beer and enjoyed the show in front of me.

Once we had separated Dave and Bruce, Ian, Bruce, Lee, Jimmy and Chubb jumped in Ian's motor and left. We were supposed to be going to Nuremberg that day, but the rest of us were definitely not in a fit state to drive the camper van, so we stayed for one more night in Frankfurt. A couple of hours after the boys had gone, three girls from Tamworth approached us called Nicky, Nieves and Kayleigh.

After talking to them for quite a while, the girls asked whether we'd guard the shower door while they showered. Being the gentlemen we were, we agreed. Once the girls had gone inside, Paul wrote a sign out saying 'PEEP SHOW: 1 Euro for a limited time only'. I sat with the sign announcing the show to all who passed, but most people just laughed and carried on going. All except this little French lad called Cedric.

The girls had finished in the shower and were getting dressed when they noticed this strange-looking lad peering through the door. They told him to fuck off and thanked us for the help, and they told us that if England got to the quarter-finals they would come back to Germany to meet up with us. We said our goodbyes to the Tamworth trio and carried on lounging on the pavement.

That night we were back at the Brazilian bar by the riverside, drinking strawberry punch. There were twenty Brazilian birds doing that arse-shaking dance, but no blokes could dance with them. We knew how to change that. Paul and I Georged up along with Dave – arise George the Fourth. Dave said he felt like a twat, but he changed his mind when the three of us had twenty Brazilian girls all over us. Which just goes to show it isn't who you are, it's what you're wearing.

After several hours of dancing with these semi-naked Brazilians, Dave, who was wearing some weird carnival head-gear, shouted, 'OUR NAME IS ON THIS CUP, STAN!' I raised my drink and carried on dancing with the girls.

I woke up the next day really hanging and knew the only way to sort myself out was to have another beer. The first couple were a real struggle, but I got through them. Two hours later the other lads woke up. Paul said, 'How many beers have you had?' 'About six! Why?' I replied. 'Cause you're meant to be driving to Nuremberg today. Great, I'll have to fucking drive now,' Paul said. Before we left, Steve emptied the toilet bucket. Dave wanted to watch the contents coming out and proceeded to throw up when he saw log after log nose-diving down the drain. We jumped in the vans and we were off...but oh no, we weren't.

Paul couldn't start the camper. Every time he tried there was this horrendous bleeping sound but the van wouldn't start. Two hours later, Steve saw the steps of the camper van were still down, 'I wonder if we lifted the steps up, would it help?' He said. We lifted the steps, Paul turned the key and the van started. 'The fucking steps!' Dave said, 'Why didn't you think of that Stan?' At this point I could barely make out the difference between day and night. We were on our way.

Chapter 4

Gatecrashers

We arrived in Nuremberg at about 6 pm. We followed the signs to the stadium and there was a campsite right next to it. The thing was, how would we get the two vans into the campsite? I had a plan. The lads parked just out of view of the camp hut by the barrier gate. I went into the office dressed as St. George and all three of the staff smiled and told me I had been on German telly and in the papers.

They all wanted photos with me, and as I was posing with them, a car trying to get out beeped his horn. The manager pressed a button on his desk and the barrier lifted. The car drove off and the manager went to press the barrier button again. I quickly grabbed his arm and shouted, 'Come on, my friend – one more photo!' I turned him away from the view of the window as the roar of two engines whizzed through the perimeter. The manager tried see who it was, but I gripped him round the neck and said, 'Smile!'

I left the office and went to find the lads. The campsite was based in the middle of a forest and only 400 yards from the stadium – it was perfect and it was free. I found the lads and they were beaming from ear to ear. 'Never mind the "Great Escape", we've just done the "Great Entry",' I said.

The following morning, we found out there was a game of cricket arranged – England versus the Trinidad and Tobago fans at a local park. We hadn't been invited to play in the cricket match, but agreed among ourselves to 'George-crash' it and take over. We were leaving the campsite when a Hummer limo with different England decals on it pulled up. Everyone was round it like flies to shit. 'Take no notice, lads – he'll never outdo the Georges,' I said, but before I'd finished my words, the lads were off to talk to the driver and have a look inside.

The driver and owner of the limo told us his name was 'Dex' and that a load of lads from England had hired his limo for the World Cup. I said, 'You're getting paid and you get to see the World Cup? Not a bad life if you can get it.' 'Not only that, I drive the guys around in the day and have the evenings off,' Dex replied. We dragged Steve and Paul away from the limo and went to the cricket match, knowing we would shortly be the centre of attention once more.

We arrived at the park where the cricket match was being held, strode up to organisers and said, 'Alright boys, we're here ready to play!' One organiser said, 'No, mate, you're alright – we've got enough.' What we didn't know was that Mark 'Chappers' Chapman from Radio 1 had been asked to captain the team. He stepped forward and said, 'Oh yes, the press will love it – can you play in the suits?' 'Of course,' I replied. 'Then you three are in the team!' said Chappers.

By the time the match was about to start there were hundreds of people there, mostly English who had come to see England beat the West Indies at cricket. I just hoped we wouldn't let them down. Before we started we gave a live interview for ITV, and I mentioned that we'd written a song for the match. The reporter asked us to sing it live, and Paul and Dave looked horrified − it was a song I'd made up and they barely knew the words. We gave it a go anyway and sang my new song, which ended with the line, 'And then we'll do the Crouch Robot!' followed by the three of us doing the infamous Peter Crouch goal celebration. Everyone was wetting themselves, and even the interviewer was laughing as he handed back to the studio.

We lined up and sang the national anthems and the Mayor of Nuremberg, who was the guest of honour, was introduced to all the players. When he got to me he smiled and said, 'Very nice outfit − a crusader, I think? And what do you think of our city?' 'We absolutely love your city − you should be very proud of Kronenbourg! It's fantastic.' Oh no − I'd praised his city but I'd called it by the name of the drink I'd been getting wasted on every day! I waited for a response, but the mayor just looked bemused and carried on.

All the English lads in the starting eleven, huddled together with a camera man in there as well, as I delivered my team speech to build morale, which ended in a chorus of, 'IT'S COMING HOME, IT'S COMING, CRICKET'S COMING HOME!'

England fielded first and eventually got the Trinidad and Tobago team out for 85. The England captain Chappers was delighted and said, 'We've got some good batsmen − we can do this no problem.' He then left as he had another radio thing to do, so the event organiser took over as captain and put us three at the bottom of the order. By the time Dave went to bat, England were 75 for 7. The captain said to Dave, 'Right, just try to get the other guy the strike and let him win the game for us. Just don't get out.' Easy enough instructions, we all thought. The bowler unleashed his first delivery, Dave let fly with the bat, and the ball was caught by a fielder near the boundary. He was out, and I was next in to bat. Surely the script was written that I would help England to victory.

'Take your cape off – it'll get in the way,' Dave said. I ignored him. As I stood at the crease all I could think was, 'Stan, there's hundreds of people watching, the world's cameras are watching. It's your chance to be a hero.'

As the ball reached me I swung my bat and completely missed the ball…and then my cape swung round and took the bails off. I couldn't believe it – what a fucking disaster. I was out C.B.W (Cape Before Wicket).

As I trudged off, Paul was walking towards me. He stopped when I reached him and said, 'Right…if I hit the ball, what do I do?' Jesus, he really didn't know how to play. I told him, 'If you hit it just start running and don't stop, like Forrest Gump.' Ten behind and two Georges out in two balls…now Paul, George the Second, stepped up to bat to save the day. The bowler rushed in and delivered, Paul swung the bat and hit the ball, not high but hard and low. The other batsman was screaming at him to run – there were a good two runs to be had. With all the England fans screaming, 'RUN!' off Paul went. They were safely in for one and turned around for an easy two. Quality – Paul had done it, he'd got two runs on the board, saved the embarrassment of the Georges, and got the main batsman on strike. Or so we thought.

As Paul touched his bat on the crease for two, he then carried on running back for a third. When I'd told him to run and not stop if he managed to hit the ball, he had taken me literally. The fielder, who was almost walking back with the ball, lobbed it to the bowler, who knocked the bails off and ran Paul out. Everyone looked on in horror; had he really just done what we thought he had? Oh yes he had.

After the game the media wanted footage of us three with the T&T players, as we stood there posing for the cameras, we heard loud music and a car beeping behind us. We looked round it was that guy Dex driving across the pitch in his limo. The media people immediately dumped us and went over to Dex to film him and his motor. What a bastard, stealing our thunder! We went over to where he'd parked, right in the middle of the cricket pitch. Dex said, 'Those outfits are great – I could get you lot to help advertise my cars for the Euros.' The cheeky fucker, wanting us to help him and his business!

When we arrived back at the camper, there was a cooler box filled with beer plugged in to our electric point. We thought it was a welcome pack or something, so we all opened a can up and started drinking. Dave got cracking with the barbecue and then these Manchester City fans came over and said, 'All right boys, hope you don't mind – we plugged our cooler box into your point. We're in the tents next to you.' I stood up and said, 'Sorry, mate – we thought they were a welcome hamper and we've nicked a few, but don't worry, we've got loads in the van so help yourselves.' Steve mumbled something about giving stuff away. I said, 'Take no notice of Mr Angry, he's as tight as fuck,' at which they just laughed.

That night in Nuremberg, we drank in the bars near the red light area, where there were blocks of flats with girls in each room. We left the bar and went to have a look around one of them. There were lots of dodgy, seedy, dirty old men wandering around on the ground floor, so Dave fitted in perfectly. We didn't stay for long and once again hit the bars. It was about 4am when we got back to the site to find a few of the City boys still up.

An hour later, after listening to a hilarious CD of Manchester City football songs, and playing the Scotland World Cup song 'We Have A Dream' as loud as we could to screams all around the campsite of 'TURN THAT FUCKING SHIT OFF!' we were joined by a couple of lads from Barnsley. We all sat around the fire, and one of the Barnsley lads asked, 'Where'd you get the wood from?' We all looked him in disbelief. I said, 'Where did we get the wood from? We're in the middle of the Black Forest. Where the fuck do you *think* we got the wood from?' The Barnsley lad said, 'Oh,' and then followed that gem up with, 'What about this weather? It's like being abroad.' This geezer truly was the thickest bloke I'd ever met, and I'd met a few.

I had to respond to his last comment and said, 'Fuck me…I thought I *was* abroad. I'm sure that was the English Channel I crossed to get here, but maybe not. It must have been the River Thames and I must be somewhere in the South of England. All this time I thought I was in Germany!' All the lads were wetting themselves, except these two from Barnsley who just looked totally blank.

It was about 6am and there was just me and two City lads left. One called Danny said, 'Here, Stan, have you got any food in your van? I'm starving.' I replied, 'Yeah, do you want a ham sandwich?' He did. I went into the camper and started making a sandwich for him.

'Giving our stuff away again, are we?' Steve said. 'The man's hungry and he wants a sandwich, fucking hell Steve it's only a sandwich,' I answered sternly. But he wouldn't let it go and said, 'Well he ain't paid for it, has he, so why should he have any of our stuff?' I lost it at this point. 'Right,' I said, and put my hand in my pocket. I pulled out a load of coins and threw the lot at Steve. 'Here's your fucking money, you tight cunt!' 'No, I didn't mean…' he said but I cut him short and said, 'This whole fucking trip you've been a miserable bastard, you'd think you'd paid for everything and you're that tight you won't give fuck all away.' Dave told us both to calm down. I finished making the sandwich for Danny and slammed the door as I went outside to drink until I passed out in my deckchair.

Chapter 5

I don't bat
for both sides

The next morning, we headed out of the camp to pick up some food for the barbecue to feed the rest of the S.E.C.E.F crew who were arriving later that day. On our way out there was an almighty row kicking off between the campsite owner and about 30 English people. It turned out that all these people had pre-booked to stay at the campsite, but the manager wasn't letting them in because the camp was already overfilled thanks to loads of people being there who shouldn't have been.

We left to go and get our shopping. We were gone about an hour, and when we returned to the campsite, fuck me, the situation had got even worse. Someone had smacked the campsite owner who'd then called the police. When we got there people were being arrested for fighting with the police and some geezer had cut a great hole in the fence. All the cars at the back were driving through the gap to get in.

We left the potential riot and went for a swim at the pool

that was right next to the ground. It was wall-to-wall crumpet, all in little bikinis. We spent the rest of the day lounging in the sun drinking beer and looking at all these heavenly female bodies. HAPPY DAYS!

Ian called at about 3pm, saying they were about one hour away from us, so we reluctantly left the pool and went back to the camper to start the barbecue. Dave cooked the food and Paul went to meet Ian and the returning lads to show them the gap in the fence, which they drove through to join the rest of us. Along with Ian were Jimmy, Bruce, Lee and Kev who was Lee's older brother. They were shocked to see how well we all looked, especially me.

The camp was buzzing now, with the new arrivals, and while all the excitement was going on, Dave said, 'We thought we'd go out this morning and buy some food for you all, as a sort of welcome to Camp S.E.C.E.F.' Then Bruce commented, 'I hope that food has been paid for out of the whip you nicked'. It seemed he was still stewing over the whip money that Dave had spent in Frankfurt.

Dave went into the camper and I followed him. 'Take no notice of him, Dave,' I said, but Dave didn't speak. Instead he picked up a sausage and wiped it on his arse crack. He then went back outside and cooked more sausages, making sure Bruce got the one with extra sauce on it. I was almost sick as I watched Bruce tuck into his banger; if only he'd known that it had just been banged up Dave's arse.

That evening we went into Nuremberg. We went to about three different bars and were on our way to another when someone mentioned doing a whip. 'Well as long as fucking Dave ain't got it! Hang on, he's still got two hundred from the last whip! Why don't we start with that?' Bruce said. That was it: all hell broke loose. Dave lost it and started going mental at Bruce. Obviously Bruce was not backing down either.

After ten minutes of arguing Dave, Ian, Jimmy, Lee, Steve and Kev went off leaving me with Bruce and Paul. It had taken about six hours for the S.E.C.E.F group to be split in two. The three of us found this rough-looking bar with all the windows blacked out. 'Come on, let's get on the cocktails tonight lads!' someone shouted, and we ordered pints of Long Island Iced Tea which had a kick like rocket fuel. We knew we were in for one hell of session drinking shit like that.

We'd had about two pints and were sitting outside with six German lads when this English fan staggered past us, fell over the table, and just lay there in a heap. We picked him up and sat him on a chair. The bloke's name was Paul, he was from Birmingham, and he looked like he had just arrived from the 1970 World Cup. He was wearing a union jack hat, a shirt and shorts that looked like his dad had passed them down to him. He was hammered.

At midnight the barman told us we were not allowed to drink on the street any more, as it was the law, but that we could carry on inside. We got up with ten German lads and even Paul the Brummie managed to get to his feet and follow us inside. By 2am everyone was smashed and having a mental party; it was boiling inside the bar and most of us blokes had taken our tops off and were dancing on the tables. The barman told us he was locking the door but the party didn't have to stop. A LOCK-IN! Fucking brilliant.

About 5am, after everyone had been drinking Long Island specials, a few boys were starting to flake but not me and this guy Horst, who was in the German Army. He had a shaven head and was built like a brick shithouse. At 6am the barman told us it was time to go. I opened the door and the sunlight almost blinded me – it was like coming out of a coal mine with all the blacked-out windows. My eyes had adjusted to the daylight when I realised that there were a load of coppers standing in front of me: it was a raid.

I got out the way of the forward-rushing police. We all stood outside about for about five minutes, and then the old bill came out with the barman in handcuffs. All of a sudden Horst grabbed my arm and cuddled me. I thought he was being matey so I cuddled him back and said, 'We must do this again, Horst – it's been mental!' Horst then held my arms, looked me in the eye and said, 'You will now come to my house for sex, Stan?' I thought he was taking the piss and said, 'Fuck off you wind-up merchant,' but Horst said, 'No, Stan, I really want to fuck you'. Paul heard all of this and was laughing his head off as he said, 'Yeah, go on Stan, you know you want to!' I wasn't laughing, though – I knew Horst was serious and he wanted to bum me. I tried to pull away from Horst, but his grip on my arms grew tighter. Eventually I said, 'Listen, Horst – I'm not gay, you're wasting your time with me. Why don't you ask Bruce? He takes it up the shithole!' I just wanted this twat out of my face. 'But Stan, if you want you can fuck me?' I then angrily told him to fuck off, but he was still grabbing me by the arms. Bruce came over to us holding up Brummie Paul, who grabbed Horst and said, 'I love you fucking Germans, you know how to party!' Horst let go of my arms and that was it – I was off with Bruce and Paul following me shouting, 'Hang on, Stan, your boyfriend wants you!' They were pissing themselves laughing.

When I woke up later that same morning, a few of the lads who hadn't had a lock in at a German gay bar were already up.

By George

I sat down, opened a beer and told them about the night before, and the boys were crying with laughter. Once everyone was up we went to the swimming pool and there were more women than the day before, but the sight of Ian and Lee bombing off the diving board didn't really attract the female attention we craved.

Later we held an S.E.C.E.F swimming race, but Steve and I decided not to take part. Steve did the starter's orders and I filmed proceedings. Steve shouted at the top of his voice, 'On your marks...Get set...GO!' As the boys entered the water, half the pool water came out, covering me and Steve. It was hard to see who was winning from all the splashing and chaos being caused by arms and legs, but after twenty metres Paul was in the lead. He was gliding through the water when from nowhere this woman bobbed up out of the water. Surely she would stop Paul's surge towards the S.E.C.E.F swimming champion and let in Jimmy and Ian, who were close behind him. But when he reached the woman, Paul just swam straight through her, almost knocking her unconscious, and carried on to pass the finish line and take the title of S.E.C.E.F swimming champion.

After relaxing by the pool, we went back to the camper and all the boys went to the fans' park, except me and Bruce. We got absolutely smashed beyond belief; Bruce was that pissed he decided to climb (somehow) up on top of the camper and was dancing in just his shorts singing. 'You're simply the best!' I think he was singing it about England, but may have been directing at me (if it was, thanks Bruce, I love you too). It was shortly after Bruce almost falling off the van for the tenth time, that Ian, Dave, Lee and Paul returned, it was time to go to the match and time to George up again, I can't even remember getting into my suit as I was that pissed.

With Bruce, Paul and me Georged up, we eventually reached the ground after the usual thousands of photos. We met up with several old friends who we had met on previous England trips, including the lads from Yarmouth who were part of the famous 'Yarmouth Yellows' and our old friend Bully. Bully was a top bloke who had been with us in Switzerland when England beat Argentina. We took our seats, front row behind the goal, and Bully joined us.

Sometime in the second half I went to get some drinks, and all the drinks staff were tapping each other and pointing at me. They all wanted photos with me. They told me I was very famous in Germany and that I'd been on all the TV stations. One little photo shoot got me four free beers! I got back to the lads and gave out the drinks. I looked up and saw I was on the stadium's big screen – the match camera had picked me up. The boys bundled on top of me to get themselves on the telly, Bully covering virtually everyone with his Bromsgrove flag. At last we had seen ourselves on telly, but what I didn't anticipate was how many others had also seen us.

As we walked away from the stadium, after seeing England beat Trinidad & Tobago 2-0, we had to once again go through the madness of hundreds of people wanting to have their photo taken with us. After what seemed endless photos, I started to feel really rough, like I was going to collapse at any minute. I never told the boys how I was feeling and just carried on trying to smile for the cameras, but inside my whole body was aching and felt wrecked.

We got back to camp and everyone cheered and Dave said, 'Here he is – the most famous George of all! Stan, I've been telling these boys all about you here in Germany and they can't believe that someone could drink as much as you have and still be alive to tell the story. You want a beer?' I looked at him and said, 'I just want a cup of tea, I'm fucked!' I walked into the camper and collapsed on the sofa. I was completely dehydrated but after reviving myself with two cups of tea, I checked my mobile. I couldn't believe it – I'd missed 230 calls and texts from people back home who'd seen me on telly. I dived out of the van and said, 'Right, now I'm ready for a beer!' A stranger and handed me a beer like my life depended on it and said, 'Hello mate, I'm George, nice to meet you.' I said, 'I'm George as well, but I'm off duty now. Cheers for the beer mate!' 'Right, come on boys. England just won, so let's go and have a party!' I screamed.

When we got to the town, all the boys went for a Chinese and I went to an off-licence to get some desperadoes. When I walked in, I spotted Scouse Jamie and his mates. Three of them were shouting like mad at the Indian guy behind the counter, while the others were filling rubble sacks with beer from the fridges. 'Eh, alright Stan? We owe you one, what you drinking?' Jamie said. 'Desperadoes, mate.' I answered 'Any Desperadoes in the fridge, Steve?' Jamie asked, and Steve filled a sack with Desperadoes for me. Jamie handed me the sack and said, 'Enjoy, Stan, have a good one mate.' I took the sack, threw it over my shoulder almost Father Christmas, and went back to my mates.

On my way, I bumped into the Man City boys and I told them about the Scousers robbing the beer from the shop. 'Fuck me, do you Cockney fuckers pay for anything?' they said, 'We've just seen all your mates running away from that Chinese restaurant, they had their food and then all of them fucked off without paying!' I just laughed and eventually caught up with my lads, who when I found them were dancing in the street throwing beer all over the place.

I don't bat for both sides

That night in Nuremberg there was a fantastic atmosphere and we partied long into the night with the Trinidad & Tobago fans, who while they hadn't brought the greatest football team had definitely brought some of the liveliest fans, who were all well up for it.

The following morning, which happened to be Kev Mark's birthday, we packed everything up as we were heading to our next destination – Cologne for the Sweden game. We all agreed that rather than drive to Cologne we'd go back to Frankfurt, park outside the campsite and have a party that night by the river bank. We decided to be a bit cultured and visit the place where the Nuremberg Trials for Nazi war criminals were held. As we walked in, we were met by a load of English radio reporters looking for comments from England fans. They approached Ian and said, 'Hello mate, want to do an interview for Radio Four?' Ian swiftly replied, 'Fuck off, talk to him!' pointing in my direction. The interviewer got the comment he wanted – I talked for about ten minutes about the education of future generations, never forgetting the atrocities that had happened during World War Two. I knew who the listening audience would be and made my interview as serious as I could, and when I finished the lads gave me a round of applause and the interviewer couldn't thank me enough.

We all did the tour, some a lot quicker than others. Paul and I took our time as we were both interested in the Second World War; we even tried to get down to where the gallows were to get the ultimate photo – a St George about to be hung – but we couldn't figure out how to get there, which was probably a good thing, because if you give Paul enough rope, he will hang himself.

Chapter 6

Michael

We arrived back in Frankfurt and made our way to the campsite where we had started. We all got showered and changed and were just about to set off when Steve said, 'Is that guy watching us? He's been walking up and down that bank for ten minutes looking at us.' A few of the lads approached this strange-looking guy and asked what he was up to.

The bloke watching us was a 23-year-old Bulgarian living in Frankfurt and he was infatuated with everything about England, especially the fans. He was very badly dressed with a shirt that was way too big for him and dodgy chino trousers on with trainers. His name was Michael. We asked Michael to join us for the evening but he said no as he hadn't any money. We then offered to buy drinks for him, and he excitedly agreed. We went to walk into town as we'd always done, when Michael said, 'Why don't you take the Tube?' We followed him around the corner and there it was; the Tube station. We all glanced at each other, especially me, Steve, Dave and Paul, but said nothing.

Michael

Once in Frankfurt square, Kev needed the toilet – big mistake, especially on your birthday. As he locked the door, we listened as he started pissing and then we all started kicking and rocking the portaloo to fuck with poor Kev in it. When he got out he had piss all down his trousers – the only reason we'd stopped was that the police thought that we were mindlessly vandalising the loo, but they just laughed when they heard that someone was in it.

After Kev and his Tardis incident, we went to the riverbank and the Brazilian bar. I asked Michael what he wanted and he said, 'I don't drink alcohol, could I have a Coke?' I told him they didn't sell Coke but they did do non-alcoholic cocktails. I got the barman to do a cocktail with orange in it – and alcohol, of course – and gave it to Michael. His eyes lit up, 'That's *wunderbar*,' he said and quickly started sucking at the straw as if the drink was going out of fashion. Jimmy then said, 'Michael, you can have mine – I don't drink cocktails unless they've got alcohol in them.' He gave Michael a lemony cocktail. This boy was drinking for Bulgaria and I was impressed. Dave left early as he had to pick his girlfriend up from Düsseldorf airport in the morning, leaving the rest of us to carry on the party with our new friend Michael...but where *was* Michael?

As I looked around, I spotted him lying face down with his arms and head hanging over the edge of the concrete bank. At first I thought he was throwing his guts up, but no. My new sidekick stood up holding a lilo in his hands and shouting, 'Stan, I have found my bed for the evening!' Then he proceeded to start imitating shagging movements on the lilo. The whole crowd, which was mainly English, were pissing themselves at the sight of this drunken little man from Bulgaria shagging a lilo.

By George

Half hour later, whilst talking to my mate from West Ham, he said, 'Stan, what's your Bulgarian mate doing now?' I looked and there was Michael walking slowly down the jetty, towards five swans in the river. 'Michael, what the fuck are you doing?' I shouted, 'I am catching us dinner Stan, I will kill it for you!' Bruce ran down and grabbed Michael, telling him he couldn't kill a swan. Michael seemed quite disappointed and said sorry to me for not catching my dinner.

Michael had a few more drinks before the alcohol finally hit him. He sat down, closed his eyes and passed out. He'd only been unconscious for about ten minutes when this Irish prick walked up to him and poured a drink over his head. I charged at him and shoved him to the floor saying, 'What the fuck do you think you're doing?' He got up and said he was only having a bit of fun. 'OK,' I said, 'So you won't mind if I have a bit of fun at your expense?' I grabbed a nearby pint of lager and tipped it straight over his head. The twat just looked me in the eye, turned and walked off with his mates. As they walked away, all the English fans were singing. 'One-nil to the England!' and 'No surrender to the IRA!'

I re-joined my mates who were all gathered around Michael with their trousers and pants down, mooning for photos with the now comatose Bulgarian, so I joined them. You can't miss an opportunity to humiliate someone, can you? When the bars shut, I had an idea and the lads agreed. The idea was to take Michael to Cologne with us. We picked him up, got him in a taxi and took him back to the camper. 'We're all going to be up for kidnapping tomorrow when someone realises Michael's gone missing,' Steve said. I tried to reassure Steve, saying, 'Technically it's not kidnapping as he agreed to come out with us – we just forgot to tell him how long he'd be out with us for!'

Michael

I was still up and drinking when Dave got up at about 5am moaning about Lee, saying it was like lying next to 'Spit the Dog'. Lee's chest infection was worse and his breathing was like a constant barking sound. Dave jumped in his van and went off to get his girlfriend from the airport.

The hardest days were the ones where you had to drive to another city, and obviously it was even worse for the lads who were actually doing the driving. That morning seemed much easier than other journeys, though, as all the lads were in hysterics at the fact that we were setting off and with an unconscious Bulgarian asleep in the back of the camper. I could hardly speak, I was laughing so much as we drove further away from Frankfurt. We got to within about 30 miles of Cologne when Michael wearily opened his eyes. 'How are you feeling, Michael?' I said. 'I feel terrible, Stan. I can't remember going home last night.' The boys were laughing hysterically. It was time to drop the bombshell. 'You never went home, Michael; you've come with us to Cologne for the next England match!' I sort of worded it like he'd agreed – well, I'm sure he would have if we'd actually asked him. 'Stan, I cannot be in Cologne! I have an exam on Monday! I must be in Frankfurt!' Michael said, which sent everybody into fits of laughter. Paul suggested we put him on the train when we reached Cologne, so we dropped him off at the station to make sure he got on the right train. Michael turned and said, 'But Stan…I have no money!' 'Don't worry about that, Michael – you're an England fan and the deal is that while England are still in the World Cup all public transport is free!' 'Really? I have not heard of this…' he replied. 'Oh yes, Michael, we haven't paid for anything yet!' I told him. As we approached the guard checking tickets, I stopped and put on the top half of the George suit as a distraction. It worked and Michael got through without a ticket.

Before Michael left, he told us that we were the best friends he'd ever had and that he'd never forget us. As we waved Michael off, I felt a lump in my throat and as he went out of sight, I just couldn't hold it in anymore and burst out laughing again.

Chapter 7

The camper van of love

At the van and Lee said, 'You ain't going to believe this – we've just had Dave on the phone and he's only just picked Nessa up.' 'Hang on, her flight got in at 10am and it's now 2pm! Why was he so late?' I asked. Ian couldn't wait to tell me. 'He only went to the wrong airport!'

Dave had driven to Düsseldorf Airport but Nessa had landed at Venlo, which was in Holland. Not only had he gone to the wrong airport, he'd gone to the wrong country! Bruce especially enjoyed the story, as when we'd been in Chicago in May 2005, he'd travelled with us to the airport in Chicago only to be told that he'd booked himself on a flight from a different airport. Which Dave had obviously never let him forget. Now the tables were turned!

We went to find somewhere to stay. After twenty minutes we saw a large hostel, so we drove in and followed the road around until we came to a beautiful open grassy area with lots of trees and wildlife running around. Another camper van had followed us in. The passengers got out and the man approached me. 'Hello, my name is Karl and this is my wife Greta and our son Helmut,' he said. After chatting with the couple they invited me into their camper to have a beer. Helmut asked his Dad to play football, leaving Greta and me alone in the camper. She started to come on to me, and as she was a very attractive lady in her mid-thirties, I didn't mind the way her chat was going. Karl waved to his wife through the window and she waved back with her left hand, while her right hand played with my cock under the table. I just smiled back at him out of the window, trying not to show my pleasure. I was getting close to the point of no return when her son walked in. 'Mummy, can you play football with us?' he asked. She let go of my cock and said, '*Ja, ja* Helmut.' Then Karl walked in. 'Stan, you have some great friends – do you play?' I almost choked on my beer and said, 'Whenever I can, Karl!' I got up and walked out.

Ian turned up with Dave and Nessa. Nessa actually looked very happy – probably a lot happier than she'd been when Dave had finally picked her up. We sat around drinking for a while and then these two German fellows came walking up to us shouting and screaming. 'Right, what's the problem mate?' I asked. 'This is protected land – you must leave now, before I call the police!' one of them said. 'Call the police? It was the police who escorted us here as we've got nowhere else to stay!' 'The police told you to stay here? No, they would not do that,' he said. 'We arrived at our campsite and the Czechs are still there so we can't go there until tomorrow. The police told us we could stay here for one night only,' I told him. The guy said, 'I will have to call the government, you must have permission from the government.' 'Please go and ask them and remember to tell them that the police brought us here,' I said. He walked away and I reckoned we had about twenty minutes before the police turned up and moved us on. We were parked on protected land and there was no way the government would allow that. But the council geezer soon returned, smiling. 'My English friends, I have spoken to the government and they have allowed you to stay for one night, but you must take all your rubbish away with you. Is that OK?' he said. I couldn't believe it – he'd believed every word!

We went to the city centre where all the pubs and streets were packed, it was brilliant. Nessa and I found a bar serving cocktails and decided to try and drink our way through the whole list. There were about thirty different drinks on the list, but we were up to the challenge, and we'd had six each when Ian walked in. 'Alright, fancy a cocktail?' I said. 'Fuck off, that's a woman's drink that is!' Ian replied. 'Just try one,' said Nessa. We ordered Ian a cocktail which the barman dressed up with tinsel, fruit and even a sparkler. Ian took a swig and declared, 'That's fucking lovely!'

Outside it was all kicking off with the police, the English and a load of Turks. There was a bit of a stand-off until Del Boy off *Only Fools and Horses* intervened – sorry, I mean Ian. The crowd parted to let him through and this great big geezer walked straight through the crowd, cocktail in hand with the sparkler still going, oblivious to the fact that there was a fight going on. We all went back to the cocktail bar – what a night we had in there, we were all hammered and covered in more decoration than what was in our glasses. Two lads from Northern Ireland joined us and called my Da up, as he was having his 65th birthday party back home. They wished him happy birthday, then broke out into some song about the Orange men. At 5am, with only me, Bruce and Lee left standing, we walked back to the camper. 'That's it, I can't walk any further,' Bruce announced. He climbed over a railing and laid down in the bushes and said, 'This will do me for the night.' 'What's it like, Bruce?' I asked and he replied, 'Well comfortable.' I climbed over, lay down next to him and went to sleep. The next thing I knew, Bruce was shouting, 'Come on Stan, the taxi's here!' I got up and asked, 'How did you get a taxi? What did you tell him, "the bush, Cologne"?' Anyway, we told the taxi driver where we wanted to go and he proceeded to drive about 200 metres before stopping. We were already at the camper van and he charged us five Euros for the pleasure!

The following morning we left, with the guy from the council and two policemen watching our exit. We saw two camper vans with England flags and decided to follow them. After about half hour, they turned off the road along a dust track, and we soon saw a load of campers, tents and cars stretched out along the River Rhine. We saw a space straight away next to another camper, but there was a small table and a tent taking up all the space. 'Stop the van, were parking here' I said. Bruce stopped the camper and we jumped out, unpegged the tent and moved it out of the way. We put the tent back up nearby, Bruce parked the camper, and we set up camp.

Dave started talking to this guy whose red van was next to us. He shouted, 'Stan, this blokes from Dunstable and his sister lives in Slip End!' 'Hello mate, my name's Andy,' he said. 'Hello I'm Stan – what's your sister's name?' I asked. He told me her name was Hilary and she lived in the old farmhouse. 'Fuck me, what a small world. Not only do I know your sister, but I used to squat in that house before she bought it!' I told Andy. My last memory of the squat before we got evicted was of someone having a shit on the floor, but I didn't mention that. 'Who's staying in that camper?' I asked. Andy replied, 'Young lads from Doncaster, here they come now!' I saw five lads walking towards us from the river. 'Alright lads? We're your new neighbours,' I said. They said hello back and went into their camper. 'Miserable bastards,' I thought, and carried on drinking with Andy and the rest of my lads.

An hour later, an eastern European geezer and his family walked through our camp and started giving us all dirty looks – they then got into the small tent, which we had moved on our arrival. The bloke then came out again and told us to be quiet. I told him that if he wanted peace and quiet he'd better move to a place where there weren't 5,000 England fans. He started going mental and I asked him, 'Where are you from, anyway?' 'HUNGARY!' he shouted and Ian immediately yelled 'SECEF!' The Hungarian man looked at Ian blankly so Ian said it again, as did the rest of the lads. They'd remembered what I told them – that 'secef' meant 'fuck off'. Obviously it didn't really mean 'fuck off' – it wasn't even a Hungarian word – but after being told to 'secef' for about the fiftieth time, the bloke packed up his car and drove away. His wife shouted something at me as they left, which I believe actually *was* 'fuck off' in Hungarian.

With all the commotion we hadn't noticed that our neighbours from Doncaster had surfaced and were sitting outside their own van having a beer. 'Fuck that, lads – if we're going to be neighbours we're going to get pissed together!' I told them. The Doni lads were Yeom, Robs, Crawf, Chubb and Flips. About 2 pm, Ian said, 'Right, I ain't sitting here all afternoon just getting pissed. I'm cultured. I'm going to walk into Cologne, who's coming?' Steve, Bruce, Paul and Kev agreed to join him. This reminded me of the time in Chicago, when we were all sitting on the end of the pier and Ian was hanging out of his arse after being out on the piss the night before. That time he said 'Right, I'm not sitting here all afternoon getting pissed. You see that big building over there [pointing at the Sears Tower]? I'm going to climb it.' Off he went. We had visions of Ian scaling the Sears Tower like King Kong, but he just used the stairs.

Later on, as Jimmy, Andy and I sat in our deck chairs drinking, Andy pointed something out. 'Stan…is that two girls making out in the river?' I looked and two girls were indeed pleasuring each other in the river. 'Quality! Beer and a lesbian show, it doesn't get better than this!' I said. The girls stayed in the water for about half an hour and then came walking towards us. As they reached us I said, 'Hello girls, would you care to join us for a beer?' They did. I introduced us and Lee, who had joined us. They introduced themselves as Hilda and Imogen, and said they were from Finland. After chatting to them for a while, I asked, 'Were you playing with each other in the river?' They looked at each other and laughed. Hilda said, 'Oh you saw us, did you? Did you enjoy what your saw?' 'Well I'd sooner join in than watch, but I suppose you're not into men?' I replied. 'Of course we are into men,' said Imogen. 'Yes, we're girlfriends but we often have a man or two sleep with us!' 'So do you fancy a foursome now, with me and Jim?' I asked. 'Yes, why not but where?' said Imogen. 'In the camper van, we can shut the curtains' said Jimmy. 'But we don't mind people watching!' Hilda replied. 'That's it, I'm coming to watch this!' said Lee and all five of us went into the camper.

When we were inside Jimmy went to grab Imogen, but she pulled away. 'Do you not want us to put a show on for you first, to get you excited?' Imogen said. We excitedly agreed. With me and Jimmy standing next to each other and Lee sat in the passenger's seat, the girls started to do their stuff. 'Right, how about letting us have a go then?' Jimmy asked after a couple of minutes. The girls, still holding and touching each other said, 'OK, but you must be ready for us now!' I was more than ready, but Jimmy seemed to be having a bit of trouble. 'Look, I can't do it with Lee sitting watching me!' he said, and told Lee to fuck off. After Lee had reluctantly left, Hilda said. 'Still nothing is happening, Jim…do you not want to fuck me?' Jimmy was in panic mode by this point, and he went into the bathroom and started to wank himself silly. I was pissing myself and shouted, 'Come on, Jimmy – for Queen and country!' 'Fuck off, Stan – you're not helping!' replied Jimmy. 'Oh well, we must go now' said Hilda, who was obviously the boss in the relationship. I grabbed Imogen and said, 'What about us getting it on?' 'Maybe later!' she said, and with that they were gone. I couldn't believe it!

We spent the rest of the afternoon drinking with the Doni lads – they'd all gone for an afternoon sleep and couldn't believe what they'd missed, but they didn't miss the opportunity to take the piss out of Jimmy. We'd made up a special song for him: 'Jim Allsop Allsop, his new name is Floppy Flop, we know he can't get it up, Jim Allflop Allflop'. Genius. About 7pm, the two girls came back with more Finnish girls and a load of Swedish blokes. They all wanted to play us at football and of course we were up for it, so we grabbed a load of English blokes on our way to the pitch next to the camp. Turned out these lads were in the Army, and they were based in Germany. We all lined up and sang our national anthems and by the time Sweden kicked off, it was virtually dusk. We'd only been playing ten minutes when Imogen walked up and started to kiss me – of course I forgot all about the match and we left the pitch and lay down on the floor. 'I told you "maybe later",' she said.

We were so busy that I didn't even hear them stop for half time, but eventually I realised Dave was screaming. 'Where is he? Where's my fucking captain? You normally can't shut him up and I haven't heard him at all. Where the fuck is he?' Imogen and I separated, and I went up to Dave and the rest of my team and said 'Sorry, I was just getting it on with the Swedish right back'. Everyone looked horrified. 'It's OK, it's that Finnish girl from this afternoon!' I added. Everyone laughed and also looked a bit relieved.

We kicked off the second half and I ran to the corner, where Imogen was waiting. She pushed me onto the floor and was just about to get on top of me when the next thing I knew she was gone. Someone had rugby tackled her straight off of my cock. What the…? Who the…? Then I found out: It was Hilda. 'She's my bitch, fucking leave her alone,' she said. I didn't argue – I'd had my bit in the first half. I jogged away and tried to get involved in the match…I just had to find out where the ball was in the darkness.

The match ended 2-2, and we lost on penalties. We agreed to have a rematch the following day and invited everyone back to our camp for a beer. With Dave's van blasting out the tunes, our camp area was rocking. 'You got anything to burn around here, Stan?' asked one of the Army lads. 'I've got the very thing. Follow me down to the river. Earlier that day, we'd seen some Germans making a tepee out of branches, to use as a sun shade, so I thought why not use it as a fire. Another army lad, Spud, joined us with his firelighters and it wasn't long before the tepee was a roaring fire.

The camper van of love

An hour after we'd started the fire, Ian, Bruce, Kev, Steve and Paul came back. They told us that they'd got lost and had then seen a massive fire start. 'That's got to be Stan's handiwork', they thought, and followed the fire home, like the three wise men following the star to baby Jesus. The boys were shocked when they found the camp they'd left was now rave central. Bruce came up to me and said, 'I'm going to sleep now, but if any of these birds are up for it, send them into my tent and I'll give them a right good pounding.' He got into his tent and zipped it up. Of course I then had a chat with Hilda about winding Bruce up, and she agreed. She went to Bruce's tent, unzipped it and put her head in and said, 'Bruce? I want to come in and fuck you, Bruce…'. We were all cracking up and waited for Bruce to drag Hilda in and give her in his words 'A right good pounding.' 'Fuck off. I'm trying to sleep so just leave me alone,' came the response. We couldn't believe it, Bruce, who reckons he's always up for the ride, was too busy sleeping? Surely that couldn't be right.

I woke up at about 10am, fell out of the van and had a beer with Ian and Andy. Ian told us a story about Bruce from the night before, and suddenly everything fell into place. On their way back Bruce had been busting for a shit, but had nowhere to go and hadn't been able to hold it in. Just like Chubb, he'd shit himself. We fell off our chairs backwards laughing – no wonder Bruce declined the offer from Hilda!

About 1pm, we all trudged out to the football pitch to face Sweden again. We all lined up to do the national anthems, but as Sweden were just finishing theirs, six riot vans turned up and all the coppers got out in full riot gear. Someone had called the police and informed them that there were two large groups of English and Swedish fans meeting on a field for a prearranged

47

fight. Once Dave explained what was actually going on, the police stayed to watch the match. It all ended 2-2 again, just like the night before, and true to form England lost on penalties.

After the match Paul took the camper to fill up the water supply – but when he came back there was massive dent in the rear side boot door. He'd driven off without locking the door and had driven right into a big tow bar on the back of another vehicle. That was the deposit on the van gone, then. Later that day, as S.E.C.E.F, the Doni boys and the Army Lads sat round drinking, our friends Luke and Tony turned up and so did a TV crew wanting an interview. The interview started with me saying, 'Day twelve in the Big World Cup house and England are still in it'. Cue the rest of the lads singing 'WE'RE NOT GOING HOME' while the camera panned around all of them. It was match day and our third and final group game against Sweden. Bruce and I Georged up for the match and although it was only a ten-minute walk from the train station to the ground, it took us nearly three hours to get there. It was endless; everyone had seen us on the TV and everyone wanted our photo.

Eventually we reached the stadium and went our separate ways as for this game we were not in the same area. I was supposed to be sitting on the third tier, but decided to try my luck getting into the VIP area. As I reached the entrance, I grabbed an English bloke who was with his son and said, 'Does your son want a photo with me, mate?' 'Of course!' he replied. 'Let's get one with all the German security, that'll look great,' I suggested. We walked towards all the VIP security staff, who stopped whatever checks they were doing and started pointing at the famous St George who was approaching them. I got to where they were all standing and said 'Before I take my seat,

48

could I please get a photo of the best German security staff with myself and my nephew?' I was pointing towards the young English lad. I stood in the middle of about thirty security staff, who were almost fighting each other to get close to me. After several pictures, the lad went off with his dad and I turned towards the VIP entrance. They just let me through without asking to see a ticket!

I saw a spare seat in the second row. That would do nicely! I looked up to where I was supposed to be sitting, in the gods, and thought to myself, 'what a result!' Until, that is, I heard a voice say, 'Excuse me mate, I think you're in my seat!' I looked round and this English bloke was looking at me. 'I know I am mate, to be honest I've blagged my way in here. How about you sit down and I sit on your lap?' I said hopefully. 'I ain't being funny, mate, but I've just paid a tout six hundred pounds for this seat and I ain't paid all that money to have fucking St George sit on my knee,' he said sternly. I thought that was fair enough, so I got up to look for another seat. I eventually found one, but true to form I spent the majority of the game in the VIP bar – and, true to form, England drew 2-2 with Sweden. We'd won the group and now faced Ecuador in the last sixteen.

I left the stadium and met Bruce, Lee, Dave and Ian. 'Where were you? I kept calling you, but you didn't answer!' Ian shouted. 'I blagged my way into the VIP area, what the hell are you talking about?' I replied. 'You twat,' said Ian. 'All the WAGs were sitting in the seats where you were supposed to be!' I couldn't believe it – all of sudden my VIP blag didn't seem that great an idea. I could have had the world's media at my feet, surrounded by the Wives and Girlfriends of the England team. Gutted.

Dave and I got off the tram in the city and the boys carried on going towards the campsite. We met up with Nessa, Paul, Kev and Army Andy; they were all steaming and it didn't take me and Dave long to catch them up. I spoke to a Swedish bloke and we swapped shirts. 'Nice gesture, Stan' said Dave, but actually I'd swapped because my shirt was soaking with sweat and his was dry. It was fine until Paul flew at me, trying to rip the shirt off my back and screaming, 'What are you wearing that shit for? Get it off you wanker!' Andy grabbed Paul, but he was insistent. I'd also been given a blow-up hand with the Swedish flag on it, and Paul grabbed the hand and launched it into the direction of the Swedes. He completely missed them, of course, but he did knock half a dozen drinks over. He was going mental – he jumped onto a table where a bloke was dancing, took his shirt off and threw the geezer off the table. Paul raised his hands like a boxer winning a fight. Dave told him to calm down, but Paul just got Dave in a headlock and started choking him. He eventually let go and ran up to a woman in her late fifties. Surely he wasn't going to start on her? He didn't – instead he tried to kiss her and she tried to kiss him back. She was as drunk as Paul, though, and neither of them could properly stand up straight, never mind plant a kiss on the other.

We staggered back to the site at about 7am, and I noticed that all the army tents and the Army Lads' minibus had gone. 'Andy, where's your boys? They ain't gone without you, have they?' I asked. 'No mate, were leaving at two in the morning,' Andy replied. 'Andy, it's 7am…they've gone without you!' I told him. 'Oh SHIT. Oh well, I'll just have to stay with you lot!' Andy announced.

We got to our camp and found some German guy pissing on a tent with an English flag on it. 'What the fuck do you think you're doing, you bastard?' I screamed and started chasing him through the campsite. I only chased him for about ten seconds, mind you, as I could barely walk, never mind run. I went back to our camp and Paul and Andy we're standing by the tent laughing. 'What's going on?' I asked. 'Dave's shagging Nessa.' Paul answered. It was so funny, each time Dave pumped himself into Nessa the tent moved. We stood and watched for all of thirty seconds and then it was over. Dave must have had some Viagra to last that long.

We opened the camper door and there asleep on the sofa was a lad from Caddington called Anthony – but we called him Scuz. I didn't even know he was coming over. Andy got into the camper and was soon asleep on the sofa opposite Scuz, and seconds later I too passed out. I was woken by Ian going mental outside shouting, 'Well if he don't get up in a minute, were going without him!' I thought 'Shit, we must be on the move again', so I opened the door and said 'It's alright, I'm ready to go!' and got into Ian's motor. 'What are you doing, Stan?' Bruce asked. 'I don't know. Where are we going?' I answered. 'Well we're going home and you're staying here,' Bruce then told me. They were actually trying to get Kev up! I got out, flopped onto a deckchair and passed out again. I woke up and to find Andy sitting next to me looking somewhat the worse for wear. 'Will you get into trouble for being late back to base?' I asked. 'I'm in deep shit,' he replied. I then said, 'We're driving to Dortmund today, why don't you come with us and then get a train back to your base?' Andy agreed. Dave came out of the camper and said, 'You've outdone yourself this time, Stan. You've already kidnapped a Bulgarian and now you're going to get a bloke court marshalled!'

Before we left I said goodbye to the Doni lads, who were still in their camper. I said we'd call them when we got to Stuttgart. We also said goodbye to Scuz, who was going home, and to Luke and Tony who were staying in Cologne. By the time we left the makeshift campsite, it was deserted. Days before you couldn't drop a pin for at least a mile between campers, cars and tents and now it just looked like a big field on the banks of the River Rhine. But did that field have some stories to tell!

Chapter 8

Sweaty socks

It took about three hours to get to Dortmund, and we drove straight to the main train station and dropped Andy there. We then drove into the city itself looking for a spot to park the vans. We found an ideal place outside the stadium in an empty car park and headed into town. Brazil were playing Japan the next day so we expected Dortmund to be rocking, but how wrong we were. It was unbelievable, there wasn't a soul anywhere and the whole place was like a ghost town!

We walked for about half an hour and eventually found a bar with all the windows steamed up. We knew that meant people, and people meant a party. I opened the door and looked in – but the whole bar was full of Jocks! 'Shit,' I thought. My worst nightmare had come true – no pubs open except the Scottish bar! We walked in, to a chorus of, 'We hate England, we hate England'. Steve shouted back, 'Fuck off you sweaty cunts' but that just made the Jocks sing louder at us. As I stood at the bar waiting to be served, Steve said 'I ain't putting up with this,

By George

I'm going to smack one of them in a minute.' We were outnumbered ten to one and to start a fight would have been suicide. Besides, I don't like hitting people in skirts and most of the Jocks were wearing kilts. We got the drinks and went over to where Dave and Nessa were sat. Shortly after, I went outside for a fag on my own, and seconds after lighting my fag I was joined by about ten Scottish fans who started chanting at me. I stood there laughing in their faces. One of them charged up to me and said, 'What you laughing at, you English pig?' That was it: no more. I lost it – especially as the guy who was having a go was a Welshman! 'I'm glad you didn't call me a sheep or you'd probably want to shag me!' I answered back.

The Jocks who were with him all started laughing at my quick response, but strangely enough he wasn't laughing as I let fly with a tirade of one liners – never raising my voice or saying anything in anger at the now cowering Welshman. It didn't take long before they were buying me drinks, whilst I told them about my antics as St George. 'Let's get some photos with Stan, the greatest Englishman' said a big six foot three Jock who looked like Joe Jordan. I even swapped shirts with one of them for the photos. After a few hours we were all pretty pissed, when Steve came up to me. 'We're going in a minute Stan, pub's about to close and it'll be nice to get away from all these sweatys.' 'Fuck off, Steve – they're sound,' I replied Steve turned his back and walked back into the pub.

The Scottish fan I had swapped my shirt with for the photo then told all his mates to be quiet as he had something to say. 'I tell you this, I hate England and hate all Englishmen, so don't kill me for what I am about to say, my Scottish friends. I want England to win the World Cup for that Englishman standing there,' he announced, pointing at me 'The greatest Englishman that ever lived and I'm proud to call him my friend, STAN THE MAN!'

I could feel tears welling up and was waiting for someone to give me my Nobel Peace Prize, but all I got was a chorus of 'We love Stan the Man, said we love Stan the Man'. At this point all my friends came out of the pub and I left with these mad Jocks still singing my name as I disappeared into the darkness of Dortmund.

I woke up the following morning to the sound of car horns – and it didn't sound like just one or two. I opened the door and found the once-empty car park was full of Brazilian supporters. The noise was deafening with every vehicle blasting its horn. People out on foot were either blowing horns or beating drums. It was an amazing sight and sound and I was just glad I didn't have a hangover. Then again I never got a hangover, because I never sobered up.

Dave had already taken Nessa to Mulheim, which was of course where we had to drop the camper off. Yes, after fourteen days it was time to say goodbye to our trusty camper, but first we had to clean it. Paul, Steve and I made the inside look brand new, but as good as the inside looked the problem was outside with the big dent in the side door. We couldn't clean that and we had a deposit riding on it. No one expected to get anything back, but I'm not one to say goodbye to any amount of money, especially when it was over a thousand Euros. We arrived at camper hire place and I went into the office and was greeted by the manager. '*Guten Tag*,' I said 'I am here to return a camper van we hired from you,' I added. The manager looked at me and said 'It's Stan, isn't it? Mulheim's favourite Englishman! How has your time in Germany been, Stan?' he asked. I couldn't believe it – the guy remembered me! 'I have had a fantastic time and may I say that using your vehicle has helped make this the best trip ever,' I replied. I was really creeping up to this guy. 'I'm glad you have had a good time, Stan; we have been watching all the games and we have seen you many times on German TV. We will now go and check the van together, yes?' he said. We had purposely left the damaged boot door open, as you would have clearly seen the damage if it was shut. The manager went straight into the van and said, 'My God, have you even used the van, Stan? It looks like new, better than when we gave it to you! I think you will be receiving all your money back, after I check the outside.' We walked around to the good side and then to the rear of the camper, the manager was nodding his head in approval of the condition of his van. He got to the damaged side, looked in the boot, and grabbed the dented door as if to close it. At this point I banged my hand cheerfully on the side of the van, put my arm around the manager and said, 'I'm really going to miss this van, I feel like I'm leaving my home!' He let go of the door, which remained open, and said, 'Come on, let us go and sort your money out for you.' Both of us headed off towards his office. Steve and Paul were speechless. Once in his office, he counted out the money and handed it to me. I shook his hand and got out quick.

Dave picked us up ten minutes later and once the rental place was out of sight, I told Dave that I'd got the whole deposit back. Dave nearly crashed the van. 'You got it all back? Fuck off, I don't believe you.' He soon believed me when I pulled a great wad of cash out of my pocket! That night in Mulheim we all got well and truly pissed. When the bar closed we made our way back to Dave and Nessa's hotel and to where the van was parked. We got to the hotel and had to decide who would share the spare double bed in Dave and Nessa's room and who would sleep in the van. I told everyone I was claustrophobic and they believed me. Paul then said he'd sleep in the van that night and Steve agreed to go in the back of the van down to Cologne the next day to meet up with Luke and Tony.

The next morning, after having a nice shower, a lovely fry-up and a nice cup of tea, Dave, Nessa, Steve and I were all in great spirits when Dave shouted, 'FUCK, PAUL'S STILL IN THE BACK OF THE VAN!' We'd forgotten about Paul. I ran to the van, where I found some old geezer talking to it. Paul had been shouting and banging and the bloke must have thought he'd had been kidnapped (well he wouldn't have been the first person we'd kidnapped on this trip). I opened the back door, glad to see that Paul was alive. It wasn't the lack of air I was worried about, it was the stench of unwashed clothing and everything else that I thought would have killed him.

Chapter 9

Blind leading the blind

We dropped Nessa at the right airport, then it was off to Cologne to meet Luke and Tony and then on to Stuttgart. Once there we drove straight to the city centre. We'd picked up a map of the city and we spotted a green area on the map and made our way to it. It was a lovely park and the location was brilliant – not only had we found a nice secluded area, it had its own train station and two swimming pools.

We jumped on the train and made our way back to the city centre's main square, where they had set up a fans' park. We settled on the steps outside, along with hundreds of other England fans. Within an hour of being there, a good couple of thousand had turned up. We called the Doni Boys, as promised, and twenty minutes later they arrived too. There was a cracking atmosphere in the square, until some German dickhead started giving a load of grief to a couple of England fans and a bit of a scuffle broke out. We knew what was coming next. The old bill had been waiting in their hundreds around the corner for something to go off and that was it – they made a huge line in front of all of us, so no one could go anywhere. A few England fans who had been sitting at tables in the square started lobbing the chairs at the police, but this just led to the coppers closing ranks and completely blocking everyone in. We all waited for the baton charge, but then heard a voice over a loud hailer: 'You all have ten minutes to leave this area or we will arrest all of you'. The crowd just started singing England songs as a sign of defiance, but behind the police lines we could see coaches already pulling up.

We decided to go and as we were leaving the square the ten-minute warning was up and anyone who hadn't left the police circle was being dragged out and stuck on to the buses. As we walked away, we were approached by a female German reporter after an interview. Crawf shoved me out the way to be interviewed and the woman said, 'Have you enjoyed Germany since you have been here?' 'Yes, I have had the best time of my life!' said Crawf. She then asked, 'What do you think of the people in Germany?' Crawf responded: 'I heard a statistic before I arrived that 45% of German women have hairy armpits, but I haven't seen too many women with hairy armpits so I think that statistic is wrong!' The thing was, Crawf was deadly serious. The reporter didn't know what to say and walked away stunned. Everyone ripped the piss out of Crawf for his ridiculous interview.

We found a place called The Rock Bar and went in, but as I walked through the door the doorman grabbed my arm and told me I couldn't take my drink in with me. I finished the Desperadoes I was drinking and he took the whole bag – with at least eight bottles in it – from me. 'I will give them back to you when you leave,' he said. 'Yeah, of course you will!' I laughed.

I soon forgot about the Desperadoes when I discovered that the club was rocking. Most of the boys had already latched on to a girl – there were hundreds in the club. It must have been six women to one man, happy days! I was soon grabbed by this German woman with short brunette hair and those sexy office secretary glasses – her hands were everywhere and I also let my hands do some wandering. We'd hit the jackpot. The whole night was spent with all the boys going from one girl to another.

The night went so quick and before we knew it, the DJ was playing the last tune. As I was leaving the club, the doorman grabbed my arm and said, 'I think this is yours?' He handed me my lucky bag. I couldn't believe it – the best club and best doormen. We knew we were going back there the next evening.

In the morning I was asleep outside on the grass when I felt a sharp prod in my back, and I opened my eyes to see two policemen. 'What the fuck do you think you're doing?' I shouted. 'Oh, I am sorry to disturb you. You are English? We thought you were eastern European gypsies.' They walked off and I went back to sleep.

When we all woke up, we decided to go to the swimming pool, but then Crawf rang. 'Ay up, Stan – where are you lot?' After chatting, Dave and I jumped in the van and within twenty minutes found the Doni Boys parked in a massive car park. Crawf was driving as usual, and he followed Dave back to our parkland area. We'd been driving for about ten minutes when we saw the *Sun* newspaper's bus with gorgeous models on it. Obviously our eyes were then fixed on the other side of the road and not on the turning on the left which we should have taken. 'Shit, we missed the turning, Dave! Oh well, don't worry, just take the next left and we'll be alright.' I confidently said. Dave took the next left turn, but we found ourselves on a dual carriageway. Dave, clearly still pissed, was in no fit state to be driving on a main road, so he pulled off at the next exit and headed back towards the city centre.

We were merrily driving along when I got a bad feeling in my belly and instantly knew I was in desperate need of a shit. 'Dave, you've got to stop somewhere,' I pleaded. Dave replied, 'Where the fuck am I going to stop, Stan? It don't look like there are many fields around here, you're just going to have to wait.' I don't think Dave actually realised how desperate I was and all I kept thinking was that I wasn't going to do a Chubb or Bruce in my pants. We stopped at a set of traffic lights and I couldn't cope any longer. 'That's it Dave, I'm going to have to shit on the street, I can't hold it anymore,' I blurted out. 'You can't shit on the street! There's cars and people every-where, you'll get nicked!' Dave responded. 'Why don't you use the Doni boys' toilet in their camper?' For once Dave had come up with a great idea. I jumped out and ran doubled over to the Doni Boys' camper. 'I need to borrow your toilet!' I yelled. 'No way, Stan! None of us shit in the toilet, that's the Doni rule,' said Crawf. 'You let me use that fucking toilet or I'll shit on the floor here and now,' I said, trying to sound forceful, but I knew too much shouting may well trigger off the explosion which was imminent from my arse. Flips could see the desperation on my face and he shouted to the boys in the back to open the door. The door opened and I flew in. 'You can't use the toilet Stan, that's our changing room!' Doni Chubb said. I ignored him and went into the toilet. As my bum hit the seat, the shit just flew out of me. After the initial rush from my arse, I looked around and it was indeed their changing room – there were loads of toiletries and it smelt like the perfume department in Boots. As I stood up, Crawf pulled away from a junction – I fell backwards into the shower and the shower came on. I'd turned it on and wasn't sure how to turn it off again, but all I did know was I was getting drenched. I eventually turned the shower off and opened the door. 'What the fuck have you been doing Stan?' asked Robs, 'You're fucking soaking!' I told them what happened, but they didn't believe me. I didn't care whether they believed me or not, I was just relieved I hadn't joined the BBC (Bruce and Chubb Club)!

We eventually found the parkland and all went to the swimming pool down the road from us. As we were queuing to get in, Robs told me about his night before. 'You remember that blonde-haired bird I was chatting up, the one with the gimpy-looking boyfriend?' 'Yes,' I said. 'Well they were staying on the same concrete car park as us lot, so I got a taxi back with them and you'll never believe it, the blonde bird only sucked me off in the back of the taxi with the boyfriend in the front!' Robs said proudly. 'Aye, and you'll never believe this, Stan,' Flips said. 'She's only standing right behind you!' We turned around and there she was with her boyfriend, it was a priceless moment, maybe not for those involved. 'Hello, have a good night last night?' I said to her, trying not to laugh at this poor girl who clearly wanted the ground to open up and swallow her.

Paul and I got talking to the alleged gimpy boyfriend, who turned out to be just the blonde girl's friend. They'd travelled over together from England but we didn't tell Robs, as he obviously thought he was going to get a smack in the mouth at any moment and it was hilarious watching him squirm.

At 5pm, as we were leaving the swimming park, Ian phoned – they had just arrived in Stuttgart. Dave and I went to meet them in the city centre. With Ian were Bruce, Lee and my nephew Ricky. Ian followed Dave on what was a simple route back to our base camp – just as long as Dave didn't decide to go the wrong way down a dual carriageway, that is. 'DAVE! YOU'RE GOING THE WRONG WAY!' I screamed – he'd reverted back to driving on the left. Dave turned the steering wheel to get back on to the right side of the road and we flew over the central reservation. It was like something out of the *Dukes of Hazzard*, but Dave's van certainly wasn't the General Lee and neither was Ian's motor.

When we got back to base, Ian jumped out and screamed, 'Were you trying to fucking kill us or something? We were on the wrong side of the road!' 'Look, I don't know what I'm doing half the time,' replied Dave. 'You don't know how hard it is spending every day with Stan. We drink all night and then he has me driving all around the fucking city all day meeting people, I don't think I can go on'. Everyone laughed, knowing that what Dave was saying was so true and they would have all been in the state he was in if they'd been with me for two weeks.

While Dave was trying to compose himself, Paul phoned and told me they were in the Chinese restaurant down the road and that they had a surprise for me. As I walked in and went to the garden area at the back, there stood three of the army boys: Kenny, Taff and Spud! 'Fucking hell I don't believe it, I didn't think we'd see you again after the Andy incident! By the way, what happened to Andy?' I asked. Kenny told me that after

By George

Andy had turned up nearly a day late, he'd been told that he was banned from leaving base for any more of the England games and had to stay and do chores. 'He's absolutely gutted, and he's going to be even more gutted when he knows we've met up with you,' Kenny said.

That night we went back to the city centre to find The Rock Bar, but none of us could remember where it was. Luckily Bruce started chatting up a German girl who was a tourist information representative out for the night. She took us to this bar called L'Oasis, where they were playing real hardcore house music and everyone was going mental. She then led us through the back streets until we reached where we wanted to be, The Rock Bar. I left my beer bag with the doorman again and went in. Once again the place really was rocking and it was full of horny women. Every time I looked around all the boys were getting off with different girls! Everyone got absolutely wrecked that night, especially Luke and Crawf who passed out and had lit candles and beers placed onto their heads while they slept. We left at 6am, having to carry Paul who was in a virtual coma, but everyone was excited as later that day we faced Ecuador in the last sixteen. You could feel the apprehension amongst the lads – apart from Paul, who couldn't even feel his legs.

After having few pints and a bite to eat, those of us with tickets made our way to the ground. Once Bruce, Paul and I put the George suits on the 200-metre walk from the entrance to the ground took us nearly two and half hours due to the usual barrage of photos. England beat Ecuador 1-0 to reach the quarter finals – we now faced Holland or Portugal, who were playing their game later that night. As the three Georges walked away from the stadium the celebrations on the streets were fantastic, someone had laid out a massive England flag which was causing a tailback as no one would walk on it. No one except us, of course – the three of us strode across the flag, which had been signed by hundreds of people, and lay down in a row. Cue the onslaught of photographers.

The streets were thinning out the nearer we got to our camp, but all of a sudden from nowhere appeared Michael from Frankfurt. 'Michael, what are you doing here?' I asked 'Stan, I travelled down yesterday looking for you guys and I thought I was never going to find you. I need to give you my phone number so we can stay in touch.' He gave me his phone number and said 'I have to go, Stan – my bus is leaving in fifteen minutes.' He was gone. He'd travelled from Frankfurt to Stuttgart to give me his phone number? The bloke was mental, for fuck's sake we'd kidnapped him and he still wanted to be friends!

Back at camp the boys didn't believe us that we'd met Michael until we showed them us in a photo with him. I noticed Dave with his feet in a bucket of water. 'What's wrong, Dave?' I asked. 'Stan, I'm falling apart at the seams, my feet feel like they're on fire and to top it all my bollocks are chafing like hell,' Dave said. 'Try some of this, it's a herbal cream for sore skin and chafing,' Ian said, passing him this small tub of cream. Dave took the cream and quickly rubbed a load into his balls. Seconds later he was screaming – Ian had given him Tiger Balm, which when applied to the skin gets very hot. We were all crying with laughter at the sight of Dave hopping and jumping about like he was standing on hot coals, which I guess is what his bollocks must have felt like. The next thing I knew Dave's got his bollocks out for all to see, dipping them in the bucket of water.

By George

After Dave's bollocks had cooled down, we went to eat. It sort of had that last meal feel about it because Ian, Bruce, Ricky and Lee were going home first thing in the morning and this time Paul and Steve were going with them. The meal tasted even better when Portugal beat Holland and thanks to a record number of bookings and red cards, the Portuguese would be without three of their star players for the quarter final, including the very dangerous Deco.

Dave and I went back to the camp to see the others off, especially Paul and Steve. We'd been used to all the others coming and going but Paul and Steve had been there from the start. I turned to Dave and said 'Oh well mate, it's just you and me now for a week, so there's only one thing to do. Let's go and get hammered, we're in the quarter final!'

We got to the city and headed straight to The Rock Bar, as there was no better place to party, but when we got to the door it was all locked up. We asked a German man passing and he told us that most of the bars closed early on a Sunday. I didn't even know what day it was. 'You might want to try the L'Oasis bar – I think that's open until 1am,' he said, so we made our way there. We soon spotted the Doni boys, who were also leaving the following morning, so we said goodbye to our new close friends. We walked into L'Oasis and the tune playing was a remix of my favourite rave anthem of all time, 'Playing with Strings'. I just started going off my head and screaming at Dave. 'That's it, Dave! Our name is on this cup!' Luke and Tony were also in L'Oasis going off their heads, until Luke once again passed out and snored his head off. I noticed this cute little German girl dancing across from me and she was staring, so I went over to her and started to chat her up. I stayed with her for the rest of the night, until the bar closed. She left with her friends but gave me her number – Dave and I were going to be in Stuttgart for another couple of days, so I was definitely going to call her.

Chapter 10

Just the two of us

We'd been walking around trying to find anywhere we could get a drink, but there was nowhere. We came across a bar with a rainbow flag outside, which signified it was a gay bar, but we didn't care less – we'd found somewhere else to have a drink. The doorman gave me and Dave a strange look as we entered, but we went to the bar and I soon got chatting to two girls, Frani and Adrea, and a bloke they were with called Nick. They were from Switzerland, but they lived in Stuttgart. It wasn't long before each beer we ordered was accompanied by a chaser, and our new Swiss friends were more than keen to join in. There were only about twenty people in the bar, but with the drinks fully flowing and the music pumping it was turning into a right party atmosphere.

Whilst talking to Frani – who I really fancied – and Nick, I looked around to see Dave dressed in pink cowboy gear dancing around with Adrea and three of the gayest looking blokes I'd ever seen. After a couple of hours everyone knew me and Dave on first name terms – we could barely remember our own names at this point! Then Nick asked whether we fancied coming back to his apartment for a few more drinks. 'Are the girls coming back as well, Nick?' I asked. 'Yes, they both are – especially Frani!' he answered, giving me a cheeky smile. So we went to Nick's apartment, which had a fantastic lounge area with really expensive leather sofas and a huge 50-inch television. We had hit the jackpot. 'Do you want beer or shall I get the spirits out?' Nick asked. 'Skip the beer, its spirit time,' I replied. Nick got out a bottle of vodka and a bottle of Jagermeister. We had shot after shot and everyone was getting very loud, until some geezer with a shaven head appeared from nowhere in his underpants, screaming at Nick. Dave got up, put his arm round this bloke and said, 'It's alright mate, calm down and come and have a drink with us!' I put my drink down at this point and was ready to jump up as I thought the geezer was going to belt Dave. The bloke looked at Dave, said one word to him and walked off and I assume went back to bed. 'Who the fuck was that?' I asked. 'My flatmate Ricardo, he's from Brazil,' Nick answered. 'What did he say to me?' Dave asked. 'He called you a wanker!' replied Nick, which started everyone laughing.

Nick opened the second bottle of Jagermeister and I asked him how long he and Frani had been together. He started laughing, as did the two girls, and I sat there trying to work out what was so funny. 'Me and Frani are not together, we just work together,' Nick said. 'She's not really my type, if you get my drift!' I just looked at him. 'What I mean, Stan, is that *you* would be my type!' Shit – it was Nuremburg all over again! This fucker was going to get me pissed and bum me! Or maybe he'd bum Dave, that wouldn't be so bad. That would be quite funny. 'Actually, I also think you're Frani's type, Stan! I think Frani really likes you…' Nick said. I turned and looked at Frani and she started kissing me. The next thing I knew, Nick had got a camera out and was taking pictures of me and Frani getting it on. It all got even more strange when Nick wanted to film us having sex with his video camera. I declined his offer.

'Is it alright if I sleep in that empty room?' I asked and Nick nodded. I went into the bedroom and could hear someone walking in behind me. I prayed to god it wasn't Dave and thankfully my prayers were answered. It was Frani, who was already undressing on the way towards me and the large double bed. It didn't take long before we were both naked and in bed together.

I woke in the morning looking up at the ceiling and feeling pretty good about life. I turned to look at Frani and there she was…looking like Dave! 'What the fuck are you doing in the bed, Dave, and where's Frani?' I asked. Dave opened an eye, looked at me and said, 'I don't know. After you two went to bed together I fell asleep on the sofa. I woke up and looked in here and there was you and her lying asleep together, so I got in between you and went to sleep!' I got up and looked in the other bedrooms and found Nick in bed asleep, but no one else was in the flat.

About 11am Nick and Dave got up, and we sat in the lounge drinking a cup of tea. Dave asked whether Nick had a washing machine, and whether he'd mind us washing some of our clothes as we'd been in the same lot of gear for two weeks and hadn't been able to wash anything. 'Of course, where are your clothes?' Nick said. 'They're in the back of my van,' Dave answered. 'Feel free to use my machine' Nick said. We were both so grateful – it had got so bad that Dave had suggested that we swap underpants, as it would have the feeling of a new pair!

We went and fetched our stuff from the van, and when we got back to Nick's, he said, 'I've got to go out in a bit and get some stuff for the barbecue later'. 'What barbecue, Nick?' I said. 'I'm having a barbecue this afternoon and then we're going to the Fans' Park to watch Switzerland against the Ukraine,' he said. 'You and Dave will be staying for the barbecue, yes?' 'We'd love to stay,' I answered.

It was about mid-afternoon when the first of Nick's friends turned up – including Frani, who seemed a little embarrassed but soon relaxed with the aid of a drink. Nick's friends were so friendly and I couldn't believe it when they asked if we knew the English Knights from the TV. I told them we were the English Knights and they all wanted photos with us. Unfortunately the only items that we hadn't brought to wash were the George suits, big mistake!

We left Nick's flat about an hour before kick-off, with all his friends singing, 'We're red, were white, were fucking dynamite, Switzerland, Switzerland!' – it was a song I'd taught them. After watching Switzerland lose on penalties, Dave and I headed into town, while our new Swiss friends went home. We'd arranged to go back to Nick's in the morning to collect our clothes before we left Stuttgart. It got to about midnight and we already knew that plan of an early night was out the window – we'd ended up back in L'Oasis and were drinking as heavily as we had when we first arrived in Germany. Being pampered for a day had given us wings.

We left L'Oasis when it closed and didn't expect to find too much else open. We'd been walking – or should I say stumbling – around for a while when we came across a little bar called Sinatra's, full of mad Italians celebrating their win earlier in the day. A geezer was singing on the bar – he was absolutely crap,

By George

but me and Dave were cheering him like crazy because he looked like our mate Pete Dimmock. Next thing this ropey old bird gets up on the bar with him wearing just a bra, knickers and fishnet stockings. The crowd were encouraging her to strip off and it didn't take long before she whipped her bra off. Everyone cheered as she threw her bra into the crowd and she was encouraging people to have a feel of her tits. She was obviously the singer's bird, as he seemed to get the right hump and got off the bar and sloped outside.

The people in the bar got stranger and stranger – this old bloke walked in wearing shell suit bottoms with his arse hanging out and this red Indian medallion on his hairy chest. He looked like Jimmy Savile on acid. In the corner another bloke and his wife sat there staring over their glasses at all the people in the bar. We were standing there laughing at all the strange characters when I felt someone dancing behind me. I turned around and there stood this fucking He-She – Dave was pissing himself. 'Fuck it', I thought, and got the He-She to pose for a couple of photos. After all, I'd already had my photo taken wearing a Scotland shirt, so I was beyond caring.

Sinatra's closed at 6am and Dave and I left the lunatics – but not before they gave us some excellent wrestling action. Jimmy Savile seemed to be trying to kidnap the singer's bird, and it was hilarious. We slept at the park for about three hours and then collected our clothes from Nick's flat before leaving Stuttgart.

Chapter 11

Hostel

We drove back to Frankfurt and met up with our Bulgarian friend Michael. We'd decided to spend that night in the van and the next night in a hotel, so Michael took us to a hotel that he knew. It had an eerie feel it was more like the Addams Family house! A small lady in her sixties spoke to Michael in German, eyeing me and Dave up, and once the room was all sorted for the following night, we headed into town with Michael.

We sat in a bar drinking cocktails – Michael ordered Coke and said that the last time he'd had drinks that looked like ours, he'd lost several days of his life! He then asked if we would like to go to a place called Rudesheim with him the following day, and as we had no other plans we agreed to go. The following morning, we went to the hotel. The landlady showed us to our room, but there were bars on the windows and it smelled like there was a dead body in there. Dave didn't care and collapsed on his bed, and all I needed was a good shower. I got into the shower and turned it on, but nothing happened. I then noticed there was a token machine on the wall to run the water, but I didn't have any tokens. I left the room with a towel wrapped round me to look for the landlady and I could hear music playing at the end of the corridor. I opened the door and there was an old record player playing. 'Hello, is there anybody here?' I asked, but got no answer. I turned round and standing there was the landlady with a carving knife in her hand! I proper shit myself. 'What are you doing in my room?' she asked. 'I need a token for the shower, but I couldn't find anyone,' I replied. She walked past me into her room, still wielding this knife, and got two tokens. 'One for you. One for your friend. Will you be wanting lunch?' she asked. 'Er…no ,we're OK thanks,' I answered.

The landlady from hell went back down the stairs and I went back to my room. I'd only been in the shower a couple of minutes when the water stopped running – the bloody thing was on a timer! I put the other token in and finished washing myself. About 12pm, Dave woke up and wanted a shower. 'You've got to ask for a token,' I told him, so he went off to find the landlady. 'Fucking hell, she went mental that we'd used both tokens!' he said when he got back, before showering as quickly as possible.

On our way out to meet Michael, the landlady appeared in front of us. 'Are you going out already?' she asked, blocking our way to the exit. 'Yeah, we're going to meet our friend…' I said. 'First you must meet my family and our other guests!' she told us, pushing us into the lounge. First she introduced this skinny bloke who was her husband – we said 'hello' and he just nodded back. Then there were these two Ukrainian girls who were about thirty sitting in the corner of the room. 'Hello, are you here for the World Cup watching the Ukraine?' I asked. They didn't answer but the landlady said, 'No, they are always here, they never leave!' We got out of there as soon as we could.

When we got to the station, Michael got his ticket and said, 'Are you not getting a ticket?' 'No, Michael – public transport is free for the England fans, remember!' I replied. 'I have not heard of this...if you don't have a ticket they will give you a fine,' he said, but we ignored him and boarded the train when it arrived. After 45 minutes, we saw the guard coming. 'Right, Michael, we'd better move seats quick,' I said and moved through the carriages away from the guard. 'Stan, I thought you could travel for free? Why are we running from the guard?' 'We're not running, Michael, were escaping,' I replied and we burst into the *Great Escape* tune, laughing as we did. By the time we got to the last carriage, Michael was visibly shaking. 'It's alright – if he gets too close we'll climb out the window and run along the roof of the train!' I said. Dave was pissing himself, but Michael looked very anxious.

The guard was within two carriages of us when I slid the window down, and I was halfway out of the window when the train started slowing down to pull into the last station before Rudesheim. We got off the train, walked down the platform and re-boarded. We pulled away from the station and twenty minutes later we were in Rudesheim. We wandered around the old town, then Michael asked, 'Would you like to see Rudesheim from above the town? We could walk up there, it doesn't take long.' 'Now hang on, Michael – you asked us out for the day, you didn't say anything about going fucking hiking!' I said, but Dave reckoned it'd be nice to see a bit of the real Germany rather than spending all our time boozing. 'We'd love to see it, Michael – lead the way, he added.

By George

Michael led us out of the town and into a grape vineyard and then just kept leading us up and up and up. It seemed never-ending and we must have been climbing for about an hour when eventually Michael announced, 'OK, we are here!' I was just behind Michael and Dave joined us about a minute later, wheezing. He turned round to see the view and said, 'That's it? You made me walk up fucking Mount Everest to see a fucking load of hills and a lake? I was cracking up. 'But Dave – this is the real Germany!' I said, taking the piss. 'Fuck the lot of it, I'm going back to the pub.' Dave started to make his way back down the hill.

We found a pub at the bottom of the hill and after a while Dave said 'Michael, I didn't mean to offend you back there, but come on, do I look like I need to walk up a fucking hill? I'm shot to pieces anyway being on the piss with Stan constantly and that nearly killed me.' 'It's OK Dave,' Michael replied, 'I just thought you would appreciate seeing the view. Maybe we should have taken the cable car…?' Dave almost choked on his beer. 'The fucking *what*? Please tell me you're joking!' he yelled. 'No, they do have a cable car, but I thought you wanted to walk so I never mentioned it,' replied Michael, straight-faced. I was in fits of laughter, but strangely Dave didn't see the funny side! I'd just about recomposed myself when Nikki from Tamworth called. Nikki, Nieves and Nieves's cousin Liam were landing in Cologne the next day at 7pm. I said we'd meet them at the train station and hung up. 'Stan, I hate to tell you this but we're in Frankfurt, not Cologne!' Dave said. 'I know, but we can drive to Cologne in the morning, set up camp on the river Rhine again then meet up with the girls when they arrive,' I replied. 'Oh, great – so you mean I've got to drive again? You carry on making plans and then just tell me where I've got to take you!'

I could tell he was being sarcastic so I just said, 'Nice one, Dave, I knew you wouldn't mind.' Dave didn't answer.

It was early evening and we were relaxing in the beer garden when Michael said, 'If we want to get the last train, we'd better leave now – it goes in ten minutes!' We were fifteen minutes' walk from the station. 'Ten minutes? Ten fucking minutes? You've had me hiking up the fucking Himalayas and now you give me ten minutes to get back to the fucking station?' Dave roared. We finished our drinks and ran out of the pub. The train was at the platform when we arrived – we could make it! Or so we thought. We ran through the station but we somehow ended up on the wrong platform, and by the time we'd run back through the underpass and up the stairs the train was pulling away. 'Why the fuck didn't you tell us that the last train was going a bit earlier?' Dave screamed. 'You never asked, Dave,' Michael answered. 'It's OK, there's another train in about one hour,' said a guard standing near us.

We eventually managed to get on the train and after ten minutes, the carriage door opened and the guard walked in and said 'Tickets'. Dave closed his eyes and pretended to be asleep. Michael looked petrified as he handed his ticket to the guard, his hand shaking as he did. The guard clipped it and gave it back to him. The guard then looked at me and said. 'Ticket please?' 'No, you give me a ticket,' I replied. 'No, you give me a ticket…' he said. 'No, you give *me* a ticket,' I demanded. The guard looked at my England shirt, said 'Fucking English!' and walked off.

The following morning after we'd had breakfast, we left the hotel from hell, made our way to the van and headed back to Cologne.

Chapter 12

It wasn't me

When we got to Cologne we went straight to the makeshift campsite by the River Rhine, but there was no one there. 'Fuck this, Dave. Let's go back to the heritage site,' I said. We parked up in the hostel car park this time, rather than on the protected land, and went to get a shower before heading into the town centre.

There were about two hundred teenagers in the main foyer of the hostel, obviously away on a trip. They all made their way into a large canteen area, so we followed them and joined the queue. The dinner ladies looked a bit suspicious as they served the food up to us, but no one said anything – they probably thought we were teachers or something. After eating, we showered and went into town.

At 9pm I got a call from Nikki, who had just arrived at the central station along with Nieves and Liam. I met them at the station and we jumped on the tram with their luggage and made our way back to the heritage park. We threw their cases into the van, got back on the tram and headed back to Cologne and to where Dave was drinking. The pub and was going mental – someone had put an England football CD on and the whole place was singing and dancing. The party was in full swing and everyone was getting completely off their faces, especially Liam who seemed to be getting well hammered a lot quicker than everyone else. At least he was enjoying himself.

I started talking to a German girl from Cologne, whose name was Heidi. She was in her early thirties, with brown hair, and she was quite plump with massive tits. She was with two friends, a really big girl called Anna and another one who looked like Ken Dodd! While I was chatting up Heidi, her friend Doddy was trying to pull Dave. It was hilarious watching Dave trying to hide behind people while this really ugly bird was looking for him – it was the funniest hide and seek game I'd ever seen! Eventually Dave came over to us and said, 'Look, I ain't being funny but I've got to get out of here. Your friend is scaring the shit out of me.' I was laughing my head off, but knew I'd be doing a runner if she was coming after me. 'It's OK, Dave. We shall go to another club and leave her here.' Heidi said. We just about got Liam to understand what the plan was and we left. We came across a gay bar and went in. The bar was to our right and the DJ booth to our left, leaving plenty of space to dance. I was dancing with Heidi when Liam (who to be honest at this point didn't have a clue where he was) charged onto the dancefloor. He was wearing army-style shorts and a vest top and he obviously caught the eye of the DJ, who cut the tune he was playing and put on 'YMCA' by the Village People! Liam started doing all the actions and was soon surrounded by about twenty men, clapping and cheering him on. It was hilarious.

By George

When the song eventually finished, the crowd gave Liam a huge round of applause and all started hugging him. We were cracking up at the all the gay blokes who were clearly trying to pull Liam, who eventually re-joined us. 'These Germans are so friendly, I love them!' he announced. 'Yeah, and they really want to love you,' I said, laughing. We agreed – for the safety of Liam's anus – to finish our drinks and move on to the next club.

Heidi asked if we had been to any World Cup matches, and I told her we'd been to all the England games. 'I was at the game against Sweden, here in Cologne,' Heidi told me. 'How did you get a ticket?' I asked. 'I didn't have a ticket, I work at the stadium!' she answered and produced a FIFA stadium pass. 'Would that pass get you into all of the stadiums?' I asked 'Yes, I think so,' Heidi answered. Anna then went into her handbag and pulled out another pass – she was also a steward. I couldn't believe it.

Later on that night, while Heidi and Anna went to the toilet, we plotted to get our hands on the passes, so Nikki and Nieves could use them to get into the England game in Gelsenkirchen. The plan was that I'd go home with Heidi, and once she was asleep I'd get her pass and head back to the others. Dave was the next part of the plan: he was going to dance with Anna, while the girls would grab her pass from her bag. What could possibly go wrong?

Heidi and Anna came back from the toilet and we took them onto the dancefloor. While we were dancing I glanced over at Nikki, who nodded to indicate she'd got the first pass. The rest was up to me. I asked Heidi if she wanted to go back to her place and she agreed, so we went to get a taxi and Anna came with us. I assumed we'd drop her off before we reached

It wasn't me

Heidi's place, but I was wrong. The taxi stopped outside some apartments and Heidi said, 'OK, this is where I live.' Before I got out of the cab I went to give Anna a peck on the cheek. 'What are you doing, Stan?' she asked. 'Just saying goodnight, like any proper gentleman would,' I replied. 'But this is also my home – we live together!' she told me. Anna reached into her bag to get her keys – but she couldn't find them. She then emptied her bag onto the doorstep, looked up at me and said, 'Your girlfriends have taken them, haven't they?' 'No way – why would they take your house keys?' I replied. 'Because they wanted my pass, and it was attached to the keys!' Anna screamed. 'Stan, how could you? I thought you liked me!' Heidi cried. 'I do like you, and I'm sure my friends haven't taken your keys,' I replied, but she was having none of it. Yet again, thanks to my friends, I too would be having none of it!

When I got back to the others, they'd already put the tents up on the heritage land. 'Fuck me, Stan – that was quick,' Dave said. 'Did you get it?' 'No, Dave. Thanks to you lot not only nicking the pass but her fucking keys as well, I didn't get anything!' I answered.

The next morning we'd all been up for about an hour when Liam fell out of the tent. 'Morning Liam, how you feeling?' I asked him. He answered by projectile vomiting everywhere before collapsing on the floor. 'I feel fucking awful. I need something to sort me out,' Liam groaned and then threw up again. 'No, Liam, what you need is beer and you'll feel OK again,' I reassured him. Liam looked at me as if I was mental, but could see that I was sitting there already drinking Desperadoes and said. 'You got any more of those, Stan?' I gave him a beer and he had about three mouthfuls before being sick again. 'That's great, mate – now keep drinking,' I told him. Fair

81

play to him, he kept drinking through the pain barrier. 'Do you know what, Stan? I don't feel too bad now.' He opened another beer and necked it straight down.

For the rest of the day, we continued to drink, sunbathe and watch the world go by. As we lay in the sun, Nikki said, 'Those rabbits are amazing. People are jogging and riding bikes past them, but none of them run away. Look, some of them are literally lying down.' 'That's because they're special rabbits,' I said. 'They breed them so they're not afraid of humans, it's brilliant how they do it,' I added 'Really?' Nikki said. 'Honestly – go over to them and bet they won't run away,' I told her. Nikki and Nieves approached the rabbits and not one of them moved. 'That's unbelievable!' Nieves said. 'Can we pick one up?' 'You silly cows! Special rabbits? They don't move when you go near them because they've all got myxomatosis!' I said. The girls got closer and saw that all the rabbits had bulging eyes. Most of them were nearly dead. They screamed and ran back to where we were sitting.

About 5pm, Ian arrived after driving back from England with only Jimmy and Lee. 'Where's Paul and Steve? And where's Bruce?' I asked. 'Steve's coming over tomorrow with Luke and Tony, but I don't think Paul's coming back,' answered Jimmy. 'He's got black spots on his tongue and the shakes well bad,' Floppy added 'Fuck me – it sounds like he's got the plague!' I said. 'Where's Bruce, though? Surely he's not missing the match, is he?' I asked. 'Don't mention fucking Bruce to me. We went to pick him up this morning and it turns out his missus found a condom in his shirt pocket and went mental, accusing Bruce of shagging while he'd been away!' Ian said. 'He told her someone must have planted it on him for a laugh, but she didn't believe him. Then she went fucking mental, smashing his computer up and everything,' he added. Dave was cracking up and said, 'Oh, I love it! Bruce has been caught out!'

After we'd all finished pissing ourselves laughing, we went into town to watch Germany v Argentina on the big screens. I think the whole of Cologne came out to watch the match, and the place was buzzing in anticipation. Within an hour, Dave was dressed in a German shirt, German hat and German sunglasses and his face covered in the black, yellow and red stripes of the Germany flag. With his white shorts, he looked like a tennis player on acid. Before the match started, a couple of other boys from our home town, Danny and Adam, turned up having just arrived in Germany – and what a time to turn up. That evening in Cologne, after we'd all watched Germany beat Argentina on penalties, the place went fucking mental. I'd never seen scenes like it and we were right in the thick of the celebrations. We knew this party would be going on all night.

While we were partying with the Germans, Jimmy pulled a German girl and although she was well hammered, she was also well fit, which made the fact that Jimmy had managed to pull her even more unbelievable! She was obviously into Albert Steptoe lookalikes! She didn't speak a word of English, which was probably a good thing for Jimmy because if she'd actually understood his chat-up lines, she'd have been off. Eventually she fucked off without him – she'd obviously sobered up.

By 2am there was only me, Danny, Adam and Dave left and we found an underground club playing hardcore! I slipped into the club without being searched, which was a bonus, as I'd smuggled a bag of Desperadoes in with me. A few hours into our mad raving session, the bouncer approached me and accused me of drinking my own beer. He had a pretty good case; he pointed out that I was the only one in the club drinking from a bottle (everyone else had plastic glasses) and that they didn't sell Desperadoes in there. It was a fair cop, but he told me I was OK to carry on drinking. Top man.

We left the club at about 6am and made our way back to our lovely parkland campsite. As we staggered through the walkway into the park, we saw that a motor had parked on the grass. Behind it was this tent thing that I can only describe as the Tardis. 'Fucking hell, Dave – even Doctor Who's turned up to watch England!' I screamed. We were shouting and singing and the people who were in the Tardis appeared. No, it wasn't Doctor Who – it was in fact Kev, Steve, Mark and his brother in law. I stayed awake for about hour drinking with Kev and Steve, before my body shut down and I fell asleep were I lay on the grass. I'd only been asleep for about two hours when I heard Ian screaming. 'Come on, get up! We're leaving now!' Once everyone was up, we jumped into the motors and set off for Gelsenkirchen and our date with destiny.

Chapter 13

They think it's all over

We got to Gelsenkirchen and went straight to collect our tickets for the match. Once I was out of Dave's van I Georged up, to add to the atmosphere, and I was getting cheered and hooted at by all the England fans in the car park. As I queued for my ticket, you could feel the excitement building all around. When I got to the front of the queue, the girl distributing the tickets smiled and said, 'Here he is, our most famous fan! Keep up the good work, mate!' I walked back to where the vehicles were parked and Lee told us that he'd spoken to Kenny, one of the Army lads. They were at a campsite in Gelsenkirchen.

I jumped in the back of Ian's motor and stood up so I was sticking out of the sunroof. We drove through the car park and the sight of St George got everyone clapping and cheering as I went by singing, 'Keep St George In My Heart, Keep Me English'. I was waving my arms like a conductor until Ian hit the main road and flew around a corner, almost causing me to fall out of the bloody car.

By George

We got to the campsite, where Kenny was waiting for us, and we drove through the site with me still waving out of the sunroof. Loads of people were taking pictures and cheering, and as we approached Kenny's mates I saw a play area with its own rip cord. I jumped out of the car, got onto the rip cord and flew past everyone, raising my fist for a bit of show. But I wasn't slowing down! As I hit the end of the cord, I was literally flying. I tried to make a cool landing, but I ended up going arse over tit and landing in a heap on the dusty ground with everyone laughing their heads off.

After my poor impression of Superman, the lads and I made our way to the stadium. It took about half hour on the tram and once we were there Dave Georged up as well, moaning that his suit stank of stale sweat. I wasn't surprised; it had been in a bin bag for over a week.

As it happened, that was the first and last time Dave ever wore a George suit at an England game, as inevitably England lost on penalties yet again. As I watched Portugal score the winning penalty, my head sank into my hands and my heart sank with it. We were out. It's strange, the numb feeling you get and how you drift into a different world – and then we were brought back down to earth by screaming Portuguese supporters. We hadn't heard a peep out of them the whole game, but now their noise was deafening. The sound of victory…but we wouldn't be making any more noise at this World Cup. I tried to leave several times, but the disbelief of another penalty shoot-out loss had glued me to my seat and my legs wouldn't work. Once I did get up, I could see grown men crying their eyes out all around. It was more like a funeral than a football match, and then it hit me: it was my trip's funeral. My wonderful time was over, it was dead!

They think it's all over

I walked aimlessly away from the ground, and a TV crew who'd filmed me on the way in rushed up to me. 'Could we get you on camera again please?' they asked. 'Yeah, no problem,' I said. 'We don't want an interview,' they explained, 'we'd just like you to walk away from the camera. It'll make for a great exit shot on our programme.' That was my last camera action in Germany: a lonely knight walking away from a lost battle. The reporter yelled, 'Thank you, that was brilliant!' and I turned, looked at her and waved, then disrobed. Wearing the suits had been a laugh, just as Paul had promised, but now it was over.

Just a few minutes after I'd disrobed, I was wandering towards the station to get the train back to the centre when I heard a voice: 'I hope that's not the last we've seen of St George?' I turned around to see my good friend from the F.S.F (Football Supporters' Federation), Ken Malley. I'd sung my World Cup song that I wrote to Ken and the other F.S.F people on the streets of Belfast and they'd helped push my song by putting it in the England v Argentina Three Lions programme. 'Hello Ken!' I said. 'I don't think we'll be wearing these again, mate – we only did it for the World Cup,' I added. 'That's a pity, Stan. We've got some nasty little trips coming up in Eastern Europe and I tell you what, you boys walking around in that gear really takes the edge of the situation and puts a smile on people's faces, even the police,' Ken added. 'I don't know...maybe we'll see. This result ain't even sunk in yet,' I replied and made my way towards the station.

I thought about what Ken had said and realised he was right. Without the suit on I was just an ordinary fan, but as St George everyone wanted to know who I was and it changed how everyone saw me. And after waiting over an hour for the tram, there was only one thing for it: put the suit back on! Soon I

By George

was shouting, 'Excuse me! St George coming through! My horse is waiting for me and he hasn't had a drink all day!' (*I* hadn't, more like!) The crowd parted, it was unbelievable.

When I got to the platform, it was absolute chaos. Every time a tram pulled up, it was packed and no one could get on, then the next rush of people would come down the stairs and it was the same carnage on the next tram. I made my way right to the end of the platform, as I thought it might be easier to get on, but when the next tram turned up it didn't matter what carriage you tried to get on. It was a free-for-all. But something always seems to happen when I'm wearing a George suit, and sure enough when the next tram pulled in I saw that the driver and his colleague in the cab were pointing and laughing at me. I was about to give them the two-finger sign when they said, 'Hello, you are one of the Crusaders from TV? Would you like to ride in the tram with us?' 'Yes, mate! That would be great, cheers!' I replied. It was quality travelling in the driver's cab – the carriage behind me was packed to the rafters and everyone in it looked very uncomfortable. I had a spacious, nicely air-conditioned cab to myself!

After ten minutes, the driver stopped the tram. A load of people got off and walked in front of the tram to get to some bars on the other side of the road. The driver started to pull away and an English fan ran in front of the tram. He didn't look like Superman and as the tram hit him and sent him flying off to the left, it proved he wasn't Superman, just a twat. The driver stopped the tram and he and his colleague jumped off to see if the guy was OK. The bloke was still lying on the floor, screaming, but not as loud as his mates were at the driver. I was certain a fight was going to break out any second. I stood there alone in the cab and then I thought 'fuck it', so I pulled the door to, eased the throttle forward and the tram started to move. I'd only gone about twenty metres when the driver's colleague ran up to the tram, banging on the door and screaming at me to stop. I thought about really opening the throttle up and going for it, but instead I eased it back and pressed the red stop button.

Quite a crowd had gathered by this point and they were all laughing as the driver's colleague hauled me off the tram. I told him I was only having a laugh, but he said he was calling the police. I wrestled free from his grip and ran to the bars across the road – the people having a drink couldn't believe they'd just seen St George driving a tram and a few of them thought it was me who'd run the bloke over. Then the police turned up. The tram hadn't moved since I'd driven it and I could see the driver explaining to the police what had happened, then pointing in the direction of the bars. That was the quickest I've ever got out of my suit and by the time the police got to the bars, the tram-driving St George had vanished. Once again I'd had a lucky escape.

That night we all sat around the camp fire. By this point I was just drinking for the sake of drinking, so I said goodnight to the couple of army lads who were still up and went to sleep in a tent. I was just closing my eyes when I heard a voice screaming my name – it was Dave, and he wasn't alone. He had a Moroccan girl with him. 'Stan, where are you? I've brought someone who wants to meet you,' he said. I got up and she looked me up and down and said. 'Who is this? You told me you knew King George!' 'This is him!' Dave said. 'No. King George has a silver head and red cape,' she said. 'I don't fucking sleep in the stuff!' I replied, and went and got my suit. I only put the tunic, cape and headgear on but her eyes lit up. 'It is

you, King George!' she said – she was like a female version of
Michael from Frankfurt, obsessed with England fans. Dave and
I went to sleep with this Moroccan girl lying between us, and
I hoped we'd given her the (K)night she was after!

Chapter 14

Auf Wiedersehen

I got up the following morning with one thing on my mind: get the fuck out of here and go home. For me the war was over. We said goodbye to all the army lads and to the Moroccan girl, who cried as we left. I actually thought the whole campsite was going to cry. We wound down the windows in Dave's van, turned the stereo right up and played Vera Lynn's song 'Auf Wiedersehen, Sweetheart'. People were waving their arms above their heads as we went past and inside I knew it was over. Or was it?

We got to the junction of the main road and Dave said, 'Can I just say that I've had the best time of my life – all thanks to you, Stan!' 'It's been the best for me as well and wouldn't change a bit of it – well, except having to go home,' I replied. Dave paused as we sat at the junction and I knew what he was thinking. 'Dave, whatever you decide is good with me. Turn left for Calais or right for Munich, you decide!' I said. Then I closed my eyes and heard the indicator ticking – and then I felt the van turn left.

By George

We got to Calais ferry port and we were not alone: there were thousands of cars and people all trying to get home. We queued for two hours before we even got to the passport control booth. Dave gave the official our passports and the customs officer with her asked to check the back of the van. I got out and walked around the back and opened the doors for him. The smell of damp sweaty clothes nearly knocked us both off our feet. He looked at the shit piled in the back and said 'OK, you can close the doors – if you are smuggling anyone, they are already dead!' We then drove to the ticket booths and I went to get our ticket out of the glove box, but I couldn't find it. Dave eventually found it amongst the crap on the dashboard. 'What the fuck's happened to this?' he asked. 'I used that to write my songs on,' I replied. The boarding ticket had bits missing and it was covered in writing. Dave handed it to the woman at the barrier. She struggled to read through the scribbles to see our booking, and then she said, 'I'm sorry, but this booking ran out two weeks ago. I cannot let you board the ferry as you do not have a valid ticket. Drive your vehicle over there and stop.' Dave drove the van to where she'd pointed and we got out, at which point Dave went ballistic. 'That fucking wanker Bruce – he sorted the ferries out and once again he's fucked us over!' 'What the hell are you doing now, Stan?' he asked, as I spread my duvet on the floor, lay down and started drinking Desperadoes. 'If we can't go, I'm going to get pissed right here in the sunshine,' I said, and Dave sat down with me.

About two minutes later, Ian pulled up and shouted, 'What's going on, boys?' 'They won't let us on the ferry. Our boarding ticket ran out two weeks ago!' Dave shouted back and with that Ian, Jimmy and Lee started singing, 'You're not going home, you're not going home, you're not going, you're not going, you're not going home!' before driving off to get their ferry. All of a sudden a Land Rover pulled up and two customs blokes jumped out. 'NO, NO, NO!' they screamed, 'You cannot be here, you must go!' 'We haven't got a ticket,' I explained. 'That does not matter, follow us,' one of the blokes said. We followed him to a queue of cars which were boarding the next ferry. He spoke to the guy taking the tickets and we boarded to go home.

When we got home, we went straight to S.E.C.E.F'S official headquarters, the Social Club, and I Georged up to see what reaction I would get. There were big cheers and handshakes from everyone in the club — their returning heroes (or fools) were back. Two hours later, Lee and Jimmy walked in and couldn't believe we'd got back before them, and at about 9pm Nessa turned up to get Dave. I gave Dave a massive hug and the lump in his throat almost took my eye out. He was leaving to return to normality. As I hugged him, he whispered, 'Why didn't I turn right?' I stepped back, looked at him and said, 'I can't believe you didn't, my friend'.

The next day was great as I got to see all my family again, especially my two little girls, Ellie and Lucy, and of course my Mum. My mum was the most wonderful person in my life and had always stood by me. She'd been so proud to see her son in all the newspapers and on the TV and had loved hearing all the stories from Germany.

The World Cup soon became a wonderful memory, as minds were set on the travels to come, starting with trip to the unknown: Macedonia.

Chapter 15

Here we George again

Two months later and with my George suit perfectly repaired by my Mum's best friend Babs, the now official seamstress to the M.I.G..S, we were ready to tour once more.

We arrived in Macedonia and walked out of the airport to complete chaos. There were hundreds of locals almost wrestling English people into what only I can describe as banger-racing cars. We were having a fag when we noticed Alan Smith, the ex-Arsenal player, being pushed into the back of this old banger. It probably wasn't quite what he was quite used to – and then he had to get out anyway, as the car wouldn't start! A few locals then bump-started it, he got back in, and Smithy was on his way.

We tried to get in a car which did say 'taxi', but were forced to take two of the shit motors which were clearly not taxis. I got in a car with Chubb, Paul and Jimmy and as I went to undo the window, the handle came away in my hand. I looked at the driver but he just shrugged his shoulders. As we drove towards the hotel, we must have passed about six cars that had broken down, with English fans standing at the side of the road. We couldn't work out why the authorities had let such shit-heaps onto the roads, and then we realised they didn't. We drove past a scrapyard filled with motors – the locals were getting any old car that would run, knowing planes from England were arriving and they could make a fast buck off the England fans. I liked their style.

We got to the hotel and asked the driver how much, but he gave me a blank look. He jumped out and spoke to his mate who'd driven Ian, Dave and Lee, and they eventually asked for the equivalent of about forty quid. We paid up and from their faces you could tell they'd made more than they'd paid for the car!

After lobbing our bags in our rooms, I went to reception and asked how far it was to the city centre. 'You cannot walk. You will be mugged or killed! You must take taxi,' he answered and rang two taxis for us. When we arrived in the town, we had to walk through some shitty market and all the boys' faces dropped: it was clearly a mugger's paradise. As the lads walked through cautiously with their hands in their pockets, I crept up behind Ian and put my hand in his pocket. 'What the fuck?' he screamed. Luckily, I knew what would follow and ducked before the big swinging right hand connected. Around the city centre perimeter there was armed security to make sure only the right people entered. We were having a drink when some kids came up to us begging and trying to sell pebbles with paint on. One kid, who was about eight with a fag in his mouth, came up to us holding a baby no older than three months. He asked Chubb for money but Chubb just told him to fuck off. The kid didn't understand and then tried to give Chubb the baby – we were cracking up at Chubb struggling to get this kid to leave him alone.

That night, after drinking all day and telling hundreds of begging kids to fuck off, from nowhere this troop of dancing girls appeared in black uniforms and started putting on a dance show. They were wild cheers of approval from all the England fans and a loud chant of 'Get your tits out for the lads!' Which of course they didn't, but Paul did! He stripped down to his pants and got past the security surrounding the girls. He was wildly gyrating while trying to grab hold of these beautiful women – but it didn't last too long. Three security blokes grabbed him and launched him into the tables. Everyone watching dived out of their chairs and started trying to get the three security geezers. The girls stopped dancing and made a barrier to protect the three bouncers, who were shitting themselves. Meanwhile, Paul picked himself up and continued to dance, oblivious to the fight which he had created.

The following morning was match day and with me and Paul already Georged up, I told the lads, 'We're not getting taxis, we're marching'. Everyone decided to join us. The security on the gate didn't want to let us out and kept saying, 'Taxi, Taxi, Taxi'. We all replied, 'Fuck off, fuck off, fuck off' and pushed past onto the main road. It wasn't far to the city centre, probably a couple of miles, but Chubb was moaning immediately. Walking is not one of Chubb's favourite pastimes. After walking for ten minutes and with the city centre now clearly in sight, we ran out of path to walk on. There was a long bridge leading over a dried-up river, but no room to walk along the edge, so we decided to go under the bridge and come out on the other side. We stumbled down the hill and once on level ground it soon became apparent that we were not alone. There were dogs roaming free, donkeys drinking from a puddle and hundreds of people – this was their home. They looked as shocked to see us as we were to see them. Their houses were just bits of wood with a plastic sheet as a roof. It was unbelievable to see and it really made me think about what we had. But then again they had more than we did – they had donkeys. I approached a geezer standing near the donkeys and said, 'Can me and my mate go on the donkeys?' He looked blank. I then gestured like a jockey riding a horse and held out the equivalent of five pounds. He soon understood. In no time this bloke and his mate were dragging the donkeys through this makeshift campsite with me and Paul on the donkeys' backs. People were coming out of their shacks waving and clapping as George One and Two paraded around. Mind you, the donkeys stank to high heaven! As we dismounted kids were mobbing us and they followed us on the rest of our walk into the city centre.

That night as we walked along the river to the stadium, we bumped into our good friends the Yarmouth Yellows, who as always were well represented. We reached the ground and I soon realised that what Ken Malley had said to me about dodgy European trips was absolutely true. There was a massive police presence and they all looked as moody as anything, until they saw me and Paul. Instantly they started smiling and laughing and shouting things at us – and they completely ignored the England fans who they were meant to be checking. We had loads of photos with the police, who allowed us to hold a couple of batons, pretending to hit them. We eventually got into the ground ten minutes before kick-off and met our mates from Stoke, Rob and Twat (to this day I don't know what his real name is!) Rob was absolutely wrecked and as we were standing with them laughing and taking the piss out of Rob, he fell forward. He was so pissed that he didn't even know he was falling, until his face broke his fall on the concrete steps of the stadium. There was blood everywhere and Rob looked like he'd been hit with a sledgehammer. 'Fuck me, Twat – you'd better get him some help,' I said. We got Rob back on his feet and Twat carried him out of the ground at the back of the stand.

It was half time when Dave shouted, 'Fuck me – it's Michael!' I turned around to see Michael from Frankfurt, still in the same shirt and trousers he wore at the World Cup. 'Michael! What are you doing here?' I asked. 'Hello, Stan – I have travelled by bus from Germany to give you something.' He then produced a paper which had a picture of me dressed as St George at the World Cup. 'You've travelled all this way to give me a paper? Are you mental?' I asked – we couldn't believe it. 'Where are you staying?' Dave asked. 'I don't have anywhere to stay…could I stay with you guys?' We couldn't say no.

While we chatted with Michael, Rob from Stoke came back, still covered in blood, with Twat in tow. 'Did you not get him any help then Twat?' I asked. 'Nah, I just dumped him on the floor outside and got a drink, he's alright now'. He certainly didn't look alright. Never mind – the match ended with England winning 1-0 thanks to a goal from Peter Crouch.

After the match the bars were packed with birds and whereas the night before they didn't want to know us, now they couldn't get enough of the Georges. The bars by the riverside shut at about 1am, but we weren't ready to call it a night yet. We went back to the hotel with Michael, and then Paul and I got out of our George suits and decided we'd head to a nightclub with Jimmy and Dave, so we got the receptionist to call us a cab. We told the taxi to take us to the best nightclub in Skopje and five minutes later, the driver shot down a narrow side street. You couldn't fit a fag paper between the car and the houses and he was going faster than he had on the main road. Dave was in the front, telling him to slow down before he killed us all. The driver just laughed hysterically, then he pulled out a bottle of brandy and took a swig. He offered all of us a drink and we all declined, even me! 'This quick way!' the taxi driver shouted. 'Yeah, fucking quick way to die!' I shouted back. A dog then ran into the road and stopped, dazzled by the headlights. The taxi driver accelerated and ran the dog clean over. He slammed his brakes on, got out, picked the dead dog up and threw it in his boot. We all sat there mortified at what had happened. He got back in the car, looked at Dave and said 'Dinner' whilst rubbing his belly! We drove for another couple of minutes before the car came to a stop. The driver pointed to this derelict looking building and said 'Club', dancing in his seat. We didn't care what this place was like – we just wanted to get out of his car. After we'd paid him, he screamed off, nearly running a group of people over.

We paid a girl at the door and then went up a narrow staircase to the club. It was without doubt one of the biggest shitholes I'd ever been in, and I've been in a few. It was big enough to hold two hundred people at a squeeze, but there must have been five hundred people in there. You could feel the floor bowing beneath you and I thought, well, if I'm going to die I'm going to die drinking so I pushed my way to the bar. I bought four bottles of beer, which cost about £16 – I knew it was overpriced, but we weren't getting a drink anywhere else. We stood together crammed in like sardines, and then suddenly the people nearest to us moved away to be replaced by about

By George

ten blokes, who weren't coming to ask us to dance. We all stood back-to-back looking at these nasty geezers. The one in front of me had 'Hooligan' Tipp-exed on his black shirt, and he pointed at it and shouted 'HOOLIGAN' at me. 'Yeah, that's a lovely shirt mate! Where can I get one of them?' I said. Then a few more of their mates joined them: we were fucked.

We were still close to the bar, so I said 'Boys, do you want another beer?' 'I've still got some here, Stan.' Paul said. 'Yeah I know, but if we're going down fighting, two bottles each will take out more of them than one,' I told him. I turned to the bar and a bloke of about 25 in a smart suit next to me said, 'Are you English, my friend?' 'Yes mate,' I replied. 'And where in England are you from?' He asked. 'London,' I answered. 'My father has many properties in London. Kensington. Knightsbridge,' he told me. 'Your dad is doing alright for himself,' I said, 'what's he do for a job?' 'He is – how you say – the Mafia!' the geezer replied. 'Oh great – we've got every hooligan and his dog wanting a piece of us and now we've got the Mafia to deal with as well!' I shouted. 'What hooligans?' the guy said. '*Those* fucking hooligans,' I replied, but when I turned round to see the group of blokes who'd looked like they wanted to kill us, they'd all gone! 'My English friend – if you are with me then you are my friend and no one will harm my friends,' the son of the godfather said!

I introduced my mates to my new found Mafia associate, Goran. 'Are these your friends?' I said pointing to the three big blokes in suits with him. 'No, they look after me. Would you like a drink?' he asked. 'Yes mate, that would be great,' I answered. He raised his hand to the barman, who came straight over and served him. I never saw any money change hands. One of the big blokes whispered in his ear after an hour. 'I must go now, but can I ask – how much did you pay for your beer before we met?' After I'd told him, he called the barman over and spoke to him. You could see the barman was petrified. Goran turned to me and said, 'Stan, all of your beers will now cost one pound!' 'Top man, Goran – a pound a beer? That'll do me!' I replied. 'No, my friend – one pound for four beers!' He shook my hand and left with his three bodyguards.

The rest of the night was spent dancing and drinking very cheap beer, before we left the club at about 6 am. We were going up to our rooms in the lift when Paul started play-fighting with Dave. Dave was hammered, so Paul easily pinned him. We got out and Paul pushed Dave onto the floor and hit the ground floor button – were on floor 14! We were all laughing, watching the lift head back down with Dave still in it. We laughed even more when the lift came back up and Dave couldn't get out – the lift doors had jammed shut and then the lift buttons didn't work! Dave shouted and screamed as he looked through the little glass window – it reminded me of Jack Nicholson in *The Shining* but without the axe. An hour later Dave finally managed to get the door open and went to his bedroom, only to find Michael asleep in his bed. It wasn't the best end to the evening for Dave and the next day wasn't going to be much better.

We had an evening flight back to Heathrow via Vienna. We didn't have much time for the changeover in Vienna, and as we checked in, Dave said, 'Has anyone got my boarding pass?' 'You had it when we left Skopje, Dave...don't tell me you've lost it?' I said. Yes, he had. Dave spoke to the girl checking everyone's boarding passes, but she informed him that if he didn't have a boarding pass, he couldn't get on the flight. We checked back along the path Dave had taken from the other plane, but there was no sign of it. Chubb and I boarded the plane, and shortly after so did Ian, Paul, Jimmy and Lee – but not Dave. 'What's going on with Dave?' I asked Paul. 'They've told him now everyone's boarded they have one spare seat left and he can buy that if he wants!' Paul answered. Me and Chubb started pissing ourselves. Five minutes later Dave, looking very gloomy, boarded the plane to rapturous applause and many comments. He just stuck two fingers up at the entire plane, which just got a bigger cheer. 'Dave, how much did it cost you to upgrade to your own seat?' I shouted. 'Two hundred fucking Euros!' Dave shouted back before the stewardess told him to be quiet.

Chapter 16

Battleground

Our next match was taking place in Croatia – we landed in Vienna for a connecting flight to Zagreb and had to wait about an hour. We got talking to a MK Dons fan, who told us he was their top boy. While chatting, this Russian skinhead came and stood in front of me and Jimmy and started gesturing us to have a fight with him, shouting, 'Bounce, Bounce!' He then pulled out a bottle of vodka – it was nearly empty but he downed the lot. When he'd finished we gave him a round of applause – he was absolutely wrecked.

When our flight was called, we went to board our plane and Russian Ronnie, as I was now calling him, followed. 'You go to Zagreb?' I said. 'No Zagreb, Moscow!' he struggled to answer. 'OK – you come with us', I said and ushered him towards the check-in desk. We went through the gate with Ronnie following…surely we couldn't smuggle this fellow on the plane, could we? We got to the steps of the plane and Ronnie walked away from us, not back to the terminal but under the plane and towards the runway before a security vehicle spotted him wandering around aimlessly and drove to grab him. Two blokes jumped out and guided Ronnie back to what they thought was his flight. Ronnie had other ideas, though, and decided to smack one bloke before being wrestled to the floor by the other. They then frogmarched him into the terminal. I can only assume that Ronnie didn't get on any flight that day, let alone the one he actually wanted!

After we got to our hotel, we went to a nearby pub. A crowd had made a circle and was cheering and taking pictures – I went to the front and saw my mate Bully from Bromsgrove rolling around on the floor with a bulldog! I dived on the floor as well – St George and a British bulldog? What a photo opportunity! What I didn't notice was that the little black bulldog had taken a liking to my red cape and was doggy-styling my back. Everyone was cracking up as I struggled to push this randy little fucker away.

We were then joined outside by a group of lads from the Yarmouth Yellows, my mate Jay from Brighton, and Andy Jolly. We'd been there about an hour, when this stinking old tramp staggered up to us and started bowing. I got out of my chair, reached my arm out and pretended to knight him, but he thought I was trying to belt him so he went for me. He was stopped by Goff and Nobby from the Yarmouth Yellows, who pushed him away sending him in the direction of the mass of English fans. The tramp waltzed straight into them, giving it all the bowing shit again, and a fan tipped a pint over his head. He threw his arms in the air, turned around, charged up to a England fan and kicked him in the back of the leg. Unfortunately, the fan he'd kicked was none other than the M.K Dons' top boy. He pushed the tramp, who went flying.

Next thing four Old Bill steamed in and gave him a few whacks before lobbing him in the back of the meat wagon.

We marched to the ground and as we got to the front gates, about 100 metres from the stadium, the stewards closed three of the entrances and tried to get all the fans to go through one. What followed was mass pandemonium. Everyone was surging and pushing and we really started to fear for our lives, especially when we saw the stewards battering people who were trying to get through the one open gate. Then, to our disbelief, that gate was closed as well. We were all trying not to get pushed towards the metal gates – it was so bad that even when I took both my feet off the ground I was still carried along by the crush of the crowd. Jimmy got pinned up against the railings and I was powerless to help him. I thought I was going to have to watch one of my mates die right in front of me. People were screaming in pain and in anger, but still they didn't open the gates. An English FA official on the other side of the railings finally ordered them to let people through, which they did, but only after they'd got the riot police in line to give everyone who passed a good whack.

Eventually all four gates were opened and we surged into the perimeter of the ground. Once in I met up again with Andy, Dave and – thankfully – Jimmy. We walked towards the stadium, only to be stopped in our tracks once again, not by a metal gate but by a three-deep line of Croatian riot police! As more fans pushed to get in, another crush started and this time we were being pushed towards the police. They stopped everyone getting through until about twenty fans picked up a crash barrier and charged the Old Bill with it. All hell then broke loose. The riot police started whacking everyone and anyone. All the people at the front were desperately trying to get back, but for most their efforts were in vain. I was only about six feet away from the riot police and was trying to hold my ground when a geezer in front of me turned round, looked at me and said, 'Go on mate, get in there – you're dressed for it!' 'It's not real fucking chain mail, mate!' I replied, but he still pushed me towards the baton-swinging police. I was right at the front and certain I was going to take a good crack over the head when a riot copper raised his baton at me, then stopped. He looked me up and down and then whacked the bloke next to me. It was like what I was wearing had saved me.

All this went on for about ten minutes, until everyone backed off. We were then made to walk single file through the police lines. As I walked through the riot police, one of them put his baton across my chest. I turned and looked at him and he said, 'Nice suit, mate.' It was the copper who'd gone to hit me, but didn't. I smiled and said, 'I like your outfit too, mate!' Then I went into the ground.

The match itself was a disaster, with England losing 2-0. It had been a shit week all round, as the Saturday before we'd been held at home 0-0 by Macedonia.

Chapter 17

Lock in

My next trip was a jaunt to Amsterdam with Ian, Dave, Jimmy, Paul, Lee, Chubb, newly-single Bruce, Kev, Mark, my mate for years Richard Adams, Alan Payne, Dale Evans, Ian's son and my nephew Ricky and his mate Sam. The first day we all got absolutely slaughtered and for a few of the lads it meant that day two, match day, was going to be a non-starter.

We decided that a pub crawl to the Heineken brewery was in order but Jimmy, Bruce, Dale and Richard couldn't even make it to the first pub, never mind the final destination, and they all went back to bed. After five hours and Christ knows how many drinks, we eventually arrived at the brewery. We'd worked out that as the tour cost 10 Euros and everyone got four beers whilst on the tour, it was cheaper than the beer in the bars.

Everyone, even Chubb with his gammy leg, sprinted round the brewery claiming their free pints. When we got back to the start, we each paid another 10 Euros and did it all over again. We went round three times and tried for a fourth, but the security guard saw how pissed most of us were and asked us to leave.

Back at the hotel, Paul and I went to change into our George suits and Dave and Kev went next door into their room. We got into our suits and went next door – Kev had gone and Dave was in the bathroom. Kev had left the key in the door. We pulled the door to, locked it and stood outside Dave's door. When he eventually tried the door, he found it was locked, so he phoned the guy on reception, who agreed to come up and open the door. But before he arrived, we unlocked the door. When he got there, he opened it, telling Dave it hadn't even been locked, and went back downstairs. Once he was out of sight, of course, we crept to the door and once again locked it. Seconds later Dave again tried to get out of his room, but to no avail. He then twigged that someone was behind it and started screaming our names – we wanted to laugh, but didn't. Dave again phoned reception, and again we unlocked the door. The same bloke turned up and again simply pushed the door open. Dave then left with the receptionist, who locked the door behind them. We'd been hiding around the corner and we then noticed a soaking wet mattress, where someone had pissed the bed! So we opened Dave's door, carefully picked the mattress up, changed it with Dave's and put the sheets back on before heading off to meet the others to watch the game.

As we left the stadium after the match, I heard a voice. 'Eh up, Stan! How's it going kid?' It was Doni Flips with Crawf, Robs, Podge, Brownie and Boats, who we'd met in Doncaster after the World Cup. We made our way back to the city and at 2am ended up in a lap-dancing bar. The bar was thirty foot long with stools all along it, and there were topless girls dancing on the bar. The only trouble was, they wanted 10 Euros a pint! While talking to Paul and Crawf, Boats – who was steaming – was also getting a lap dance. I don't know if he even knew it was happening, but when the girl finished her dance she asked Boats for the money. But Boats was skint. She then signalled to these two huge bouncers, who flew over and grabbed Boats. 'Crawf, your mate's in a bit of bother!' I said. Crawf tried to sort the situation out, along with the other Doni lads. It soon became clear that if the boys didn't pay 80 Euros for Boats, who the bouncers had now let go of, he'd be taken outside and given a right good hiding. They had no choice: they couldn't let their mate get a kicking.

While they tried to sort out this first bit of trouble, however, Boats was busy creating more havoc! He'd ordered 10 pints of lager, and Paul and I were cracking up. That round was going to cost 100 Euros! The rest of the Doni boys went fucking mental, but it made no difference. The bouncers were still holding the first lot of cash they'd given them, and they didn't even ask Boats, they just told the Doni boys they'd get a kicking if they didn't stump up another hundred for the beer. Reluctantly they paid, then they all wanted to take Boats outside and give him a beating themselves! But by this point Boats had disappeared.

I got up the following morning and charged into Dave's room, and to my delight, there he was fast asleep on the pissy mattress we'd put there the night before. He never mentioned the mattress – he must have thought he'd pissed the bed himself!

Chapter 18

Jesus was born here

'WHERE THE FUCK ARE YOU?' Chubb screamed down the phone at me. 'I'm out at a club. Why, where are you?' I drunkenly asked. 'I'm outside your fucking house, waiting to take you to the airport!' 'I'm on my way, Chubb, see you in ten,' I quickly answered. I'd gone out with my mate Ben and had completely forgotten about Chubb picking me up. We were off to Israel.

When we arrived, Paul and I put the telly on while we unpacked. To our surprise, there was my mate Preston doing an interview from a bar. 'And how many beers do you intend to drink today?' the interviewer asked him. 'Probably twenty or more. Come and see me again in three hours!' he answered. 'Twenty beers? I'll bring an undertaker with me if you drink that much!' The interviewer was shocked. 'Bring who you want, as long as they get the beers in,' Preston replied. Good man!

We made our way down to the two main bars by the beach, the Buzz Bar and Mike's Bar. There was a carnival atmosphere and why not, England was in town. The whole of Tel Aviv had either come to join us or had come out in their cars just to get a look at us. The Israeli people loved the English fans and more than helped make that pre-match party day go off with a bang. With the party in full swing, temperatures in the eighties and gorgeous girls everywhere, there was only one thing missing. It was time for me and Paul to George up.

We got changed in the toilets of the Buzz Bar. When we came out we were mobbed like never before. They went crazy for us. We spent the next six hours doing TV interviews and photo shoots, and they even arranged to film us on a passing open-topped bus while thousands of people lined the street. I felt like royalty.

After the game, which was awful and ended 0–0, we headed back to the Buzz Bar. The place was going mad, with English and Israeli fans alike singing and dancing along to an England CD that just kept repeating all night. We were still dressed in our St George outfits, and when we looked across there was someone we recognised, but we couldn't remember where from. He was mid-forties and he was having the time of his life. He saw us and signalled for us to join him. 'Alright boys, long time no see! Well, actually, you two are impossible to miss. Where's the other George?' he said. 'You mean Bruce? We're meeting up with him in Barcelona,' I answered. 'I don't mean to be rude, but I can't remember your name or where we've met,' I added. 'You don't remember me? I was in Nuremburg with you boys on the cricket pitch,' he told us. 'Oh, you were in our cricket team?' I asked. 'No, I was the bloke driving my limo across your cricket pitch! It's me, Dex!' he said and burst out laughing. 'I fucking knew I'd seen you before, it was you trying to steal our thunder!' I said, laughing.

111

By George

We stayed with Dex for about an hour, and then Chubb appeared absolutely wetting himself. 'What's so funny Chubb?' I asked. 'It's, it's, it's…' he managed before he started laughing again. 'Oh for fuck's sake, it's *what*?' 'It's Lee, he's pulled a bird!' Chubb said and burst out laughing again. We left Dex to see exactly what the hell Lee had pulled. He was getting off with this tall blonde bird, who was a couple of inches taller than him. We couldn't see what Chubb found so amusing, but then we realised: she was a dwarf and she was so small that she had to stand on a chair to reach up to Lee's face. We started cracking up and when Lee lifted her off the chair and she dragged him to the bar, we were in fits of laughter watching a munchkin leading the Michelin man.

Later on, Ian told me and Paul that he was going on a trip to Jerusalem at 7am, and asked whether we fancied it. 'Fuck that, I'll only just be getting in then and I don't think they'd appreciate us turning up in our George suits. We may get our heads cut off!' I told him. Ian left and went to bed. We eventually rolled in at about 5am, but still had no intention of going to Jerusalem.

The following day, Ian went to Jerusalem on his own (God help the Palestinians, I thought. What'll they think when they see the size of him? Goliath has turned up again for a rematch?) and we met Dave and Lee before they went home. When the boys had gone, I headed down to the beach with Paul and Chubb. A waiter came over and took our order, and as we were all up for a session we ordered a pint, a shot and a cocktail each. I went to use the public toilet and there were two tramps outside. One of them, who stank of alcohol and piss, asked me for some money. I thought 'Fuck it, I'll probably end up drinking with him later' and gave him the equivalent of £10.

He tried to cuddle me, but I resisted the offer and went in the toilet. When I came out, the tramps were knocking the shit out of each other (it wasn't the greatest scrap I've seen, but certainly one of the funniest) and I couldn't understand why. Then two police officers turned up and broke the two tramps up – apparently they were fighting over some money that someone had given them. I thought it was a good time to leave and re-join the lads.

A few hours later, I asked Chubb a question, but he didn't answer me. 'Are you listening, Chubb?' I asked. 'No – I'm watching that bird wank that bloke off on the beach!' Chubb replied. Paul and I looked and she was indeed wanking him off, with her hand up his baggy shorts. The girl looked straight at us, smiled a sexy smile and carried on, looking at us while she tossed the fellow off. Eventually they got up, she gave us a cheeky wink, and they walked away. 'Right, I'm off to the toilet,' Chubb declared. 'Yeah, to knock one out no doubt!' I said.

After spending five hours on the beach, it was time to go back to the hotel to get changed for another night out. The waiter brought over our bill and gave it to me. 'Fuck me, are you sure that's right? That's about £350 in English money!' I said. 'Yes, you and your friends have had many drinks today,' the waiter said. To be fair, he wasn't wrong.

After getting changed we staggered into Mike's Bar and met up with Kev from Luton. 'Where's Ian? He hasn't gone home, has he?' Kev asked. 'No, he's on a day trip to Jerusalem on his own. We couldn't be bothered,' I answered. Five minutes later Ian walked in grinning from ear to ear, chest out. 'Alright you fuckers, what sort of day have you had?' he beamed. 'You don't want to know, it's been mad, we've been on the piss all day.' I told him. 'What about your day? How was Jerusalem?' I then

113

asked – he was clearly itching to tell us. 'Mental, fucking mental!' Ian answered. I doubt if one of the most historic Biblical sites in the world had ever been described by anyone as mental before, let alone 'fucking mental', but it had now. 'Oh yeah mate? What did you see?' I asked, trying not to laugh. 'Everything. Fucking everything. I even saw the hospital that Jesus was born in!' We all started laughing. 'The fucking *what*?' I managed to ask, tears rolling down my face. 'The hospital Jesus was born in, I saw it!' Ian said, seriously. 'Let me get this right – that was all bollocks about the inn, the stable and the manger? He was actually born in a proper hospital?' I asked and burst out laughing again.

There was a cracking atmosphere in Mike's Bar that night with everyone partying hard. Chubb, who'd kept up with me all day, couldn't go on and went back to the hotel. I walked back with him as I needed to get some money. I headed back to the bar, but never made it as Paul and Ian came sprinting towards me. 'What's going on?' I asked. 'We're off – we ain't gonna be here tomorrow, so were skanking the bill!' Ian said, and off they both ran. There was actually no one chasing them – the bar people probably hadn't even noticed them go – and it then hit me. 'Hang on, you bastards! I want another drink but I can't go in there or I'll get lumbered with the fucking bill!' I shouted. But they were gone and so I had to join them, ending both my night and my time in Israel.

Chapter 19

Not a pretty sight

We arrived in Barcelona for the Andorra match and the one thing that instantly hit us was the temperature. It was fucking freezing. We'd come from 80 degrees in Israel to sub-zero temperatures in Spain. Dave, Lee and Jimmy arrived with Lee's mate Johnny from England and Bruce was due to join us that evening. Once we checked into our hotel on Las Ramblas, we headed up to Barcelona's stadium to do the tour. The tour was decent and the stadium impressive, but none of it compared to the club shop – or should I say what happened in the club shop.

Paul and Chubb came across a mannequin modelling a skintight Barcelona body top. Next to it was a picture of Ronaldinho wearing one of the tops, and we wondered whether if Chubb put one on he too would magically have the figure of Ronaldinho. We urged Chubb to try on the top and he duly obliged. He got some strange looks as he stripped to his waist in the middle of the club shop, and some even stranger looks as he wrestled to get the top on. Eventually we squeezed him into it and we were in hysterics – it was so tight that it was pulling his arms in so he looked like a trussed-up chicken. After we'd taken a few photos of poor Chubb, he went to take the shirt off. But there was a problem: the shirt was well and truly stuck!

I was on the floor laughing, as he struggled and tried to get the skintight shirt off his bloated body. After five minutes, Paul tried to help along with two other England fans, but as much as they pulled it was stuck tight. Chubb started panicking and said it felt like the circulation was being cut off from his body, but we could do nothing but laugh at the situation. One of the English guys who'd tried to help then went to the payment counter and came back with a female assistant. After a few more attempts, Chubb lost it, screaming, 'Just cut the fucking thing off!' The assistant took Chubb to the desk, got some scissors and started to cut the shirt up the side, just enough so Chubb could then free himself. The assistant then told him he would have to pay for the top. Chubb went mental. 'Pay for it? I didn't want it in the first fucking place and I certainly don't want it now it's almost fucking suffocated me!' he raged. Once again I was crying with laughter. The girl then called the manager, who was joined by a security guard. They weren't letting Chubb go without paying, so eventually he parted with 25 Euros and the girl put the ripped shirt in a bag for him. Chubb was not impressed.

We went back to Las Ramblas and found a little Irish bar. After a few hours, Ian got talking to some lads who claimed to be top hooligans – of course he then wanted nothing to do with us, as we cramped his hooligan style. I decided to teach him a proper lesson, so I went to the bar, ordered a pink cocktail with all the trimmings and even a lit sparkler, and took it to him. 'Here you go mate, here's your drink,' I said. The four blokes he was with looked totally disbelieving – this big geezer had been telling them all about his so-called hooligan days and now he was drinking a pink cocktail! It was priceless. 'Fuck off, that ain't my drink!' Ian shouted. 'Well it's what you've been drinking all day,' I said and walked off. Strangely enough, Ian joined me very soon after.

All the lads went to eat in the Chinese restaurant opposite the Irish bar, but I stayed. I got talking to a guy who asked me if I was on my own. 'No, mate,' I said, 'I'm with a group of lads, we all get on really well and they're all over there having a Chinese.' I pointed to the Chinese restaurant, and all of a sudden we saw Ian throwing a screaming Jimmy out of the door. Dave then came flying out, having a go at Jimmy, with Lee and Paul trying to hold him back. Chubb casually headed in my direction. 'They're the mates I was telling you about,' I said to the guy. 'Yeah, they seem to be getting on great, don't they?' he replied and started laughing. When Chubb eventually hobbled to where I was, he told me that Dave had been taking the piss out of Jimmy, going on about him looking like Albert Steptoe. Jimmy had then said something about Dave's ex-wife, Dave went for Jimmy, and it all kicked off. 'What was the food like, though?' I said, laughing. 'Yeah, proper nice and a show for afters!' he replied. The lads carried on screaming at each other until eventually they were shepherded away in the direction of the hotel.

Chubb and I were following our still-screaming mates when all of a sudden a massive fight broke out between about eighty people. It turned out they were Newcastle and Sunderland fans. It wasn't too long before the Spanish police came in, battering anyone they could. We got in close to the building, well out of the way – or so we thought. After watching the scrap we went to walk away, but this dirty copper came up behind me and swiped the back of my legs, taking me off my feet. 'What the fuck was that for?' I said, but he just hit me again around the back of my thighs. He then went to strike Chubb, but he didn't – he must have thought he'd already hit him as he was limping.

Once we got back to the hotel Ian, Paul and Lee took Dave into the foyer to try to calm him down and it was mine and Chubb's job to control Jimmy outside. Jimmy was standing with us and then said, 'Don't hold me back.' We let him go. He charged into the foyer where the boys were holding Dave, screaming, 'Here I am, Dave!' He flew towards Dave with fists raised. 'And there he goes…' I said as we watched Jimmy run right onto Dave's fist, which sent him skidding on his arse across the tiled floor. We were cracking up.

We left the hotel and went to the Port Olimpic bars, where we met up with the Doni boys: Flips, Robs, Crawf, Podge, Yeom, Beaky and Boats. Dave was still having a row with Jimmy and Ian tried his best to calm him down, until Dave said to him, 'You fucking Allsops are all the same, think you can say or do what you want!' Ian threw an almighty punch at Dave and missed. He was about to throw another, but was grabbed from behind by Bruce. 'Whoa, whoa! What the fuck's going on?' Bruce asked. 'You better get him out of here before I kill him, Bruce,' said Ian. Dave, meanwhile, had disappeared. Then I actually took a look at Bruce, and said 'What the fuck are you wearing?' We were in Barcelona, it was almost midnight and about -3 degrees…and Bruce was wearing a t-shirt and shorts with flip flops! 'I'll tell you what I'm wearing – or rather why

Above: The figurehead was a George instead!

Below: I'm a George…get me out of here!

Above: Who said we aren't posh?

Below: 'We're on the camels and we're havin' a laugh!'

'BINGO!'… Shit, wrong game…!

Above: The Caped Crusaders.

Below: We are the M.I.G.S.

Next, we conquer Everest…

Above: S.E.C.E.F. and the M.I.G.S. on tour.

Below: Who gave them nutters real swords?

Above: Who wants to wake up with a horse head in their bed?

Below: The bar is that way…!

Above: Back Door Jack at it again…

Below: Come and have a go, if you think you're hard enough!

I'm wearing it. It's that bastard Lee. I text him before I left and asked what the weather was like and he told me it was boiling, no need for jacket or jeans. And I believed him! I'm fucking freezing and what do I walk into? World War 3.'

The whole club soon warmed up when a couple of sexy dancing girls wearing just bras and knickers started dancing on the raised platform. They were encouraging men to get up with them, but they didn't anticipate that most of the men would have less on than they did, especially Flips. Crawf, Robs, Yeom and Beaky had their tops and trousers off, but Flips was stark bollock naked! He dived on the stage to dance with the sexy dancers, but they were not impressed. The bouncer – who looked like Emperor Ming from *Flash Gordon* – came over and ordered Flips to put his clothes back on.

The drinking went on all night, and we all had these red shiny wigs on, which we regretted in the morning as the dye from the wigs was all over our faces and wouldn't come off. We came out of the hotel looking like we'd contracted some kind of skin disorder overnight, and bumped into Bruce. He was still in his t-shirt, shorts and flip-flops, but he was carrying a load of shopping bags. 'One hundred and fifty fucking quid, that's what it's just cost me to get a jacket, a jumper, some jeans and a pair of trainers. One hundred and fifty quid!' he complained, and we all cracked up.

After another session that day, we made the long haul up the hill to watch the match, but I don't know why we bothered. At half time, standing there in the freezing rain, we were drawing 0-0 with Andorra, fucking *Andorra*. The England fans were booing and screaming at the team and Steve McClaren, it was a joke. It must have worked, though, because we ended up winning the game 3-0.

By George

After the game, we went back to the hotel, Paul wanted to get out of his George suit and Ian said he wanted an early night. Me and Paul went down to the foyer where Lee, Johnny and Chubb were waiting. The others had gone straight to the Port Olimpic to meet the Doni lads.

When we got out of the lift, there was an almighty row going on between the hotel manager and a bloke who was the spitting image of Steven Gerrard, his girlfriend and this really stocky Colombian. 'Stan, this English couple have just got back and found that fucker in their room!' Johnny said. The Colombian tried to make a bolt for it, but I jumped in his way and forced him back. The Colombian looked me up and down and started saying something to me, but I couldn't understand. 'Did he get anything?' I asked the Steven Gerrard lookalike. 'I don't know, we walked in and he was going through our stuff,' he answered. The Colombian then started shouting his mouth off at me, clearly asking if I wanted a fight. I pushed him again and he came at me, pushing me back into the people behind me.

The girlfriend of Gerrard's double was screaming at the hotel manager to call the police, and he told her the police were already on their way. The Colombian understood the word 'police' and made an almighty effort to get past me and Johnny, but we once again forced him back. Johnny then turned to Lee and shouted, 'Go get the General, Lee!' At first I thought he meant the car from the *Dukes of Hazzard*, but he was actually referring to Big Ian. Lee shot up the stairs and Ian came down soon after. 'Right, what's going on Stan?' Ian asked me, so I told Ian what had happened. He listened to what I told him, then shoved the Colombian almost through the wall. 'Come on then, you thieving cunt!' screamed Ian. The big stocky Colombian had met his match. The manager screamed at Ian, 'No fighting! I call the police.' The Colombian tried to bolt past Ian, but Ian once again nearly put him through the wall – there was no way out for the robbing bastard. The Colombian then took a different approach; he started talking quite softly and slowly to Ian while undoing his jeans. A few people thought he was going to pull a weapon out on Ian, and I suppose in a way he did. He pulled his jeans and pants down to his ankles, grabbed his cock in his hand and started waving it at Ian, while using his other hand to simulate a blow job in his mouth. Everyone stood shocked at this display, as did Ian, who then turned to me and said, 'What do I do, Stan? He wants me to suck his cock!' I just started laughing – poor Ian was bang up for a scrap with this fellow, but the sight of this bloke waving his cock about had completely thrown him.

The old bill turned up and we all headed down to the Port Olimpic, while Ian headed back up the stairs. We went into the bar we'd been in the night before and the two well fit dancing girls immediately dragged me up there with them. I didn't put up a fight – well, why would you? Two almost naked beauties all over me, just because I'm in my George suit. I was in my element until Flips, who was wrecked, joined me on stage, once again completely naked. Emperor Ming was on the scene immediately and told Flips to get dressed, but this time Flips ignored him and carried on dancing. After several requests, the bouncer threw him out, being careful not to touch certain parts of Flips' body. Our motto has always been 'If one goes, we all go' so the whole group made a mass exodus to the door, where by this time Flips had at least put his pants on. We went to the next bar and this woman came rushing up to me and said, 'You come into my bar and drink! You will bring many people to my bar like that [referring to my costume]'. She dragged me to the bar and shouted at the barman, who gave me two free bottles of beer. What I didn't realise was that it was payment for my dancing skills – for my *pole* dancing skills. She forced me up onto a platform about five feet high, with a pole from floor to ceiling, and told me to start dancing. The sight of me above everyone sent the crowd wild. I hauled myself up the pole and tried to spin round it, fairly unsuccessfully I might add, but the crowd loved it.

I'd been trying to pole dance for about ten minutes, when Flips managed to pull himself up there. He lost his balance and grabbed me to steady himself, but all he actually achieved was to push me straight off the platform and into the crowd, who unfortunately were not ready to catch me. I remember falling forwards and thinking 'This is going to hurt when I land'. Fortunately for me, my fall was cushioned by this Spanish girl, but unfortunately this sent her crashing down onto the floor. I bounced up unscathed, but she lay there knocked out. Her boyfriend started trying to throw punches at me, but he was held back. My main concern was this poor girl, but I seemed to be the bar manager's main concern. She pushed me back towards the platform and then got two of her bouncers to pick the girl up and carry her to the outside seating area. 'You keep dancing and people will keep drinking!' she shouted. I started to feel like one of those bears in Russia, where they electrify the floor to make it look like it's dancing. 'Fuck this, I'm off.' I said and left with my entire group.

There are about a dozen bars and clubs down the Port Olimpic and during the course of the night for one reason or another we managed to get thrown out of all of them, except the very last one. There weren't many people in this bar, but the music was good and there was a hen party from London in there who were as drunk as we were. While I was gyrating with one of the girls, I saw Bruce in deep conversation with one of her mates at the bar. After an hour of being bought endless drinks and half a bouquet of roses, the girl went to the toilet. I then approached Bruce. 'Alright mate, how's it going? Better still, will she be going with you?' I asked. 'It's in the bag, Stan, she's coming back with me and I'm gonna give her a right good pounding!' Bruce claimed. But then the girl who was 'gonna get a right good pounding' came out of the toilet and started dancing around with Crawf. 'What the fuck? She's mine!' Bruce said. He raced over to her and tried to pull her away, but she stayed dancing with Crawf. Bruce trudged back to the bar and sat down looking as miserable as sin — well, he had just spent a fortune on this girl and got completely blown out.

Chapter 20

The idiots abroad

We arrived at our hotel in Estonia, which had advertised itself as being 100 yards from the best beach in Tallinn. After checking in, I headed straight for the beach with Paul, Dave and Ian. Chubb said he wanted to have a shower and he'd catch us up.

We got to the beach and our jaws hit the floor; we'd never seen so many beautiful women in one place at one time and there were no blokes, apart from the odd England fan. 'I've died and gone to heaven!' I said. 'Fuck this – I can't stay here,' Dave said. 'I've just got over a mini stroke and looking at all these women all day will give me a full-blown heart attack!' Dave had indeed only suffered a suspected mini stroke a few weeks earlier, and had been told to take it easy and not get overexcited. A difficult thing to do when you're surrounded by gorgeous women! Strangely enough, though, Dave stayed put.

We perched ourselves on a wall by the beach – we had the perfect view and it was nice and close to the bar, which was selling flavoured cider at forty pence a can. We'd been on the beach wall watching the women for about two hours when Chubb come ambling towards us. We all looked at him and burst out laughing – he was dressed like he was about to play tennis, with a brand new bright white top, bright white shorts, white socks pulled up to his knees and very bright white trainers. 'Fuck me, lads, it's Beasey Borg!' I shouted and Chubb told me to fuck off. 'Where have you been, Chubb? You've been ages.' I asked. 'Well, I had a couple of wanks before I came out...' Chubb replied. 'You dirty cunt,' Paul said. 'You're gonna think I'm an even dirtier cunt when you realise I spunked all over your pillow!' Chubb retorted. That was what I loved about Chubb – he had such a dry sense of humour and he could get away with saying anything to anyone, well you couldn't hit a cripple could you!

Dave and Ian went into town and after two more hours on the beach, we also made our way towards the centre. The hotel manager had told us which bus to get, but after one stop an old drunk got on carrying a bottle with no label on it. I don't think it was tap water. He sat himself down next to Chubb, who was struggling to take a clean breath of air as this bloke stank of piss. 'Oh for fuck's sake, mate, let me out – I can't fucking breathe, you smelly cunt!' Chubb said to the old drunk. We were cracking up, even more so when the drunk looked at Chubb and offered him a swig of whatever he was drinking. Chubb tore into a torrent of abuse at this geezer, but the bloke didn't speak English and just smiled – he only had two or three teeth. We pulled into another bus stop and the drunk jumped up and got off the bus. Six people in bright orange jackets jumped on; they were ticket inspectors and we didn't have tickets. I tried the old 'No, you give *me* a ticket' trick, but it didn't work. They marched us and about four locals off the bus and lined us up against a wall. Surely we weren't going to be up for the firing squad just for jumping a fucking bus, were we?

The transport police asked us all for identification. The locals showed them theirs and Paul and Chubb showed them their passports, but I had nothing so they made me stand away from the others. Paul and Chubb started singing 'You're not going home, you're not going home, you're not going, you're not going, you're not going home.' Very funny. The transport police started writing out charge forms and giving them to the locals. Once given their sheet, they were allowed to leave. Finally the only ones left were me, Paul and Chubb. They processed Chubb first and then tried to do Paul. Paul read what the charge sheet said. He had been fined £15 and if he didn't pay he'd be due in court in a week's time. Paul reacted in his usual way: 'Fuck that, I ain't going to court! I'm going home in two days!' He threw the piece of paper he'd been given back at the police and tried to grab his passport. The police then grabbed Paul to restrain him and tried to get him to sign the paper, but Paul was having none of it. I saw a taxi coming towards us and flagged it down, and me and Chubb dived in the taxi and told the bloke to drive. As we looked out of the back window, we could still see Paul wrestling with the transport police, but I didn't care: I was making my escape.

The taxi dropped me and Chubb near the old town, where we spotted Ian and Dave drinking outside a bar in the square. About half an hour later Paul turned up calling me and Chubb all the names under the sun, which we just laughed at.

The bar was packed with English fans, and I started asking if anyone had any spare tickets. These three guys from Leeds had about forty! 'Where did you get that lot from?' I asked. 'This

Estonian bloke came in here about two hours ago trying to flog tickets. We gave him a couple of whacks, pinched all the tickets he had, then told him to fuck off,' one of them explained. 'How much do you want for them? I need three,' I asked. 'Here, mate – you're English, you can have three for nothing,' he replied, before checking through the tickets to find three together. I bought him and his mates a beer and went to join my gang. Twenty minutes later, the old bill turned up being led through the bar by some Estonian bloke. He took the police straight to the three Leeds boys – it was the guy they'd nicked the tickets off. The Estonian had told the police that these blokes had beat him up, so they'd come to arrest them, but when one of the Leeds blokes told them that he was in the bar trying to sell match tickets, which is illegal to do in Estonia, the police then nicked the Estonian bloke and took him away to a chorus of, 'One-nil to the England'.

We were starving by this point, so we went to a pub that sold food and found that they also brewed their own beer on site. The waitress brought our beers over and gave us some menus. When she'd gone, an English couple sitting behind us said, 'Would you lads like to finish our meal? We've just ordered too much food.' There was a whole great big lump of pork that hadn't been touched. We accepted and they passed us the food, got up and left. Ian wasted no time in cutting the pork up for us all to eat – I think a meal always tastes better when it's free! We'd had about three beers and a lovely meal in this brewery, when we asked for the bill. The waitress handed it to Ian and said, 'There is your bill, sir, with your friend's bill as well.' 'What friends?' Ian asked. 'The couple who were sitting there,' she then said, pointing at the table where the English couple had been. 'They weren't our friends. We'd never met them before

By George

in our lives,' Ian said. 'We ain't paying for them!' 'Well I'm afraid they didn't pay for anything and you were eating with them, so you must pay,' the waitress explained. Ian went fucking ballistic. The lovely English couple had turned out to be a pair of wankers, but fair play to them for pulling it off. Eventually the waitress went and got the manager. He grabbed Ian's shoulder and said, 'You ate the food, you pay for the food.' Ian stood up. The manager, who was about five and half foot, shit himself. 'That's it – call the police,' he said. We eventually had to agree to pay our bill – along with the extra for the pork joint – and left.

When we got outside, Ian said, 'If I ever see them fuckers again, I'll kill him and his missus. No one skanks me and gets away with it!' The thing was, he meant every word of it, so all of us deep down just hoped we never bumped into them again.

The next day, me and Paul went to play for the England fans' football team against Estonia. The Estonian TV crews turned up and were all over us like a rash, as we were dressed in our George suits. We had a representative from the British Embassy and some guy from the Estonian FA as guests of honour and they walked down the assembled line of England and Estonia players, shaking each player by the hand. It felt like a proper international. When we sang the English National Anthem, the hairs on the back of my neck stood up. I was so proud to be representing my country at whatever level and sang our National Anthem at the top of my voice. We lost the game 2-0, mainly because we were playing against a load of teenagers and most of us were in our thirties, but even though we'd lost, I loved playing for my country and told them that I'd definitely play again.

That night we had a strange walk to the stadium, with loads

of people coming down from their flats to get photos with us.
We didn't mind, as most of them seemed to be the fit birds that
we'd been watching down at the beach. Some mothers even
got us to hold their babies!

We got into the ground and the free tickets we'd got off the
Leeds boys were three rows back from the England dug-out,
giving us a wicked view of the match. England won the game
3-0. We went back into old town and Ian left us at about 2am,
but called me half an hour later. He told me there were loads
of Russians outside the hotel fighting with baseball bats and
that they'd already done over a few English fans. We took his
advice on board and just stayed out all night – well, even
baseball-wielding nutters have to go to bed at some point! At
4am, Preston turned up and he was hammered. While we were
having a drink together, this English bloke got up and fell
straight through the white picket fence outside the bar. The
barmen came out and went mental, but Preston stood up and
said, 'Have you got any tools? I'll fix it.' The barman left and
came back with a bag of tools and a power drill, set it all up and
left Preston to fix the fence. I wasn't certain it was a great idea
giving Preston a fucking power drill, looking at the state of
him, but he managed to fix the fence and got a few free beers
for his handiwork. Shortly after Preston had done his Bob the
Builder act, we were joined by Dex who was absolutely
steaming. On several occasions he almost broke the fence again!
By 6am the bar staff asked us all, along with these Finnish birds
we'd been chatting to, to leave as they were closing. One of the
Finnish girls had taken a liking to Chubb and kept rubbing his
belly and cuddling him like he was a big teddy bear. As we went
to say our goodbyes, she gave Chubb a kiss on the cheek.
Chubb hugged her so tight I thought her eyes were going to

pop out and it looked like he had no intention of letting her go, but eventually she freed herself and left.

The next day we got up and went to wait for the taxis that we'd booked. The first cab pulled up and Dave and Ian went to get in it. A woman approached them and asked Dave if they were going to the airport and could she and her husband share the cab. Dave told them they could. We got the next taxi and met Ian and Dave outside Tallinn airport. Dave looked anxious and I asked him what was wrong. 'You know that couple who just got a taxi with us? Well they were only the same fucking couple that gave us that lump of pork and fucked off!' Dave said. 'You're joking, does Ian know?' I asked. 'No, he didn't recognise them. I dare not tell him, he'll go off his head!' Dave said and we both agreed to keep it to ourselves.

Ian even said goodbye to them as they went through the customs desk. 'They were sound people, weren't they Dave? Absolutely sound.'

Chapter 21

Up in smoke

We all met up at 11am at the Whitehouse pub in Luton to go and watch England v Estonia at Wembley. There was Paul, Chubb, Lee, Ian and his two sons Ricky and Sean, and we were also joined by some of my other mates, who didn't do the away trips – Michael 'Paddy' Harte, Russell Clark, Garth, Justin, Scotty and Mole. Ian left early with Sean, leaving me to look after Ricky.

After the pub we went to the off licence. Everyone bought at least eight cans apiece and I got a bottle of Sambuca and a bottle of red Aftershock. We stood on the station platform, taking it turns to do swig after swig, and by the time the train turned up we'd done half a bottle of each and we then carried on going once we'd sat down on the train. We'd finished the lot before we got to West Hampstead and when we got off the train, everyone was smashed to bits and it was only 1pm.

As we stood outside the Railway Tavern, I shouted, 'Where's the fucking bag?' 'What bag?' Paul asked. 'The bag with the three

By George

George suits in, my camera and the fucking match tickets!' I told him, but no one had seen it. 'Your England rucksack, Stan? Is that the bag you've lost?' Justin asked. 'Yeah, did you pick it up?' I asked. 'I put it in the luggage rack on the train, did you not get it down?' 'Well of course I fucking didn't or I wouldn't be saying it was lost would I?' I said. I couldn't believe it: there were three St George suits, a £200 digital camera, five match tickets and a packet of fags in that bag – an expensive thing to leave on a train that was now heading to Brighton. Someone told me to ring British Rail, but at that point I was too fucked to give a shit and said I'd ring the lost property department on Monday.

On the Monday I spoke to someone and when I gave them a description of the bag and said what train I'd been on, they told me to ring the Metropolitan Police. So I called them up and was then put through to the bomb squad. After I'd given them all sorts of details about me and my friends, they told me that my bag had been flagged as a security risk by the guard on the train, and that the bomb squad had been called as it was a suspect item. The guy from the bomb squad then said that they'd stopped the train somewhere on the way to Brighton and blown my bag up! 'Did you not think to have a look in it, mate?' I said. 'Yeah, because that's a really good idea with suspect bags, isn't it?' he answered. I had to give him a description of the items that were in the bag, and he advised me to claim off my house insurance. 'But I haven't got a house...' I said and left it at that.

Chapter 22

You're not going home

Chubb had arranged to pick me up at 5am on the Tuesday morning – I hated these early pick-ups. I had a word with my mate Mark in the Rising Sun, who agreed to throw me a leaving do on the Monday night, even though I'd be coming back on the Saturday. But it meant that Chubb could pick me straight up from the pub at 5am and drive me and Paul to Heathrow, where we met up with Ian, Dave, Bruce, Jimmy, Lee, Dale and Alan.

We arrived in Moscow and it was about –5 degrees; everyone was frozen, especially me. I'd left my coat in the Rising Sun and had managed to arrive in Moscow with a Sweden football shirt on. The Russians were looking at me and I could tell they were thinking 'If he's wearing that here, it must be fucking cold in Sweden'.

We got to the Cosmos hotel and it was packed to the rafters with England fans. Some young lads from Luton came up to me and said they needed my help; the young man on the check-in desk had told them he was part of the Spartak Moscow youth firm and he wanted a 20-versus-20 no tools fight in a park near the hotel. He then told them that if they didn't turn up, he would come and batter them in their room. 'Well, Michael, I think you'd better get on a recruitment drive! I think I might be too old to fight for the youth team but go and ask Lee, he'll be up for it,' I said jokingly.

About six of us left the hotel and went to the off licence. We dared not go out on our own, as there were cars full of Russians waiting to jump the English. But we made it back to the hotel with four trolleys of beer, vodka, alcoholic energy drinks and even some Babycham for Chubb. We put all the alcohol in mine and Paul's room and left the door ajar, so people could get in when they wanted, and headed down to the foyer. I went back up to our room a bit later to get myself a couple of refills, and when I pushed the door open, there were three blokes skinning up and having a drink. I'd never seen them in my life. 'Alright mate, help yourself to a drink!' one of them said. 'Cheers, I think I will, as it's my fucking drink and my fucking room,' I told them. 'Alright mate, you must be Stan, we've heard all about you,' the guy who'd offered me a drink said. I shook their hands, grabbed a few drinks and headed back to the foyer, leaving these strangers to carry on.

The foyer was packed with English and while we were there, four right moody-looking Russians came up and spoke to a group of ten English fans. 'We are Spartak Moscow top boys, we have fifty boys outside. You get your best fifty and we fight, yes? No weapons, just fair fight, yes?' the mean-looking fucker said. One of the English lads leaned forward and said, 'Listen mate, were fucking English and there *is* no fair fighting where we come from.' He dashed a bottle over this bloke's head and it all went off – these four Russians, hard or not, were getting kicked to fuck. The hotel security came wading in whacking the English, which gave the Russians enough time to make an exit through the front doors.

No one expected what happened next. The Cosmos had erected this enormous Russian flag using red, white and blue balloons. It looked very impressive, but not any more. Two English fans had decided to run through the balloons, which were all linked together by string. As they just continued to run the whole lot came down and everyone in the foyer started jumping up and down on the balloons – it was hilarious watching the security whacking people with batons as they were trying to burst the balloons.

I went back up to my room for a refill, after the Battle of the Balloons had ended, and found Preston and quite a few others happily getting stuck into the drink. As my room was being used as a bar, I knew I wasn't going to get much sleep that night, so I stayed up drinking until they were about to open the breakfast room. I was waiting at the breakfast room doors with a few of the other lads when we were joined by a load of Japanese tourists. The hotel foyer had all these paintings hanging up that were for sale, and the tourists were looking at them. 'Do you like this one?' I asked them, 'I'm very proud of this picture – it's one of my favourites, but let me show you another that I painted which I think you will really like,' I added. 'You are the artist?' they asked me. 'Yes, I'm the biggest artist you'll ever meet,' I said – yeah, the biggest piss artist! As I showed them 'my works' they asked me how much they were. 'Well, this one is $200, a very good price for a very fine piece of work,' I told them. The guy who was very interested asked, 'Do we pay you?' and I was about to tell him that I was joking, when I stopped. 'Yes…then just go to the reception desk, tell them the number of the painting, and they will arrange the packaging.' He then spoke to one of his friends and said, 'OK, we will buy your painting!' Got his wallet out and gave me $200.

I took the money, shook his hand and thanked him before jumping into the lift and going up to my room. I was sure that I was going to get nabbed, but nothing ever came of it and the picture I 'sold' was still hanging on that wall when we left. We all struggled out of bed, Dave more than the rest of us. He'd got back from Florida on the Sunday night and had then got a plane to Moscow on the Tuesday morning. Never one to miss out on an opportunity to take the piss, I emptied Dave's water bottle and filled it with neat vodka. When he woke up, Dave took a massive swig and then almost threw up everywhere – we were wetting ourselves at the sight of him!

At the match me and Paul were joined by a guy called Jeff, who wears a horse's head to games. He was the same guy that Ian had seen in Jerusalem, when he nearly got shot for wearing it. The press loved getting photos of me on Jeff's back, like St George on his noble steed. Dave, who was sitting behind us with Ian, commented, 'There are more characters in the front row than there were at Disney!' We had then been joined by someone dressed up as Shrek in a England kit, and Bruce who had come as a Russian tank commander. A win in Russia meant at least the play offs, as the team had put a run of five wins together since the draw in Israel, and at half time there was no reason to think we wouldn't qualify as we were 1-0 up. We were already celebrating and making plans for the following summer, but the Russians had other ideas as they came out fighting in the second half and won the game 2-1. We were back in the shit.

The next day, we drank all afternoon in Moscow with two lads from Birmingham who were lugging their bags around with them as they were flying home that night. I offered to put their bags in our room until they were ready to go, and they agreed. We got back to the Cosmos and sat in the foyer drinking with the two Brummie lads, whilst Paul and Jimmy – who were both wrecked – had the fiercest, longest, maddest play fight in history. They were throwing each other across the tiled floor, rugby tackling each other, diving into the hotel foliage – if you didn't know them you'd have thought it was a proper scrap.

I saw Dex at the bar and went to speak to him. Meanwhile, the two Brummie lads asked Paul for the room key, as it was time for them to go and they wanted to get their bags. Paul went to our room with them. Twenty minutes later, the Brummie lads came up to me. 'Alright boys, did you get your bags OK?' I asked. They told me that when they'd got to the room with Paul he could barely stand up, never mind put the key card in the door. They offered to help him, but he turned nasty and whacked one of them, telling them to fuck off! Eventually they managed to get the key off Paul, got into the room, and got their bags. Paul then chased them down the corridor and dived into the lift, still swinging punches. The lads pushed Paul out of the lift and the last they saw of him, he was rolling around on the floor. I apologised and went up to the room to see Paul. He was all over the place. Bruce told me he'd found Paul outside the lifts on his back like a tortoise, unable to get up. We put Paul in Dave's room so Dave could keep an eye on him, as he was obviously a danger to himself.

By George

I woke up on the Friday to the sound of someone kicking the shit out of my bedroom door. I opened it and it was Paul. He started tearing the room apart: 'What the fuck are you doing?' I asked. 'I can't find my passport!' Paul yelled. We helped him look for it, but it was nowhere to be found. I wasn't surprised; he'd had it in his back pocket the day before, and he'd spent most of his time rolling around fighting with Jimmy and the two Brummie lads. We rang the British Embassy, who told us we needed a form from the Russian police to allow Paul to get a new visa to get out of the country. Paul went to the police station with Alan, Dale and Bruce to report his lost passport. The smell of stagnant piss in the station was unbearable and the lads were glad when the police said they would come to the hotel to take Paul's details later in the day. Paul told the rest of us to go out without him while he waited for the cops, as it was our last day there.

The police came after six hours and gave Paul the form he needed. The trouble was that the British Embassy couldn't do anything until Monday, as the visa could not be issued over the weekend, Paul was fucked and had to stay.

The following day Dave flew out about five hours earlier than the rest of us; he'd changed his flight as he wanted to get back home to watch England in the Rugby World Cup final. It had cost him £500 but he reckoned it was worth it. Meanwhile our flight back to Heathrow had a stopover in Milan, but when we went to check in, the airline representative told us that our flight was delayed and we would miss our connection. Luckily they'd managed to get us all on a direct flight with another company back to Heathrow, and we got back to London just as the rugby final was kicking off. We'd got back an hour later than Dave, hadn't missed a minute of the game and we hadn't parted with £500! Paul eventually got back to England the following Wednesday.

Chapter 23

Snow way

A big group of us travelled to Vienna for the friendly against Austria, including the Doni boys. We'd been drinking all day in an Irish bar when the heavens opened – not with rain, but with snow. None of us had seen snow like it – within an hour it was a couple of feet deep, and we decided it was time to play. What could be better? England away, on the piss and two foot of snow! We emptied out of the pub and joined in with what had to be the biggest snowball fight in history.

After an hour or so and with our hands freezing, we came across a bar which had a sign outside saying 'FREE BEER until 11pm'. We all bundled in, but it turned out the free beer was only served in half measures. We were quite happy to drink halves, though – especially free halves. As we got tanked into the free beer on offer, this woman came up and asked us all if we were red, yellow or green. It took a while to work out what she was on about, but apparently there was a sticker system: red meant you were off limits, yellow meant you might be up for it and green meant you was free and easy. Of course we all slapped green stickers on our shirts.

I went up to a woman near the bar who was also wearing a green sticker – she was Austrian and seemed quite chatty, but she never really put out any signs that she was interested. I looked to see where the boys were and Jimmy, Flips, Robs and Yeom were sitting at a table being chatted up from both sides by all these Austrian men. The penny dropped: I realised it was a gay nightclub and we were all wearing green stickers. I went to get another free drink and noticed the DJ blowing kisses at me. 'Should I stay or should I go?' I thought, but the offer of free beer was enough to sway it. Even if we'd have to spend the next few hours brushing off the advances of all these gay men.

The friendly match didn't matter to us; it was the game being played the day after that we were all interested in. Israel were playing Russia in a qualifier. We needed Israel to get at least a point, or England were all but out. The Irish bar we watched the game in was heaving and they had to shut the doors about two hours before kick-off. Israel beat Russia 2-1 that night and we were back on to get to the play-offs at least. All we now needed was a draw at home to Croatia the following Wednesday.

That night all the England fans had the party of a lifetime and celebrated long into the night – all thanks to Israel. The celebrations proved to be short lived, though, as England famously failed to beat Croatia and went down 3-2 at a rain-soaked Wembley. We were out, it was over.

Chapter 24

Right before
my eyes

M e, Chubb, Paul, Bruce, Ian, Jimmy, Lee, Ricky and my big drinking mate Meatloaf made the trip to France – the only reason most of the boys went was because they'd already paid for it before the disaster against Croatia at Wembley.

We got to our hotel only to be told they were double-booked, but they'd sorted it for us to stay in a different hotel. The hotel we'd booked was very modern and clean and the one we ended up in was a right old shithole, but we'd stayed in worse. We headed out into Paris and found a bar doing a happy hour on all cocktails until 7pm. Within an hour the barman was letting us mix our own drinks, as he could barely make a vodka and coke. It all got very messy very quickly and Ian was the first to bail out of the drinking.

We all left when the prices went up and went off to find somewhere cheaper. Me and Chubb somehow lost everyone and ended up on the Champs-Elysées. It was a good opportunity to George up, and of course I did. As we walked up this famous road, I told Chubb that I was going to run across to the Arc De Triomphe. I think deep down he was hoping I would get hit by a car, but I dodged and staggered and managed to get across the seven-lane roundabout in one piece, even pulling off some matador moves with my red cape on the oncoming cars. 'Right, now you've got to do it!' I shouted back. I never in a million years expected him to even attempt it, but he did and it was hilarious. As you know by now, Chubb is not the most graceful on his feet and cars were swerving like fuck to avoid hitting him. The sound of all the horns beeping was deafening, but Chubb kept going and he made it.

'I'm never doing anything like that again!' Chubb said. 'I think we'll have to…' I replied. 'Why's that?' Chubb asked. 'We've left the fucking bag on the other side of the road!' I told him. We ran back together, which was even worse than the first time, but we lived to tell the tale. I couldn't understand why Paris was known as a romantic city – I'd take a girl there if I wanted to dump her, not propose to her, as it was a stinking dump in most areas from what I could see.

We were well late getting to the ground for the match and as I queued in my George suit to get in, there were many other fans around who'd also arrived late. Once again, a surge started. I got pushed right to the front and was heading straight for these police wearing masks. Fuck! They had tear gas sprays and I caught the full blast of the smoke in my face. I couldn't see a thing and all I could hear was people screaming and horses running past me. I somehow managed to grab hold of a tree and didn't let go. I still couldn't see a thing and the pain was getting worse, when a heard a voice speaking English with a French accent. 'Open your eyes,' the stranger said. 'That's fucking easy for you to say mate, you ain't just been gassed!' I replied. 'No, you must open your eyes,' he repeated. As I opened my eyes, I could see that this bloke was holding another can of spray, right in front of my eyes. At first I thought I was going to get gassed again, but the guy the said, 'Antidote, Antidote.' I didn't care at that point. I couldn't be in any more pain than I was, so I let him spray my eyes and within seconds, my sight returned. 'I can see! It's a miracle…!' I shouted jokingly. The guy and his mate then proceeded to spray me in my mouth, ears and nose – basically all over my face. I thanked them for helping me, but an English fan ran up and screamed, 'Don't thank those cunts, it was their lot that fucking sprayed you in the first place George!' When I turned around, the two undercover cops had gone.

The game was awful and as we walked away Meatloaf turned to me and said, 'Fuck me, Stan, I feel right pissed off having watched that shit and I got my ticket for free. Fuck knows how you lot must be feeling after having paid £60!' While we were having a drink outside a bar, a tramp came up and started hassling Chubb. Chubb told him to fuck off, and the tramp obviously understood him. 'Me fuck off? No, you fuck off,' the tramp said and pulled Chubb backwards off his chair. We went to jump in and stop it, but it was so funny watching Chubb and this tramp having it – well, if you could call it that. I think you could say Chubb just about got the better of him, as it was the tramp that walked off first, but it was a good laugh watching them.

Chapter 25

St George of the Caribbean

Four of us went to Tobago – me, Ian, Meatloaf and a bloke called Timmy who lives in my village. We arrived in Tobago and me and Ian were one of the first off of the plane, so we went to get our bags. The conveyor belt had gone down so they were just dumping the bags on the floor outside the hatch. Four female passengers were trying to climb through the hatch to see if they could find their bags. 'Oh look, two really strong men to help get the bags through!' one said happily. 'No chance, love, it's every man for himself and I'm gagging for a pint!' I replied, and we grabbed our cases and went to get the transfer bus.

I phoned Timmy, who told me it was chaos in the baggage reclaim; there were people out on the runway trying to find their bags. I told him we'd meet him at the hotel. When we arrived, we were greeted with trays of rum punch, but by the time Meatloaf and Timmy turned up about two hours later, it was all gone as us England fans had drunk it all. Meatloaf was not impressed. We went down to the pool bar and had a few drinks, and then the four of us walked along the beach to the nearest town, which was Plymouth. When we got there, I approached one of the locals and asked him where the nearest pub was. He was in his mid-fifties and told us his name was Pumpa. He was with a younger bloke who was sitting in a sort of bus shelter, but he never spoke. While I chatted with Pumpa, I could see the lads behind him backing away and Ian said quite anxiously 'Right, come on Stan, it's time to go now. Come on!' I'd have been happy to chat with this eccentric local, but I said my goodbyes and ran to catch up with my mates. 'What's the fucking hurry?' I said. 'The hurry was, Stan, that the other geezer behind you seemed to have the right hump with you talking to his mate. He was walking towards you with a fucking great machete in his hand!' Timmy said. I hadn't noticed! As we wandered around Plymouth we saw that most of the blokes had machetes – we decided it wasn't the best place to start a fight.

Eventually we found a bar – well if you could call it a bar. It was basically someone's house with the front wall removed, a load of makeshift chairs, and a tiny bar in the corner. Meatloaf and I sat on this battered fabric sofa with springs shooting up our arses. Timmy sat on a plank of wood resting on four beer crates, and Ian took the only plastic garden chair. CRASH! Ian sat down and all four legs just snapped, leaving him on the floor with beer all over him! He jumped up, trying to look cool, but it was all in vain – the rest of the people in the bar were cracking up.

As we walked back to the hotel Timmy, who was wearing flip flops, stubbed his toe and dislocated it. He screamed as he tried to put it back in place, and we were screaming with laughter. Back at the hotel pool we got chatting with three other England fans: two Leicester City fans called Roger and Rob, and a QPR fan with bright ginger hair called Pete. As we sat drinking, we were constantly hassled by locals trying to sell us stuff. I told them what we really needed was a doctor, as my mate had a broken toe. 'No problem, man, I'll go get the doctor,' one of the locals said. He came back with this bloke who barely had a tooth in his head. 'He will fix your friend's toe for a small fee,' the guy explained. I was more than happy to pay just to see this fellow yanking poor Timmy's toe about. Timmy on the other hand wasn't so keen, but he eventually agreed as he was in so much pain anyway. The doctor put something on Tim's toe that smelt like petrol and started to pull and yank. Timmy was screaming at first, but whatever that fluid was, it had numbed his toe and the doctor was free to do his stuff. After ten minutes, he told Timmy his toe was fixed and put a bit more smelly stuff on it. I paid him about £5 and he left. I sat down opposite Timmy and asked him how his toe felt. 'It's…it's like a burning sensation now, and feels like it's getting hotter,' Timmy claimed. Of course it was – I'd sparked my lighter and found that not only did the doctor's ointment smell like petrol, it burned like petrol too. Timmy, realising his toe was on fire, quickly jumped up and dived into the pool to extinguish it. Everyone was cracking up and even Timmy saw the funny side of it as he climbed out the pool. He said he'd get me back, but he never did!

Whether it was the doctor's handiwork or my version of a deep heat treatment, Timmy was now walking about just fine. It was that good, in fact, that he and Ian hired a pedalo. The boys went really far out and could barely hear me shouting, 'Look, it's Captain Pugwash and Seaman Stains!' We soon got bored watching them become an ever-smaller dot on the horizon, so we went back to the bar. We'd been drinking for about an hour when we heard a siren and watched as one of the hotel staff raced to the beach to climb aboard a jet ski. Twenty minutes later the guy on the jet ski returned, towing Ian and Timmy. They'd gone out so far that they were too knackered to pedal back. It was only thanks to a passing fishing boat spotting them waving for help that someone was alerted to their crisis. They were both fucked from their re-enactment of *Pirates of the Caribbean* and immediately fell asleep on their sun loungers. I went to reception and got a piece of card and some scissors. I cut out the letters C.U.N.T and returned to the two sleepyheads. They were both lying on their backs, so I placed the letters on Timmy's stomach and let the hot sun do the rest. Timmy woke up about two hours later – when he stood up, the cardboard letters fell to the floor, but the word was clearly still visible on his stomach.

While the boys had been sleeping, a dumpy little English bird who was on her own had sat with us. When Ian woke up he found he had an instant connection with her: food. She told Ian that if you went into the dining room, they would cook you hamburgers no matter what time of day it was. Eventually the pair couldn't resist any longer and they both headed off to the dining room to feast on burgers. Ian came back to our room, rubbing his very badly sunburnt belly after his burger indulgence. I asked if he wanted some after sun, but he said, 'I don't use cream, I'm a man!' even though his skin was more cooked than the burgers he'd just eaten.

At night the hotel got in a load of live entertainers, but there was no need, the place was full of English fans who had been drinking rum all day and were providing enough entertainment of their own. A fire-eater was the first of the hotel's acts up on stage and he needed a volunteer, so we persuaded Pete (who was also badly sunburnt) to get up. The fire-eater swigged some liquid, then blew it out of his mouth, lighting it. Then it was Pete's turn. Pete swigged the flammable liquid, but rather than blowing it out, he coughed and spluttered, virtually setting his head on fire. The fire-eater threw a wet blanket on Pete's head to put out the flames, and when he removed it, we could see that Pete's eyebrows had also been removed.

Next up was a female singer who got me – dressed in my George suit – and a bloke called Dave, a West Brom fan, who'd been drinking on his own all day and did not have a clue what he was doing, up with her. I sang along with the woman as instructed, but Dave had other ideas and started stripping off. The crowd were cheering wildly, encouraging him to go all the way, and he did before trying to get the singer on the floor. The singer's manager raced over and pulled Dave off her, with Dave shouting, 'Get your own bird mate!' He made another grab for the girl and the hotel staff marched him away, to rapturous applause from the crowd. The singer walked off, leaving me with the microphone, so I started singing one of the songs I'd written for the previous World Cup. The crowd loved it. I sat back down with the lads, who'd been joined by this very skinny fellow – a West Ham fan called Andy. As we sat there, a local came up and asked us to try some of his home-made rum. I took a swig and passed it on, and around the table it went until it got back to me. I took another swig and passed the bottle on again. 'No, man, you can't drink it like that, you'll die, man!' the local guy said, but the bottle was passed round until it was half empty. It got round to Andy again and he just kept taking swig after swig and never passed it on – he finished the rest off on his own. Thirty minutes later and with some limbo dancers performing, Andy stood up and wandered over to the pool. He then started pissing in the pool – we cracked up watching Andy relieve himself, but the security guard was not so amused. He charged over and grabbed Andy, who stumbled and fell into the pool, dragging the security guard with him.

The next day, we had an early flight to Trinidad to watch the match. I got straight into my George suit and headed for the airport with Ian, Meatloaf and Pete. We dropped Pete at another hotel near the airport, where he was meeting his mates, and the three of us walked from there to the airport. On the way we came across a load of chained up bulls in a field – 'Ian, this would be a great photo! St George the matador!' I said and went into the field, approaching the bulls with my red cape held in front of me. The lads cracked up as one bull ran at me – it was stopped by its chain, which was six foot long and attached to a metal bar in the ground. I decided to try another. I walked towards this haggard-looking brown bull, which looked at me but didn't even move. I got a bit closer and then he charged, and I quickly realised that this fucker had a much longer chain than the others! I ran like fuck, waiting for a horn to go up my arse, but after about thirty feet the chain tightened and stopped him in his tracks. Any further and I was fucked. I decided to give up on the idea of chasing bulls, and with my heart racing, we went to the airport and on to Trinidad.

After the game, we made our way back to the airport. Ten minutes before we were due to fly, an announcement was made asking for about six passengers to report to the check-in desks. I was one of them. We asked the girl at the desk what the problem was – she couldn't tell us, but she took our boarding passes and went off into the back office behind the desks. 'Fuck this, I've got my ticket and I ain't missing this flight!' I said, grabbing my ticket, which she'd left on her desk, and leaving the other people standing there. I went through security and into the waiting area, but everyone had gone. I ran to the door leading to the runway and showed the girl standing there my boarding pass. 'If you're quick you might still make the plane!' she said and let me through. I needed to be more than quick – the little forty-seat plane was taxiing down the runway! I started running as fast as I could (maybe not as quick as when the bull was chasing me, but fast...) and luckily as I ran along (still in my full St George suit) Ian looked out of the window and started shouting for the plane to stop. It eventually came to a halt about fifty metres away, the stewardess opened the door, and the steps came down and I climbed aboard.

We got back to the hotel at about 1am and I could hear a machine-gun sort of laugh; it was Timmy. Still laughing, he introduced me to a young English couple that he'd been out with all day. 'Fuck me, it's Chubb!' I said – this guy was the spitting image of Chubb only twenty years younger. Chubb's double told me that Timmy had been smoking weed with the locals and hadn't stopped laughing since. Timmy doesn't even smoke fags, never mind weed. The only person not laughing was Meatloaf, who said, 'It's alright for you fuckers laughing, it's me that's got to sleep in the same room as that bastard!' 'No it's alright Meat, I'm staying out tonight, we're going for another smoke. Are you coming?' Timmy said. 'Am I fuck! I'm going to bed and locking the fucking door.' We'd only been gone a day and Timmy had turned into a Rastafarian.

The next day I Georged up again – we'd booked a tour that involved a bus trip round the island and up to the rainforest and a boat trip around the hotel bay. We went to the capital of Tobago, Scarborough, and everyone got off the bus to look round some market stalls. I wandered down a side alley and drank Jamaican moonshine with the local pissheads. Well, it was gone 10am! The bus then took us to somewhere called Fort King George! I was in my element. There were American tourists there who thought I worked at the fort and I was happy to give them a guided tour, making it all up as I went. After my tour, I got a round of applause from the Americans saying it was very educational! The bus then headed to another aptly-named place: Englishman's Bay. Englishman's Bay had very few people living there and as I stepped off the bus, the locals came rushing over to me thinking that I was a priest. After a couple of blessings on some of the children's heads, we got back on the bus and continued our journey around the rainforest. Finally it was time for our boat ride back to the hotel bay. For most of the trip I was stood at the front of the boat, like that bit in *Titanic*. Then we stopped to do a bit of snorkelling, which wasn't the best thing I've ever done. I put my snorkel on and jumped overboard, only to find that the weight of the George suit pulled me under. I was drowning. The guy driving the boat got a long hooked rod and pulled me to the safety of the boat – I didn't try that again! The boat pulled into a secluded bay, where we had a barbecue. I got out of my suit and went snorkelling again for two hours, unaware that the blazing sun was burning the shit out of my exposed back. Before we left, we were treated to one last jaw-dropping experience – Timmy in an England thong! He got changed behind the boat and then came out dancing in the sea. It was one of the most hideous sights I've ever seen and still have nightmares to this day, and then a woman on the trip commented on how large Timmy's packet was. I tried not to look, but couldn't help noticing Timmy constantly adjusting himself. When we were back on the boat, the truth behind what was in Timmy's trunks became apparent. 'Has anyone seen my socks?' Meatloaf said. 'Here you go, Meat!' Timmy announced and pulled a bunch of socks from his thong. Once again, Meatloaf was not impressed.

We got back to the hotel at about 7pm and my back was on fire. I asked Ian if he would put some after sun on me, but he point-blank refused and went to get Timmy. As I lay on my front, almost unable to move, I could hear the boys laughing as Timmy poured cream all over me. As the cream touched my skin, you could practically hear it sizzle, but it felt great and it was such a relief. It was only after Timmy had put half the bottle on me that I realised what was so funny. Timmy had applied the cream wearing only his England thong and Meatloaf and Ian had been taking pictures.

Chapter 26

Gotta pick a pocket or two

The first World Cup qualifying game was against Andorra, again in Barcelona, and on this trip I was accompanied by Ian, Chubb, Paul, Jimmy, Bruce, Lee, Scotty, Meatloaf, Mole Morris, Justin, Dave, Garth and his brother Colin. When we got to Barcelona we did almost exactly the same as we'd done before: we drank all day in the same little Irish bar and ended up down the Port Olimpic. We latched on to a hen party and drank with them; there was only one decent-looking bird out of the lot of them and I was trying my hardest to pull her, but while I was chatting her up, I noticed that Paul and Justin were wrestling with each other in the club. Paul pushed Justin onto the raised dance floor, grabbed his ankles and dragged him off the stage backwards. Justin's head thudded against the tiled floor and he was out cold, so Scotty picked him up and threw him over his shoulder. The girl I was talking to lifted Justin's head to check him. Whack, whack, whack – Justin hit her three times in the head, then passed out again.

Scotty took Justin outside and made him lie on a sofa, while I was trying to make sure this girl was OK. 'What the fuck did he hit me for?' she asked. 'I don't know, I don't think he knew what he was doing...' I answered. 'Are you ok?' 'Yeah, I'm fine – but I dropped my drink when he hit me,' she said. 'Don't worry, I'll get you another one,' I told her – well, I was on the pull, the least I could do was buy her a drink. She went outside to where Justin (who was semi-conscious by this time) was lying, while I went to the bar. As I approached her with our drinks, she was leaning over Justin, telling him to wake up. Justin opened his eyes and looked at the girl...smack! She thumped him in the face with her right fist, so hard that she briefly knocked him out again! She then turned to me and said, 'Think that makes us quits, don't you?' before taking her drink and going back to her mates.

The following morning I woke up and went to see Justin, who had a lovely black eye. Then Paul came running in. 'Have you got my wallet, camera and phone?' he asked. I just shook my head in disbelief. Once again Paul had lost something! It could only happen to him...or could it? Colin then came in and told us he'd had his wallet and phone nicked. The state they were in the night before, they'd have been easy pickings for a pickpocket, especially Paul who I'd found asleep on the street at 6am. Paul spent the day ringing his bank and his phone company, while Colin just got back on the drink. He'd regret that later on.

Mid-afternoon, Mole turned up. 'Where have you been, Mole?' I asked. 'I went for a walk down the beach and while I was there I entered a sandcastle competition and I came third,' Mole replied. We were in fits of laughter. We'd just about calmed down when he then told us that after the competition, he'd had a little kip on the beach wall and had then discovered that some bastard had nicked his phone while he'd been asleep. That was it: everyone was crying with laughter again.

At about 11pm, I asked if the boys were up for going to Port Olimpic, but none of them were except Colin, who at this point was slaughtered. We left the lads and went back to the hotel, as Colin wanted to change his shirt. After ten minutes Colin still hadn't appeared, so I went to his room – he'd got as far as taking his top off, but he was fast asleep on the sofa. I tried to wake him, but he was unconscious. As I went to leave, I noticed a puddle of water beneath Colin's feet: in that short space of time he'd not only passed out, but pissed himself as well. I shut the door and went back to the Irish bar with the boys.

Chapter 27

I am the one and only

Only me and Ian went to Croatia, and we had agreed to play for the England Fans' team. We met up with the rest of the team, which included my mates Dane and Keith from Torquay, Aide from Coventry and Simon from London, at 6.30am to travel to the match. Ian already knew the Traitor in Black, Dave Beverley – the Scunny fan who refereed our games. Once everyone was there, we got on a really nice coach and had a police escort. Two police motorcyclists escorted us to the edge of Zagreb and we were then escorted the three hour journey to Zupanja by a police car.

Zupanja was 250km from Zagreb, right on the Bosnian border. It had been the site of the first ever football match to be played in Croatia, which was why we were also playing there. When we arrived, we pulled up to a quality little stadium and were greeted by about two hundred people all waiting to see the England team. Before we played, the head of the Croatian FA turned up with heavy security. The

By George

security wasn't for him, though; it was for a football. Not just any football, but the football that was used in that very first game, on that very pitch. The Croatian FA had brought the football from the sports museum in Zagreb and everyone went up to have their photos taken with it before kick-off. I strode up to the top man and started having a chat with him. 'Any chance I can have a hold of that ball, mate?' I asked. 'But of course, my friend,' the Croatian official said. I picked the ball up and sort of got a feel for the weight, then looked over at Ian and the other England boys. They all looked strangely worried…well, they knew me didn't they. I looked at the crowd in the stand behind Ian and the boys and shouted, 'Lads! Shall I drop kick it into the crowd?' The boys shouted 'No!' but I dropped the ball…and then quickly grabbed it again, turning round to grin at the Croatian FA official, who had turned white as a sheet. 'Only joking, chief!' I said, handing the ball back to him.

We all got changed into our kits and I put my George suit on. As the team went out to warm up, I did a lap of honour, applauding the now well packed stadium. The whole town had shut down, including all the schools, and the crowd were applauding and cheering me on. I was proper buzzing. After we sang the National Anthems, our names were announced to the crowd. 'Number eight, Stan Stanfield!' I raised and clapped my hands again towards the main stand and was once again cheered and applauded back. I was without doubt the crowd's favourite. At half time as we walked towards our dug out, the crowd started singing 'Stan! Stan! Stan! Stan!' Of course I saluted my adoring fans; I loved it.

The game ended 5-1 to Croatia, with Ian scoring our only goal. As the referee blew his whistle for full time, the crowd invaded the pitch and I was mobbed by all the Croatian children. While they surrounded me, I had one question that I needed to ask these school kids: 'Where's your mums? Go get your mums!' Some of the women we'd seen watching the match were as fit as you like and I was hoping to meet some of them and maybe take things into extra time. But the kids didn't understand what I was asking, so I just signed autographs for them instead. I noticed Aide was also surrounded by children — Aide's black and the kids were all crowding round him, touching his skin with their fingers. They'd never seen a black man in the flesh and they were fascinated. Aide found it quite amusing!

After we got changed there was a banquet of food and free drink, and people did presentation speeches and gave out gifts. Aide, who was captain that day, handed over a Coventry City football and was given a special commemorative bottle of Croatian brandy which we drank on the bus on the way back to Zagreb. The journey back to Zagreb was a lot livelier than on the very early journey out, which was mainly thanks to the fact that people had alcohol in them. While Ian was reliving his wonder goal on the coach (I'm sure it went in off his arse) I started a song that the whole coach joined in with: '5-1, even Ian scored, 5-1, even Ian scored!' We got off the coach outside the ground and I was hammered. I went straight for a piss in the nearest portaloo, which had about five hundred old bill standing nearby. Trouble was, I could barely stand up and fell forward. My head hit the wall in front of me, which stopped me going over, but when I rocked backwards the unlocked door didn't stop me. I fell out of the portaloo and landed on my back in my George suit, still pissing. The coppers were all cracking up at the sight of me.

By George

I managed to get up but was covered in my own piss. I didn't mind in the end, thought as England pissed all over Croatia that night, winning 4–1.

Chapter 28

Lost in translation

A month later we were off to the former Russian state of Belarus, and Ian and I were joined by Chubb and Paul on this trip. We were again due to play for the fans' team, and when we got to our hotel in Minsk, we went straight to the hotel bar (which was more like a 1970s railway station café than a bar) to meet Dane and Keith from Torquay. We all got in a couple of taxis and headed off to the Belarus FA headquarters, where the game was being played. When we arrived we were introduced to the new England Fans manager, Garford Beck. Garford was a quality geezer, who I instantly got on with – he's remained a good friend of mine ever since. He wanted to get things done and wanted to get us winning, friendly games or not. The teams lined up to meet the guests of honour and officials from the Belarus FA, plus English FA representatives Dave Richards, David Sheepshanks, Gordon Taylor and the top man himself, Lord Triesman. I, of course, started having a good old natter to Lord Triesman, who thought my suit was great

161

and told me to have a good game. We got battered by Belarus 6-1, which wasn't surprising as the team we faced actually played in the third division over there. Ian once again claimed a moment of glory, scoring the only England goal. Watch out Wayne Rooney. Thankfully the 'real' England team had another fantastic result, winning 3-1.

Back at the hotel, we went to the food bar. Ian looked at the sandwiches and asked the stony-faced woman serving, 'What's that?' pointing at one of the sandwiches behind the glass. She didn't answer, so Ian repeated, 'What's that? Is it chicken? You know? Chicken?' and proceeded to make chicken noises, moving his arms to simulate a bird and walking around the foyer. The woman remained impassive, but I was laughing my head off. After Ian had eaten his sandwich, which apparently wasn't even chicken, we went to the bar. The night before there had been only a few people in there but now you couldn't get in the door, never mind get to the bar. Chubb, Paul, Dane and Keith were outside. 'Fuck this, lads we might as well go somewhere else,' I said. 'What about in there?' Chubb said, pointing to the lap dancing bar next door. The guy on the door told us it was £10 each to get in – we needed a drink, so we paid and went in. There was comfortable leather seating, waitresses serving drinks, which were cheaper than the hotel bar, and of course beautiful women taking it in turns to strip off. We agreed to stay for a bit.

After a few hours, two of the girls came over and gave Chubb him a lap dance, even though he never asked for one. When they finished they got off him and held their hands out. Chubb shook both their hands, got up and said, 'Thanks very much girls, I'm off to bed now' and left.

As Paul and I fell into our room at 5am, the phone rang.

'Hello?' I asked and just heard some woman chatting in Belarusian, so I put the phone down. Five minutes later, there was a knock at the door. I opened the door and a woman dressed in a red basque and fishnet stockings pushed past me and dived onto my bed. 'We fuck? Yes?' she asked 'Do we fuck?' I answered. 'But you speak to me on phone!' she said. 'Yeah, I thought you were fucking reception not some old brass!' Paul just lay there staring at this scantily-clad woman in our room. 'You and your friend?' she asked. 'Listen, love, unless you're giving it away for free, we ain't got no money,' I explained She understood that. 'No money? Fuck you.' She got up and walked out. I closed the door and got back into bed. 'You could have found out how much for the pair of us before letting her go!' Paul said. I looked at him in disbelief and went to sleep.

Chapter 29

Legless

We arrived in Berlin and met up with Mole, who'd travelled two days before us and saved forty quid on his flight, even though it was twenty pound a night for the hotel. Mole took us to a pub he'd found and went up to the bar. 'I'll settle my bar bill now,' he said to the barmaid. 'You've only been here two days, how have you run up a bar bill?' I asked. 'After I'd paid for the hotel it only left me twenty quid,' he answered. 'You only brought a hundred quid with you for four days?' I asked. 'Yeah…I'm a bit skint at the moment,' Mole replied. The barmaid gave Mole a piece of paper, and he turned to me and said, 'You couldn't sub us could you Stan?' Unbelievable, but I sorted out what he owed.

After two hours, an Australian bird walked in asking whether anyone fancied a pub craw. Everyone was up for it, except Mole. 'Mole, do you want me to pay for you?' I asked, and Mole agreed so of we went. It was £15 each, but we got a free drink at each bar and entrance into a club. We followed the Aussie girl a short distance to the first bar. 'You're having a fucking laugh, love!' I shouted: the first bar was Mole's local. By the time we got to the nightclub, we were wrecked. As we queued to get in, I spoke to this American fellow who was a Marine – he made us lot look sober. As I talked to him, I hadn't realised that my mates had all gone into the club. We went to go in too, but the doorman refused, saying we were too drunk. 'Don't worry mate, I know a really good bar near here,' my new Marine mate, Josh, said. We arrived at the bar and it was full of American Marines, so Josh introduced me to his mates. They were hanging on my every word and they all wanted to buy me a beer. One of them asked me if I knew Prince Charles, and I said, 'Charlie? I've known him for years! He pops in my local pub from time to time, great bloke!' Another then said, 'What soccer team do you support in the Premier League, Stan?' 'I don't, I just support England,' I answered. 'Fuck them! I support Manchester United,' he told me. 'And that Wayne Rooney, man, he fucking rocks!' he added. 'Yeah, and he plays for England!' I said. His face dropped. 'What? Wayne Rooney's signed for England? Fuck that, Stan – you're winding me up!' I was speechless.

We left the bar to go elsewhere and walked to where the taxis were parked near to a Turkish kebab shop. There were about six guys outside the shop looking at us. One of the Marines saw them looking and shouted. 'What the fuck are you looking at, boy?' The kid said something back in German and unfortunately this Marine understood German. All fucking hell broke loose and the four Marines knocked ten bells of shit out of these lads, even though they were outnumbered. With the battle over the four Marines, including Josh, jumped in a cab and left me standing there next to all these guys on the floor. I jumped into the next cab, but couldn't remember the hotel name, so I told the driver the name of Mole's favourite bar, which he knew. Sure enough, when we arrived there was Mole sitting at the bar. 'Alright mate? I thought you'd be with the others at the nightclub,' I said. 'Nah, you've got to pay for your drinks in there, so once I'd had all the free drinks on the pub crawl, I came back here,' Mole said. 'Stan…you couldn't get us pint, could you? I'll pay you back!'

The next day Paul and I bought a bottle of vodka, two bottles of Jagermeister and six cans of Red Bull and drank them in an Irish bar. Well, we didn't want to pay €7 a pint! After five hours me and Paul were smashed to bits, but drunk or not it was time to George up. We went outside and Paul tried to get into his George suit. He put his white tunic on back to front, had a wrestling match with his cape, and put his fake black boots on upside-down, so the feet were on his knees. He looked a right fucking state, but all the England fans outside the pub started singing, 'Keep St George In My Heart'. Paul waved and sang along. The pub was under a train station and Paul stood in front of the escalator and wouldn't let anyone pass; it was his escalator. As German people going home from work approached Paul, he would push them away, and each time he pushed someone the England fans watching would shout, 'OLE!' One German guy who had been pushed back three times then side-stepped Paul (quite easily) and went up the escalator, but he didn't get far. Paul rugby-tackled him from behind and then got on the bloke's back. He'd totally lost it, but he was loving the cheers from the crowd and he walked down the escalator raising his hands in the air like a boxer celebrating a victory. His celebrations were short-lived, however, as out of nowhere the German police turned up wanting to nick him. I explained to the police that Paul was just having a laugh and that he wouldn't do it again, and promised to take him back to the hotel. Luckily the police decided not to arrest him and went on their way. I turned round to speak to Paul, only to see that the England fans had lifted him up and that he was waving a set of crutches around like he was conducting an orchestra.

We fell off the train near to the stadium and started to walk. As we neared the stadium, a group of stewards approached me. 'You cannot come into the stadium because you are drunk,' a female steward said. 'No I'm not,' I replied. 'Yes you are, we have been watching you and you are staggering,' she said. 'Well the thing is, love, I'm not drunk – I broke my leg a couple of months ago and it hasn't healed properly yet, so I struggle with my balance,' I told her. She just stared at me and said, 'And your friend? Did he break both his legs?' I turned round to look at Paul: he was all over the place and could hardly stand up. 'OK, we'll allow you both in, but if we see you behaving in a drunken manner, we will remove you,' she then said. I told Paul that when we got in, we'd have to sit straight down. We somehow climbed the steps leading to the stadium – well, we crawled up half of them. We got into the block where our seats were, and I stopped as we reached the very steep stairs that led down to the pitch, but Paul was so pissed that he didn't even see the steps and went flying. I made my way down to where Paul lay in a heap – I was sure he must have broken a bone or twenty. 'Paul? Paul, are you alright?' I asked, and he lifted his head and said, 'Whose round is it?' He was OK. I got him to his feet and sat him down next to the plastic barrier that separated the German fans from us. He immediately went to sleep.

Paul slept the whole of the first half and a good part of the second. When he did wake up, he found himself sitting next to

a German lady who was about 70 years old. He was banging
on the Perspex at her and waving his fists, and after a bit she
looked at Paul and gave him a two-finger salute. Me, Jimmy and
Bruce were cracking up at Paul and his new nemesis. England
then scored another goal to make the score 2-1 to us; we all
started going fucking mental and most England fans ended up
on the floor in heaps celebrating. Paul started climbing over the
barrier to get into the German section and the stewards on
both sides rushed to stop him, but it was too late. Paul got up
and Paul fell down (it was like watching Humpty Dumpty)
right into the middle of the German fans. He was helped to his
feet – not by all the king's horses and all the king's men, but by
six stewards – and thrown out of the ground.

Chapter 30

Oranges and Georges

We arrived in Seville and got a call from the Doni lads (Flips, Crawf, Robs and Podge) who said they were drinking in a bar near the cathedral. When we found them, Flips was unconscious in a chair outside the bar, buried beneath a load of oranges. In Seville, every street is lined with orange trees, and most of the fruit was now on Flips. All the boys left at about 3am, except me and Paul – we left at about 4am and went to the nearby Scottish bar. We were both smashed when we got in there, so drinking vodka and Red Bull by the pint until 6am probably wasn't the best idea. When we eventually fell out of the pub, neither of us could remember where the hotel was. We staggered around the empty streets until we came across a load of council workers who were emptying bins and jet-spraying the streets. We charged over to them and I got hold of one of the pressure washers and started spraying the workers. They were doing their nut, but every time they got near me, I gave them another blast. All of a sudden they stopped trying to disarm me and started running after the bin lorry, which was driving up the street. Surely they weren't going to leave me with the pressure washer, were they? I then realised why they were running off in such a hurry – they were after Paul, who was driving the bin wagon! They caught up and dragged him out of the cab, throwing him to the floor. We both thought it best to leg it – well, as best we could. We managed to find the hotel and before we went into our own room, we collected all the upright silver tin ashtrays from the reception area and stacked them three high against my brother Magic's door. A while later I heard this crash of noise and said to Paul, 'Magic's awake! Come on!' There was all this dusty grey shit everywhere in Magic and Liam's room – Liam was a young lad on his first trip away. 'I fucking told you they'd do something, didn't I Liam!' Magic yelled. For once he didn't have time to moan, though, because we weren't the only ones to hear the crash. The cleaner and the manager were striding up the corridor. Me and Paul did the decent thing and ran back to our own room and locked the door, leaving Magic and Liam surrounded by what looked like volcanic ash. We could hear the manager going mental and despite Magic's protestations he made them clean it all up.

That afternoon, as I stood at the bar with Ian, Dex appeared. 'Alright Stan, have you boys booked anything up for Kazakhstan yet?' he asked. I said we hadn't, and Dex told us he'd booked to go not only to Kazakhstan for the match, but also to Dubai, India, Nepal and Mount Everest. We were both well up for it! Outside the bar, the streets were packed with English supporters on either side of the street singing and hurling oranges at each other. They then joined forces and started throwing them at passing cars and other vehicles. Already in my

George suit, I saw a bin wagon coming towards us so I sprinted up the road and jumped on the back of it. The usual singing and cheering started up as I passed by and I stayed on until the end of the street. I jumped off the bin wagon and saw hundreds of old bill getting into their riot gear. I ran back up the street and told everyone that I thought the police were planning to baton charge us, but everyone just kept throwing oranges. A bloke on a motorbike drove past and got an orange right in the face. I knew the old bill were watching and waiting for the right moment, and this was it. We heard the solitary bang of the baton on the riot shield: they were coming! I pushed Ben, Liam and Paul through the pub doors, and as we looked out onto the street the police were whacking everyone who was English. They then turned and headed for the pub, and there was no escape. The police made their way through the whole pub belting everyone at least once, and then got to the beer garden, where we were. We were certain it was our turn to take a whack, but the police looked at me and Paul and did nothing. They turned around and left.

The English fans once again started to congregate outside the pub and the Doni Lads turned up wearing bright pink Seville shirts. They'd been up to the ground to get tickets for the match and while there had bought themselves Seville away shirts. One thing you don't do on an away trip with England is buy a pink football shirt and then turn up wearing it in front of five hundred England fans, as the Doni boys found out. They had the piss ripped out of them constantly for hours, with chants of 'Does your boyfriend know you're here?' and 'Do you take it up the arse?' but to their credit, they just stood there and took it.

When we got to the ground me and Paul were mobbed by

the Spanish fans. 'I've got to get one of them suits,' Ben said. 'All them fit birds wanting your picture? I'm definitely getting one!' Since Dave had put his suit on in Germany and become George the Fourth, there had been only one other who had worn the famous suit in public to become George the Fifth, and that was my mate Duncan, who had worn the suit the previous year on St George's Day. He certainly earned the title of George the Fifth, as we both donned our suits and went into a mainly Republican Irish bar in Luton. When we walked in the old boys in the bar started singing songs at us about the Black and Tans, but we were just there for a laugh. Dunc even got one of the proper old boys to put the suit on before we continued our night around Luton.

When we got in the ground, I needed to have a shit and went in one of the portaloos. With my silver chain mail trousers around my ankles, hovering above the seat, the fucking door opened. I hadn't locked it properly. 'Do you mind, mate? I'm trying to have a shit!' I said. The guy clearly didn't mind and shouted to his mates, 'Boys, look! It's St George on the throne!' Great, I thought, why not tell everyone? Suddenly loads of people were taking pictures of me on the toilet. It wasn't my best pose ever.

Chapter 31

Whore for one and one for whore

Ian, Bruce and I took Dex's advice and booked the Kazakhstan trip. There were about twenty people on the tour, including three guys I knew from Bedford: Trevor, nicknamed Runting; Jason, nicknamed Fozzie, and Barry Fishcake, who didn't need a nickname with that surname! I walked into the airport bar and looked as amazed to see them as they were to see me. 'It's fucking Stan!' Fishcake shouted. 'Please tell me you ain't on this trip to Kazakhstan as well Stan?' 'Oh yes mate! I didn't know you were going, then again I ain't seen you for years!' I said. The three of them were just coming to Kazakhstan and going home the day after the match. When we landed in Dubai we went straight into the duty free shop, thanks to advice from my best mate Tony, and bought shitloads of drink. We were only there for sixteen hours before we flew on to Kazakhstan. At the hotel, the bloke who'd organised the trip checked us in. We had rooms with either three or four beds in them and I agreed to stay in the same room as Fishcake,

Runting and Fozzie because Dex knew Ian and Bruce, but didn't know them.

We went up to the roof of the hotel, where the swimming pool was. Fishcake and Runting took a load of beers and I took a bottle of vodka, cans of Red Bull and a teacup to drink from. The boys opened their beers while I poured myself a 'cup of tea'. The boys had barely sipped their beers when they were ordered to stop by the lifeguard who told them that drinking alcohol by the pool was not allowed. 'Here, mate – am I alright drinking my special tea?' I asked. 'Yes, you can drink, but they cannot.' So I carried on drinking my special tea for the next four hours.

About 1pm the whole group decided to go to the harbour and catch a boat across the river to go to an English bar that Jim from Southend knew. It sounded like a great idea, until I tried to stand up. I'd finished my vodka about an hour before our walkabout, but hadn't realised how pissed I was. We reached the harbour, where there were endless boats lined up. 'Boys, I'm like fucking James Bond,' I shouted, and as the boys turned round I was running and leaping from boat to boat. 'Stan, you're running out of boats!' Bruce yelled. I jumped onto a boat and leapt again to the next, but after that I had to leap to the side and just about landed on the dock.

Everyone piled into one of the boats and sat down, and the driver collected money from everyone. While he was unhooking the boat, I jumped down into the driver's seat which was below foot level. 'Stan's taking us out!' Fishcake said jokingly, but he wasn't wrong. I pushed the throttle forward and as we were now unhooked the boat started to pull away out of the dock. The real driver started screaming for me to stop, but I continued to go forward. I got about ten metres out when I saw how many other boats were on that river and thought it best to let him take over, but then I realised I'd have to reverse the thing back. I fired the throttle backwards and we headed in reverse back to the dock, but the thing was I couldn't see where I was going and crashed straight into another boat. I got out of the driver's seat before I tipped us all into the drink.

We crossed the river and walked through a market, and me and Fishcake bought ourselves some Arab headgear so we'd look the part. The rest of the group were sick of waiting so they carried on walking to the bar, leaving me with Sheikh Fishcake, Runting and Fozzie to bring up the rear. We eventually got through the market, but by that time we'd lost the others, so we walked up the road and found a hotel with a bar in it. We walked in and realised that this was not the bar the boys had been heading for. Instead it was full of Chinese prostitutes. I was still wearing my Arab headgear, and the madam running the place came up to me and said, 'You like my girls, you want one of my girls?' 'No, love, they're very nice but I'm not interested,' I replied and went to order some drinks. 'You're not interested? Fuck off Stan, you'd shag anything!' Fishcake said disbelievingly. 'Not any more, mate, I'm with someone now,' I proudly told him. 'Let's have a few drinks and if you lot want to shag something you go for it,' I said and got the drinks in. We'd been in there for about an hour when my phone rang. It was Ian. 'Where are you? We've been looking everywhere for you – we thought you'd been nicked!' Ian said. 'I'm in a Chinese brothel,' I told him. 'You're in a fucking *what*?' Ian asked. At that moment this Arab geezer walked in, wearing the same headgear as me. 'Gotta go' I said, and hung up. 'My brother from another mother!' I shouted, grabbing hold of this bloke. He gave me a bit of smile, went to the corner of the bar

By George

and sat down. It turned out he was the pimp and of course I got chatting with him; he was sound. Runting came over to me and said, 'Stan, Fishcake and Fozzie have taken a couple of these whores back to the hotel and I'm taking one now, you gonna be alright getting back?' 'You can't leave me here in this state! I'm coming back with you,' I told him.

We got back to the hotel and went up to the room. I tried the door, but it wouldn't open. 'Fishcake, open the door! I want to get my drink!' I shouted, but there was no answer. 'Fishcake? Fozzie are you in there?' I shouted, but still no answer. The cleaner came along, giving the three of us a curious look – especially the hooker. She tried her master key, but it didn't work. 'Someone is in the room and they've locked the door,' the cleaner said. 'There isn't anyone in there,' I insisted, so she called someone on her walkie-talkie and a security guy turned up, who also tried the door without any luck. He then called the hotel manager, and I pressed my face against the door and said, 'Listen Fishcake, if you're in there you'd better open the door now, there's a bit of a crowd gathering.' A few seconds later, I heard the lock turn and the door opened. Standing in front of us was Fishcake, completely naked apart from the condom on his cock. I walked past him with my eyes firmly facing skywards, and there was Fishcake's hooker naked on the double bed. Runting and his hooker followed me in, along with the manager and his two staff. I was certain we were all getting thrown out as Fishcake was still wandering around naked. I retrieved my drink and was about to leave, when the toilet door opened and out came Fozzie with another hooker. I'd seen enough, so I shot out of the door and went up to the pool on the roof. Most of the other lads on the trip were already there, including Ian, Dex and Bruce. I poured a large vodka into my teacup (I needed it after seeing Fishcake in all his glory) and told the boys what had gone on. Me, Dex and Bruce finished another bottle of vodka between us and I passed out on my sun lounger, but shortly afterwards I was rudely awakened as Dex, Bruce, Ian and Fozzie had picked up my lounger and thrown me in the pool!

Back at the airport, the security guys took a bottle of vodka and case of alcopops off me. The tour organiser could see that most of us were well pissed, so he took our passports and checked everyone in. Ian then came over to us carrying my booze. 'I've just nicked it back off the customs blokes!' he announced. 'Fucking fair play!' I said. 'Hang on, though – if we get caught with this we'll all get nicked. You can't rob booze off the customs people,' Bruce said. 'Well there's only one thing for it, Bruce. We'll have to drink the fucking evidence!' I said, and we all got stuck in.

We left Dubai at 11pm and landed in Kazakhstan at 5.30am. How they let us on the plane, I will never know. We arrived at the hotel at 7am but had to wait until 11am to check in, so we all headed down to the pool. I had a shower to wake myself up, while everyone else crashed out on the loungers. About 9am a bloke walked through, looked at all the sleeping lads and then came to talk to me. The guy looked like a military type and he was American. 'Can I ask you what you're doing here, sir?' he asked. 'What's it got to do with you, mate?' I answered. 'Well I'm head of security for the England football team and we heard there were some vagrants by the pool,' he told me. 'We're not vagrants, we're England fans!' I said abruptly. 'Well the team want to come down and have a swim and relax, but they can't while you're here as it's a security risk,' he explained. 'Listen mate, we've got as much right to be here as they have; we're guests in this hotel. If they want to come down then let them, we're their fans after all. We're not gonna attack them.' The security guy then said, 'I'm sorry sir, I didn't realise you were guests, but why are you all sleeping by the pool and not in your rooms?' I explained we couldn't get in our rooms until later and with that he left.

By 11 am our rooms were ready. I was just going upstairs when Bruce grabbed me and said, 'Fabio Capello is at the bar, with your mate Lord Triesman!' I went over to the bar, walked up to them and said, 'Hello Lord Triesman, how are you? We met in Belarus.' 'Oh hello again, it's Stan isn't it?' Lord Triesman said. We shook hands. 'Are the boys all up for it and ready for tonight?' I asked 'Oh yes, all prepared. What about you, Stan? Have you got a game arranged?' Lord Triesman asked. 'Yes, we've got a match this afternoon against the Kazakhstan army team,' I told him. 'Well the best of luck; it will be very hard playing in this heat,' he said. I then turned to Fabio Capello. The man has an aura about him that gains instant respect. 'Hello Mr Capello, it's a privilege to meet you,' I said and shook his hand and had my picture taken with him before saying my goodbyes and heading up to my room.

Later on, we got a taxi over to where we were playing the fans' match. Next door was the army barracks and their team were already warming up. The pre-match presentation show went on forever, with all these Kazakh people dressed in weird outfits (I'm a fine one to talk) doing lots of dancing. Eventually we kicked off – it was 85 degrees and we weren't used to playing in that sort of heat. We created lots of chances, but just couldn't get the ball in the net. The only time we did, Ian put the goalie in there as well. With time running out and with us 2-0 down, disaster struck, well it did for me anyway. Their goalkeeper kicked the ball out and I jumped to win the header – I got the ball cleanly but in doing so cracked the back of the defender's head as he flicked back. The referee stopped the game immediately and I had to leave the field for treatment. There was so much blood that I couldn't see out of my right eye. I was given some bandages to try and stop the bleeding, and as I sat there pressing the bandages to my head, I realised that my legs were covered in blood. I asked if there was any water so I could clean myself up, and a guy came back with a bucket of water and just threw it all over me. The doctor then arrived, in the dirtiest white coat I'd ever seen. 'Is he a doctor or a fucking road sweeper?' I asked, but I still went with him to the surgery. He sat me down and we were joined by about forty onlookers, all filming me on their mobiles. I could hear Bruce shouting, 'Let me in you bastards, that's my mate in there!' but he couldn't fight his way through the crowd. The doctor didn't speak English, but fortunately there was a girl there who did, so she translated. He spoke to her after examining the cut and she told me that it was a very deep wound and would need stitches at the hospital. 'I ain't got time to go to the hospital. I'm watching the match later!' I told her, so she spoke to the doctor again and then explained that he would clean the wound and put a plaster on my head. 'Yeah, that'll do,' I said. Just before he went to clean me up, the doctor spoke directly to me in English. 'You are a man, yes?' 'Yes, I am a man...' I answered and he laughed, taking a drag of the fag he was smoking. He then soaked a cloth in a dark-coloured liquid and slapped it on the cut. It stung like fuck and I wanted to scream my head off, but didn't. I gritted my teeth, even though my eyes were streaming, and took it like a man. The doctor then stuck a huge plaster on my head, pressed very hard and said, 'You are a man!' Then he started laughing again.

By George

We met Dex and his mate Miles at the hotel – they were going out to get something to eat so we went with them. At the restaurant Dex went to the toilet and came out dressed as Borat with a big black curly wig, large dark round glasses, a big black stick-on moustache, and of course a green mankini. We all cracked up, as did all the staff.

Back at the hotel, I saw Lord Triesman again. 'Stan, what's happened to you?' he asked. 'Unfortunately, your Lordship, there was a clash of heads at the match today and the other guy's head was harder than mine.' I explained. 'But I'm not worried, I've joined an exclusive club. Terry Butcher, Paul Ince and now Stan Stanfield have all given blood for their country!' He laughed and left to get on the coach with the England team.

With the team on their way to the match, it was time for me and Bruce to George up. When we came out of the lift, we received more attention than the England team had. All the hotel guests and staff wanted their pictures taken with us. 'We have got to get some of those suits, Dex,' Miles said. He reckoned he'd get some when he got home – we'll see, I thought. While Dex and Miles were planning to become the next Georges, I got talking to some very glamorous-looking ladies on the next table. As I chatted to them swigging my pint, while they sipped on their champagne and nibbled on their very expensive-looking food, the hotel manager came up to them and told them their cars had arrived. They said goodbye and went to get into these blacked-out motors, leaving loads of untouched food and four almost untouched bottles of champagne. It was £300 a bottle, and I wasn't letting that go to waste! After stuffing ourselves with free food and drink, we went to the game.

Whore for one and one for whore

My ticket was in the Kazakhstan end and as I got in the ground, I was grabbed by a couple of Kazakhstan army blokes. They escorted me all the way along the front of the main stand, which was filled with Kazakhstan supporters. They then pointed for me to sit in the middle of the Kazakhstan band. I sat down and was an instant hit with the opposition – I felt like a guest celebrity. As the game, which England won 4–0, went on the party atmosphere in the stand grew and I was now almost conducting the crowd, even if we didn't support the same team. I even put my headgear and cape on the band's actual conductor, which the crowd loved. I left with about ten minutes to go and as I stood up to leave, I bowed to the crowd and applauded them all. They had been one of the best crowds I'd ever been in and they cheered me all the way to the exit. What a buzz.

I met up with the lads outside the ground and we headed to a nightclub, with me still dressed in my George suit. The club was packed with England and Kazakhstan fans. I stood chatting with my mate Jay from Brighton for a while, when I saw an opportunity. There was a stage at one end of the nightclub with a microphone stand on it. I had to see if it was on, so I raced to the stage, and sure enough it was switched on. The crowd were in uproar as I started to belt out England songs, but the bouncers on the other hand wanted to belt *me* – they flew onto the stage and took me and the microphone clean out. I was frog-marched off the stage and thrown out, but I knew I'd get back in. I went round the corner and disrobed, then walked straight back in, even cheekily smiling and shaking the hands of two bouncers who'd just thrown me out.

When the club finished we said goodbye to Miles, who was travelling home in the morning and was gutted he wasn't staying for the rest of the trip. We got back to the hotel and found Fishcake, Runting and Fozzie at the bar, so we had a final drink with them and also said goodbye. The following morning, we had to get up at 7am as we were going to the Kazakhstan Grand Canyon and then staying in a remote village. We got on the bus and the co-driver introduced himself as Baghdad – apparently he was 70 years old. The driver was introduced as Basra. The warning signs were already there: this was not going to be a straightforward trip!

About an hour in, I cracked open a bottle of vodka and insisted on everyone having a swig. There were four others on the bus, who I didn't know, but they introduced themselves as Harvey, Roger, Matt and this chubby lad from Tamworth, Clubby. I took an instant liking to Clubby; he reminded me of Chubb, a right cheeky bastard who always ended up getting the piss ripped out of him. As the bottle came back to me, I said jokingly, 'Hang on, what about Baghdad and Basra?' Baghdad accepted and took a big swig and then Basra took an even bigger swig.

After two hours we arrived at a town. If this was a town, what the hell was our village going to be like? There were shacks on either side of the road and from start to finish the whole place was only about 50 metres long. I got off of the bus and went to the shop – they had beer and we cleared them out. The woman behind the counter looked like all her Christmases had come at once – I think she closed early that day! As we drove through a cutting in a mountain, Baghdad pointed and said, 'Bin Laden is up there.' 'Well stop the fucking bus and let's go get him!' I shouted. What a story that would have been, St George capturing Bin Laden! 'No, we cannot stop! There are many kidnappings of tourists here!' he replied.

Whore for one and one for whore

We drove for hours along an endless straight road, and then Basra turned left off the road and drove across the barren wasteland. We were bouncing about all over the place in the back, but he never slowed down. I joked, 'This is a set-up! Basra and Baghdad are kidnappers!' Then, two Jeeps drove straight at us at some speed. 'I told you, we're getting fucking kidnapped! I want a refund! This wasn't in the itinerary!' I said. The Jeeps were now no more than fifty metres away and didn't seem to be slowing down. Basra stopped the bus and the Jeeps drove at high speed around us and carried on going. It was a load of tourists in hired Jeeps. Everyone was relieved that it was just a load of blokes playing chicken rather than kidnappers wanting to play Russian roulette.

We reached the Kazakhstan Grand Canyon, and it was really impressive. We traipsed down the canyon and walked along with Baghdad to where the river flowed, and while the lads relaxed by the river, I found an overturned tree, which gave me a bit of privacy to have a shit. While doing my business, I heard voices to the side of me. It was another party of tourists, taking pictures of me having a dump! As we walked back up the canyon, we came across a bloke with a huge eagle, and a few of us had our pictures taken with this bloody great thing on our arm. Bruce had his picture taken as well – to be honest it was one of the better looking birds I'd seen Bruce with! We then headed off to the village that we would be staying in that night. The village had been an old KGB hunting retreat back in the sixties and when we got to the house we were staying in, it was clear that the place hadn't been used since the sixties either. There was no electricity or running water in any of the rooms, and my bathroom was filled with rubble. Basra took Dex to a shop to get as much alcohol as possible. We were going to need it. While Dex was gone, I removed the slats from his bed. Dex returned with the drink and came up to his room, where we were all sitting. 'I tell you what Dex, this might be the worst place we've ever stayed, but the beds are well comfy!' I told him, and Dex dived on to his bed – only to go straight through it and onto the floor.

The villagers prepared us a meal in the main block, which did have lights, and then left us to it. It was the perfect location for a horror movie and no one ventured too far outside after dark. But although we didn't even have the basic amenities, it seemed to add to the atmosphere of the evening and we made our own entertainment.

When we woke up the next morning, we were glad there was a full head count and that no one had been butchered in the night. I went outside and saw Basra checking the underneath of the bus. 'Alright Basra? Bus OK?' I said. He smiled and nodded back, but he had a worried look on his face. On the way back to Almaty airport we stopped at a service station and I purchased an alcoholic pink drink. We were just about to leave when a lorry pulled up with the best number plate ever – it ended in BUM, cue my arse. After everyone had taken photos of my bare arse next to this number plate, we continued to the airport. Everyone took the piss out of me, as I drank my pink drink, but it was no ladies' drink. It was hardcore and after six of them I knew it. We stopped at the Kazakhstan Olympic ski resort and I started singing, 'I'm on the piste and I'm having a laugh, I'm on the piste and I'm having a laugh' I was at this point slaughtered and the only thing going downhill was me as I walked along looking like I was in a slalom race.

Just as we reached the city of Almaty, there was an almighty bang from underneath the rear side of the bus. Basra hit the brakes, but not a lot happened. He somehow managed to stop the bus before we got to a busy crossroads, and we got off the bus and saw that the brake discs had shattered. We weren't going anywhere. Basra opened the boot, threw all our bags out, got back in and drove off at high speed with no brakes. 'Oh well, that's the last we'll see of that bus – and Basra!' I said, but half hour later, he turned up in another bus, which we quickly boarded. He drove through Almaty like Mad Max and got us to the airport just in time. At Almaty airport, we got talking to a couple of Kazakh women and asked them what they thought of Borat, but they'd never heard of him. I went to the toilet and came back out with the wig, moustache, glasses and mankini on. Everyone was in hysterics, everyone except two airport policemen (one of whom actually looked a bit like Borat). They told me to get dressed or be arrested; it was an easy choice.

We landed in Delhi at 9pm, got on the transfer bus and headed to our hotel. We drove through the very busy streets until the bus stopped and we were told we had to walk the remainder of the way. We all got off the bus with our luggage and wandered up these very dark streets. Then some wild dogs approached us, barking and growling. Everyone shit themselves, scared of being bitten and catching rabies. I'd probably be OK, I thought – my bloodstream was 100% alcohol now anyway. We turned the corner of a street and there was our hotel…what a fucking shithole! It wasn't a hotel, it was someone's house! We'd gone from sharing a hotel with the England team to staying in a place that looked like a grotty old shack. I shared a room with Ian and Bruce on the ground floor, right on the street with an iron bar to hold the door shut. But at least it was air conditioned, unlike the rest of the rooms. Even at night, it was 110 degrees.

By George

Dex came downstairs and found us sitting in the lounge watching TV. 'Alright Dex, it's not bad here is it?' I said. 'Fuck me, you've got sofas, a telly, you've even got a fucking kitchen. You bastards!' Dex said. 'The air con doesn't work upstairs and now even the fucking lights have gone as well. Fuck this, I'm moving down here with you lot.' I didn't have the heart to tell him that we were in the lounge, not our room, and said, 'Yeah, get your stuff and come down. You'll be more than welcome,' knowing full well that the owners, Mr and Mrs Patel, had given their bed up and would be sleeping on the sofas themselves.

We all went out for an Indian but couldn't find one, even though we were in India. We eventually stumbled across a Mexican restaurant, which sold Desperadoes. Happy days. After avoiding the rabid street dogs, we staggered back to the hotel and went to bed. I hadn't even closed my eyes when I heard a scream and a man shouting in the lounge. I went to see what all the commotion was about and found Mr Patel telling Dex to fuck off, as he stood in front of them in his pants. He glared at me and I just winked and went to bed.

The following day, we landed in Kathmandu at 3pm – what a place. Delhi looked like paradise as we drove to the hotel. We saw people sorting through piles of rubbish on the streets and dogs, cows and even monkeys roaming free like they owned the place. It was a real eye-opener and it reminded us all how lucky we are. When we got to the hotel I dumped my stuff and headed straight back out again with Ian, Bruce, Dex, Clubby, Brian and Toddy. We jumped in some rickshaws and were dropped off at a bar – a strip bar. Me and Dex dived onto the stage and danced around the pole until we were asked to get down as the first pole dancer of the afternoon was about to come on. We all sat there in anticipation…and then out he came. It was a geezer, stripping off and cavorting around the pole. We were in the wrong sort of strip joint so we quickly got the fuck out of there. We jumped back into our rickshaws and got them to take us to another bar. The drivers dropped us at a quality bar and we invited them all in to have a drink with us. Dex put on an England CD and the whole place was going mental. Everyone joined in when the theme from *Dambusters* came on – watching our now well pissed rickshaw drivers chasing each other around like they were in aeroplanes was hilarious.

We stopped laughing when we had to leave, though, because two of the rickshaw drivers could barely walk, never mind drive us back to the hotel, and one of them was mine and Ian's driver. I ended up pedalling the rickshaw myself, even though I was in a pretty bad state myself, but I got Ian and the driver (who slept all the way) back to the hotel. When we got there the driver still wanted money out of me, even though I'd done most of the driving!

The next day was our last day of what had already been a fantastic trip and we planned to do as much as possible, starting with a flight around the Himalayas. We got up at 5.30am and went to the airport. It was next to an army base and as we were walking towards the terminal, a siren went off. A load of us dived on the floor, with me screaming, 'Don't panic Mr Mainwaring! Don't panic!' The people around us thought we'd gone mental. The airline company was called Yeti Airlines and big Ian took great pride in posing for photos in front of the plane. Once up in the air we had a great view of the Himalayas, and of course Mount Everest, and we were allowed to go into the cockpit with the pilot. When I went to go in half the plane was screaming for them not to let me... I can't think why?

After our wonderful experience and with our feet back on

the ground, Dex, Bruce, Ian and I went for a walk around Kathmandu. We went up streets that the rickshaws never could. They were just mud strips, with holes big enough to fit cars in them and electric cables hanging just a few feet above our heads. When we saw a load of rats running down the street, we knew we were a long way from home. A bloke tried to sell us a bowl that hummed when you rubbed a stick on the rim, but it didn't work for long as Bruce poured some beer in it and it never made a sound again. The guy spoke brilliant English and he agreed to become our tour guide; we called him Dave. Dave took us to a Nepalese funeral, which was bizarre. The mourners were screaming and wailing around the body, which was just wrapped in cloth, and even though it was clearly a poor area, people were throwing money out of their windows at the body below. It all ended with them taking the body down to the river and burning it. Dave then took us to a rooftop bar, which served a drink called a Brain Haemorrhage that even I found hard to drink.

We paid Dave some money for being our guide, then jumped on some rickshaws and went to the temples, where we met up with Brian and Toddy. After seeing the temples − it's a right hippy haven − we had to get back to the hotel. We were going up to the highest restaurant in Kathmandu that evening, to see the sunset over Mount Everest. We decided to have a rickshaw race back, so the six of us lined up and we were off − except Dex, whose chain had come off right at the start. The bloke I'd picked looked young and fit, but after going past Ian (whose driver knew he'd drawn the short straw) my driver turned out to be young and fucked. We were third but losing ground on Brian and the leader, Toddy. I jumped off the rickshaw and started running through the streets − I quickly caught up to

Brian's vehicle, but when I looked round my driver was almost having a seizure. We managed to pass Brian, though, so at least second place was mine, I thought, but we missed the last turn and Brian – whose driver looked about 90 – came in second. Dex beat Bruce into last place even though he'd lost his chain at the start! Bruce came in dejectedly to the sound of us all singing the *Steptoe and Son* theme.

We travelled up to the restaurant and although we didn't actually see the sun set on Mount Everest, we sank a good few Everest beers – it was the local brew, even though it was made in London. That night Me and Bruce Georged up and went out to try and find somewhere that would be showing the England match. The closest we got to seeing any action from Wembley that night was when Dex got a picture message from Miles, who was dressed in a knight's outfit. Arise George the Sixth.

Sadly, exactly three weeks after we returned from that incredible trip, my mum passed away.

Chapter 32

The more the merrier

Our next match was in Amsterdam, and I joined Ian, Paul, Dave, Chubb, Timmy, Liam and Ross for the trip over to Holland. It was particularly special for Ross as he'd be turning 21 while we were there. While we were drinking in the Bulldog bar, two lads from Aldershot, Dale and Alex, joined us. They'd bought some serious skunk and lit a joint. They offered it around, with only Timmy taking them up on it. Timmy took an almighty drag of the joint and coughed, causing the contents of the cigarette to spray all over the floor. We were cracking up as we watched Timmy turn purple, but Dale wasn't impressed that his gear was blowing all over the street.

We stayed in the Bulldog bar until early evening, with a couple we'd met that afternoon from Bristol, Ade (who was about six and half foot and was in the British army) and his wife Amy (who had the wickedest Bristol accent – we loved it when she said 'My lovely'!) and then we went to find somewhere else to drink. We walked into a bar and saw the cellar door open in front of us, with yellow and black tape surrounding the hatch. We all walked around it – all of us except Paul, who just carried on walking and fell straight down into the cellar. He came out with his hands raised saying, 'I'm alright, don't worry, I'm alright!' Amazingly, he was. He should have at least broken one bone if not more falling down concrete steps into a cellar, but all he had was a scratch on his arm.

The following day, I woke up and could hear voices, so I opened my eyes and saw four people looking through the window at me lying there in my pants. The corridor that led to all the rooms was outside our room and Paul knew this, so he'd woken before me and opened the curtains. He was out in the corridor encouraging people to take pictures of me, the bastard.

Once I got up, Me and Paul made our way to where the England Fans match was being played. We were all changed and ready to take the field, when my phone rang – it was Anita, my fiancée. She had two wedding dates in mind and wanted to check them out with me, but on each date I was away watching England. 'At this rate we're never getting married, because you're always watching football!' she said. 'They've got the November 22nd free, but are you?' she asked. It was the week after the Brazil game in Qatar – what better place to have to my stag do, I thought, so I told her to go ahead and book it. With the wedding sorted, it was back to the football – we kicked off and destroyed the Dutch fans 6-0.

We returned to the Bulldog, where we found Ross smashed to pieces doing the truffle shuffle with his large belly for the crowd. It wasn't the prettiest of sights. As we walked to go to the match and a large crowd had gathered around a window. We thought it was a live sex show, but in fact it was Dex and Miles, dressed as knights. I went to the window and shouted to

By George

Dex: 'Arise George the Seventh!' and Miles knighted him using a dildo he'd found on the floor.

After Amsterdam Ross and Liam also bought themselves George suits, and now they needed to display them in public. What a public display it was. We were outside the Railway Tavern in West Hampstead before the England versus Slovenia match, with Ade from Bristol, and it was time to George up. The suits are meant to be one-size-fits-all, but that was not the case with Ross. When he eventually got into his suit, it looked like it had been sprayed on, and as he got down on one knee, his trousers split. 'Arise George who "Eight" all the pies!' I said, knighting him. Next up was Liam, who gained the title of George the Ninth.

Chapter 33

Planes, trains and cock-ups

Next up we were off to the Ukraine, but we weren't all on the same flight. Ian, Chubb, Bruce, Dex, Miles, Liam and I were on the second flight out that morning, with the others going out before us. Dex said it was like Division One and Division Two, and obviously we were Division Two, but as it turned out we were the only party to fly to Kiev that morning, as the flight carrying Division One was cancelled and they ended up having to fly and stay in Vienna that night. While waiting for our connecting flight from Kiev to Dnipro, the Ukrainian football team came through and got loads of abuse, especially their star player Shevchenko. We got on our flight to Dnipro, but didn't fly for long. We'd only been in the air half an hour when the plane landed at a military airbase. They marched us across the runway and locked us up in an outside holding area. They held us there without any explanation for two hours, then got us all back on the plane and took off again.

The following day I was playing for the England Fans team

with Dane and Keith. We got a taxi to a bar, where we met the
rest of the team and the two organisers, who were English
businessmen based in Dnipro. They told us they'd been
distributing free match tickets for the game and were expecting
a large crowd. A coach arrived and took us to the stadium
where the match was being played, and as we got off the bus
we were booed by the Ukrainian supporters, who were being
held back by security. We all got changed and Garford made me
captain, for which I felt very honoured. I led the team out
dressed as St George, to the sound of the hostile crowd of three
or four thousand Ukrainian fans. The teams lined up and when
the National Anthem of England started up, the Ukrainian
supporters turned their backs on us and started bouncing and
chanting; it was an amazing sight and it pumped me up even
more to get a victory for my team. After the anthems, the teams
were announced across the loud speaker system and as each
name was called it came up on the electronic scoreboard.
'Number eight for England, Stan Stanfield,' the announcer said.
I raised my arms and applauded the crowd and strangely got a
great reception back. I stripped off my George suit and was
ready for battle.

We had a really weak team that day and lost 4-1, but after
running my socks off the whole match, I received the man of
the match award – which was a big bottle of champagne –
from the Mayoress of Dnipro. After the game the coach took
us to a bar, where the organisers had laid on free food and free
drink. That night we watched England lose 1-0, but it didn't
matter that we'd lost as I stayed out all night partying with the
Ukrainians. We got on the train from Dnipro to Kiev at
6.30am and I wasn't exactly sober, after only getting an
hour's sleep. Clubby was in our carriage and having him there

certainly helped pass the time as he had to endure two or three hours of us (well mainly me), ripping the shit out of him at every opportunity.

We were about halfway into our journey back to Kiev, when the train stopped at a station. There was no one on the platform getting on and certainly no one got off, so why had we stopped? All of sudden, these market traders turned up, setting their stalls up alongside the train from one end to the other. We wandered down the platform and they were trying to sell us all sorts of crap. One trader was trying to get me to buy a bucket of fish! None of us were interested in buying anything, except Miles. We'd all got back on the train, but where was Miles? Eventually he boarded the train, but he wasn't alone; he'd brought the biggest cuddly tiger I'd ever seen. We cracked up. 'How the fuck are you going to get that on the plane, Miles?' Dex asked. 'Shit…I hadn't thought about that!' Miles answered, setting all of us off again.

We got to Kiev and went for something to eat before wandering around the town centre, where we came across a massive demonstration. None of us knew what the people were demonstrating about, but there were loads of TV and media crews around so it was time to George up and steal the demonstrators' thunder. We all suited up and started mingling with the crowd, who didn't have a clue what or who we were. We were approached by a crew from a Ukrainian news channel – the interviewer spoke English and he spoke to me. It turned out that the demonstrators were protesting about government cuts in the postal service and they were all postal workers, so I told the interviewer that we had been sent to the Ukraine as representatives from the English post office, to stand side by side with our comrades. All the boys were wetting themselves, but they all went along with what I was saying. What I didn't expect was for the interviewer to speak to the union reps, who then wanted me to speak through the loud hailer to all these Ukrainian postal workers. One rep asked my name so that he could introduce me to the thousand or so protesters. 'Wayne Kerr,' I told him, trying not to laugh. 'That's it – we're all going to get shot!' Chubb said. All the other lads were in fits at this point and it only got worse as the rep started his speech in Ukrainian. You could hear him building up to announcing my name, and then it happened...'WAYNE KERR'! The crowd started cheering and applauding and I couldn't help but start laughing. They then gave me the loud hailer, what was I going say? The camera crew zoomed in on me as I prepared to speak. 'Comrades, we are here today with you from England to let you know that we will stand with you in your fight,' I announced. The interviewer then took the loud hailer and translated, and the postal workers cheered. The interviewer gave me the hailer back, 'We in England are also fighting for our jobs. The head of the English postal service is a bastard and should be hung!' I said, not really knowing where I was going with this. The interviewer looked puzzled, but repeated what I'd said, and the crowd cheered and then all looked puzzled as well. I grabbed the hailer back for my final message to the people. 'KILL POSTMAN PAT!' I shouted into the hailer. The interviewer saw the fierce look in my eyes and then proceeded to announce in Ukrainian what I'd just said. He then started repeating it, and the crowd joined in. I raised my arms to salute the protesters, shook a few hands, and we got out of there.

We flew back to Rome to get our transfer flight back to London. We took off from Rome at 9pm, but after about ten minutes we heard an announcement from the captain. 'Ladies and gentlemen, could you please, please, please not turn on any mobile phones or electronic devices. We have a technical problem with the plane and are returning to Rome to get it checked out'. Seconds after he'd made the announcement, all the lights in the cabin went out and we could feel the plane start to slowly turn to make its return to Rome airport. The next thing, the engines almost went silent. At a moment like that the passengers were going to do one of two things: panic or find God. The whole plane did the latter. Heads were disappearing in front of me, as people started praying and the whole plane fell into silence. Cue Stan! 'We're not going home, we're not going home, we're not going, we're not going, we're not going home!' I sang at the top of my voice. It probably wasn't the song most of the passengers would have chosen to hear, but my mates were cracking up. We could see Rome airport ahead of us, but none of us thought we were going to make it as the plane was almost gliding. We landed on the end of the runway and we could see fire trucks nearby, but we just carried on rolling until we came to a stop. The stairs were wheeled up to the plane by hand and everyone got off very casually, with no sign of panic at all.

We got off the plane and walked down the runway towards the waiting buses. We then saw what the technical problem was; the plane was pissing fuel out from the underside. Safely back in the terminal, it was chaos. People were going mental at the Italian airline staff, but I was just thankful to still be alive. They told us that we couldn't fly that night and that they would get us home in the morning. We must have been the only ones happy at the situation – they were putting us up in a hotel and we got to have a night in Rome. After eating at the hotel, we all went out. While we were out, we talked about the forthcoming trip to Qatar and Miles suggested that it would be a laugh to get some horses and ride them dressed as St George while we were there, so we left it to Miles to look into.

We got back to the hotel at 5.30am and the guy at reception told us that our coach to the airport was leaving at 7am 'Can I have my passport back please?' Chubb asked, giving the guy his room number. 'That's a good idea, Chubb,' I slurred. I asked the receptionist for my passport and gave him my room number, but unfortunately I gave him the wrong one. He gave me two passports, which I opened. They were identical; the same picture of an Asian bloke, and the same name in both passports. I had been given some bloke's passport and a copy…why would anyone need two passports? I went and spoke to Dex, 'Why would someone have two passports, Dex?' Dex looked at the passports and said. 'I'll tell you why, because he's a terrorist, that's why!' 'Fuck me Dex, do you really think so?' I said, astonished. 'Definitely, mate, and I tell you what – he won't be blowing any fucking planes up in the morning!' Dex walked off with one of the passports. He wanted both but I needed to exchange one for my passport. I got my passport and joined the others. 'Dex! What did you do with the other passport?' I asked 'Fired it down the lift shaft. When we see that cunt in the morning, we should take him out. Dressed as St George. We could be international heroes after this!' Dex said excitedly and we went to bed.

In the morning, we all wearily trudged downstairs in our St George gear and sat in wait for the terrorist suspect. People from three other flights had stayed at the hotel that night and tempers were rising as young and old jostled and pushed to be at the front of the queue to get on the coach first. The first coach arrived and it was a free-for-all, but we weren't bothered about getting on so we were enjoying watching all the old people fighting and arguing with each other. Then we heard an English couple shouting at the staff. They were an Asian couple in their mid-fifties and they were going absolutely ballistic at the girl on reception. 'No it's not the airline's fault, it's YOUR fault,' the man shouted. 'What's the problem, mate?' Miles asked. 'We gave our passports to the receptionist last night and they've lost one!' the lady explained. 'Is it yours or your husband's that they've lost?' Miles asked. 'Neither – it's one of our twin boys' passports,' she said. Sure enough, sitting away from the reception desk was our terrorist bomber with his identical twin brother!

Miles and I, who are very rarely stuck for words, couldn't speak. What had Dex done? We went and told Dex about his 'suspect'. 'You've got to tell him, Dex,' I said. 'Oh yeah, what am I going to tell him? Sorry mate, I stuffed your passport down the lift shaft because I thought you were a terrorist bomber?' Dex said sarcastically, so we just kept our heads down and left for the airport.

Once we checked in, we went to the bar and started drinking again. After two or three, we were pissed again! As we sat there laughing at what had happened over the weekend, we didn't hear them announce that our flight was boarding. It was only when we heard them calling out our surnames that we knew we'd better run. The boys were sprinting and I was just about to run after them when Chubb said, 'Hang on Stan, I can barely walk at the best of times! Running when I'm pissed is out of the question!' 'It's alright, Chubb, I'll walk with you, it's not like they're going to leave without us, is it?' I said. But when we got to the gate, it was closed! 'Excuse me, we're supposed to be on that flight,' I said to the girl standing at the desk. 'The gate is closed. You'll have to get another flight,' she told me. 'But the fucking plane is still there!' I shouted as I looked out the window to see one of the ground staff carrying Miles's fucking great tiger up the stairs and onto the plane. For all our begging, they wouldn't open the gate. Me and Chubb turned around and walked away. 'What are we going to do now, Stan?' Chubb asked. 'Well there's only one thing for it, let's go get a beer and we'll work something out after that.' We eventually got on a plane to Heathrow about three hours later – I don't know how they let us on the plane as by that time we were both so pissed we could hardly speak.

Chapter 34

Got the hump

When I got to Gatwick with Bruce, Ian, Dave and Liam for our next trip, we met up with Dex and Miles. Miles told us that he hadn't been able to organise horses for us as he'd suggested, but he'd got camels instead! Once again Clubby was there too, and we all boarded the plane in economy. Except Miles, that is, who flew first class.

We arrived in Qatar, collected our bags and waited for Miles. Where the hell was he? Eventually he came through to the bag collection area and he was steaming. He'd taken full advantage of the free complimentary drinks in first class and was more pissed than I'd ever seen him. He showed us photos of him in his George suit with the first class cabin crew.

Miles had not only flown first class, but was travelling to the hotel first class in a limo, while the rest of us bundled onto a mini bus. We'd been by the pool at the hotel for about an hour when Miles came walking towards us with a carrier bag. 'Where the fuck have you been?' Dex asked. 'You ain't going to believe it,' said Miles. 'First they've left my fucking luggage in Dubai and it won't be here until tomorrow and secondly my limo wasn't a limo, it was a fucking Skoda!' Miles shouted, and all of us cracked up. 'I had to stop at a shop and buy a pair of shorts,' he added, producing the most hideous shit-brown pair of shorts with yellow stripes on them. He went off to change into his new gear and the shorts looked even worse on! Then the waiter came over with another round of drinks and asked me to sign the bar ticket. I signed and printed a name, wrote any old room number, gave it back to him and off he went. He returned about five minutes later and politely said, 'Excuse me, who do you think you are kidding, Mr Hitler? You are not in room 424?' You couldn't have written it and we all burst into a rendition of the *Dad's Army* theme tune. This went on all day long, with us all signing bar tickets with names like Osama Bin Laden, Saddam Hussein, Idi Amin, Benito Mussolini and Joseph Stalin. We were waiting for a United Nations task force to turn up, as according to us the hotel had some of the biggest war criminals – dead or alive – the world had ever seen staying there. Most of them were drinking Mojitos.

While Genghis Khan was getting a round in, Miles, who'd sobered up and then got pissed again, had passed out on his sun lounger. Bruce lifted the lounger up, wheeled him over to the pool and chucked it – and Miles – in. Two of the staff dived in the pool fully clothed, not to save Miles, but to retrieve the sun lounger.

At night, we went to another hotel with a live band playing. Miles had sobered up from the afternoon session, but within two hours was in a worse state than the other two times he'd been drunk that day. He didn't have the strength to hold his head above his waist, so he was dancing with his head on his knees. As the night went on and the drink went down, we were all on the dance floor. There were people from all over the world there and everyone was going wild. I stopped dancing to have a swig of my beer, and this Egyptian girl who was with her mates came over to me smiling. 'You are English, yes?' she said curiously. 'Born and bred and proud of it!' I answered. 'I am staying at this hotel and wanted to know if you wanted to come to my room with me for sex!' she blurted out. I almost choked on my beer and said, 'Sorry love, I'm getting married in a week's time, so thanks but no thanks!' She shrugged her shoulders and went and joined her friends.

When the bar closed, we got a taxi to our hotel and on the way taught the taxi driver some English phrases to say the next time he had an English customer. He already knew some phrases from *Only Fools and Horses* like 'Lovely jubbly' and 'You plonker', so we gave him some more. We got out of the taxi at our hotel and as we walked away, he shouted out of the window, 'You filthy cunt!' We turned round and gave him the thumbs up; he was a quick learner.

The next day, I woke up to Bruce screaming 'What the fuck have you done?' and I smiled. Dex also woke up and said, 'What's the matter, mate?' and Bruce came out of the bathroom with both of his eyebrows missing. Dex cracked up, and so did I once I got a good view of my handiwork. 'Look at me, you bastard. I look like a fucking pug dog! Oh fuck, I've got a job interview on Tuesday. They're going think I'm a right cunt looking like this!' 'They would've worked that out once you spoke to them Bruce,' I said, crying with laughter.

We went for breakfast, which for me and Dex spent crying into our fry up, looking at Bruce's glum face minus two eyebrows. After breakfast it was time to get Georged up, as two lorries had arrived and our camels were being unloaded. George the First, Third, Sixth, Seventh and Ninth all looked the part as we made our way down to the beach where the camels were waiting for us. The hotel manager, who was German, came up to us and spoke to Miles, before we mounted our trusty steeds. 'I just wanted you to know that I have spoken to the Qatar government and they have given you permission to ride the camels on the beach,' he said. 'That's great. I really appreciate you sorting this out for us,' Miles said gratefully. 'The one thing you cannot do is film the event for television or media, as this is against Qatar law and they would arrest all of you and me as well!' the manager said, sounding worried. 'All these people here with cameras, they are not the media?' he added. 'No, they're just people from the hotel taking photos,' Miles told him reassuringly. We then heard Dex on the phone. 'Hello? Yeah it's Dex, we're on the beach with the camels and we're just waiting for you to arrive.' Dex turned to me and said, 'That was Sky Sports News, they've just arrived at the hotel.' The manager looked worried. We couldn't see what the problem was, but we were told that all broadcasts have to be authorised by the Qatar government. We figured the likelihood was that no one would see it anyway, so we mounted the camels and were led up and down the beach, singing, 'We're on the camels and we're having a laugh'. Then we gave a brief interview, which wasn't easy as Miles kept swearing. 'Listen mate, if you could try not to say "fuck" every other word, we might actually get some footage that we can broadcast,' the cameraman said. We all dismounted and other people had a go on the camels, one of them being Ian. The camel he got on had the right hump.

After all the excitement on the beach we went back up to

the poolside, where we saw someone even more famous than us. It was Michael Jackson. Well it wasn't the *real* Michael Jackson, but it was a freaky lookalike and he had his son with him. 'Michael, Michael!' we screamed and he waved back. 'Chamone, mother fucker!' I screamed at him and he did a little move. He was loving it and I don't think he realised that we were taking the piss out of him. We asked if we could have our photo taken with him, and he agreed. As we all lined up with 'Michael', his son, who was about four, tried to get into the photo. Miles pushed him away and I said 'No, fuck off Miles, we want Bubbles in the photo as well.' Everybody screamed with laughter, Michael Jackson just stood there smiling, like some right gormless cunt.

As Me and Bruce walked through the main reception, the massive TV was showing us on the camels. I turned round to see Morritz, looking in disbelief at the screen. We joined the others at the poolside. 'Stan you've got to hear this,' Dex said and told me what he'd just said to the boys. Apparently Clubby had admitted that he'd been banned from Facebook because he had asked over two hundred girls under the age of sixteen to be his friend! Innocent or not, we weren't going to let Clubby live this down. When he eventually surfaced he was greeted by a chorus of, 'There's only one Clubby, there's only one Clubby! With a packet of a sweets and a cheeky smile, Clubby is a fucking paedophile!' Strangely, Clubby tried to avoid us for the rest of his time there.

Chapter 35

A time to forget, if only I could remember

O ur next match was against Japan in Austria, so we went to Bratislava in Slovakia…this is where I start hoping my missus doesn't read this! On the trip were Chubb, Paul, Liam, Ross and Ben along with Flips, Podge, Doni Chubb, Kenny, Loon, Bubba and Sick Boy. It was the England trip that never was: total alcoholic carnage. I have no memory of the two days I was there.

At the airport on the way home, the drinking went from mad to insane, all thanks to me. I bought a bottle of Absinthe and a bottle of alcoholic buttermilk and along with Sick Boy, Bubba and Loon, came up with the idea of the Absinthe Olympics. The airport was full of people, who, as the competition neared its conclusion, began to take more and more of an interest. Loon spewed up with a quarter of the bottle to go, leaving me, Bubba and Sick boy to fight it out for the medal places. It was neck and neck until Sick Boy finished the bottle and even swallowed the bits at the bottom. He was declared the champion, but I hate losing at anything – especially my specialist subject, drinking. I picked up the 15% proof bottle of buttermilk and started drinking, with encouragement from the boys. I downed it in one and with that successfully took the title of Absinthe Olympic Champion. The three of us then stood there, with me on a seat above the other two and sang the National Anthem. All the English people in the airport terminal joined in and gave me a round of applause, but fifteen minutes later I was paralytic; I don't remember getting on the plane and I don't remember getting off the plane! I blacked out for over four hours and when my mind eventually came back to me, I was on a bus leaving Luton Airport and heading back to Slip End. Problem was, I was still absolutely wrecked. How was I going to get by Anita without her knowing I was fucked?

I stood at the back gate of my house and tried to compose myself. I could hear Anita in the garden with all the kids. I had a plan. Walk in, say hello, tell her I'm ill and go straight to bed. My plan couldn't fail! I opened the back gate…and collapsed face down onto the gravel drive.

Chapter 36

Come fly with me

I travelled to the World Cup on my own and when I landed at Johannesburg, I Georged up just to see what sort of reaction I'd get. WHAT a reaction. I changed in the toilet after collecting my suitcase and then walked to the automatic doors which led out into the airport terminal. The sliding doors opened and I instantly felt like a celebrity. Cameras were flashing and it felt like there were a thousand people there. I was grabbed by a South African TV crew and immediately did my first interview on South African soil. It wouldn't be my last.

I ended up being in arrivals for over two hours, as the requests for interviews and photos were endless. I'd never experienced scenes like it. I had to get out somehow, but dressed in my George suit I wasn't going to lose the crowd. I managed to get to the toilet and told a Mexican TV crew that I'd be back in a minute. I went in and took my suit off, then walked back out. The TV crew, along with about two hundred people waiting for photos, were all bustling at the door, but as I walked past they just looked at me, not recognising me without the suit, so I legged it to the hotel.

When I woke up on the Friday morning the wait was over; Dex was arriving. Oh, and the World Cup started that day, too. I told Dex to George up when he landed and that I'd be at the gate to meet him, also in my George suit. Dex came through, Georged up, and I leapt over the security barrier and hugged my mate. The cameras were already running and the reunion of George the First and Seventh was broadcast all over the world. We did loads of interviews and were then approached by a guy doing a piece for the *Sun*. After he'd taken pictures and interviewed us, he asked what our plans were, and I told him we were going straight to Rustenburg, where England's first game was being played. 'How are you getting there, have you hired a car?' he then asked. 'We were hoping to meet someone and get a lift, but no luck yet,' I explained. 'I've got a car, if you fancy jumping in with me, I'd be glad of the company.' I was in the right place at the right time, yet again! I stayed in my George suit for the whole journey to Rustenburg, and when we got to the outskirts of the city we spotted some police in a dog van, so we stopped to ask for directions to where we were staying. I went up to the passenger window and said, 'Excuse me mate, you couldn't help us could you?' The policeman turned around and jumped out of his skin with fright when he saw me looking in at him. 'Oh my God, you scared me dressed like that!' he said. He knew the place we were staying at and got us to follow him to where it was. This was unreal; we'd got a lift from Johannesburg off a reporter and now we'd got a police escort!

We drove about three miles before he pulled into the

driveway of the hotel. We thanked the police and our journalist friend and they left, and then a lady, probably aged about fifty, came out to greet us – her name was Isabel and she was the manager at the hotel, although it was more like a safari retreat. We went to the bar (which had real swords and shields on the walls) and Isabel told us that each time we had a drink, we should write it down in the bar book then pay the bill when we left. How trusting was this woman? If we'd been those Scousers from Germany, we'd have cleared the bar and then cleared off! After a few drinks, Isabel drove us into Rustenburg and took us on a pub crawl of the town before driving us back. Now that's service! Back at the hotel bar, while I had a drink with Isabel, Dex passed out on one of the sofas. His snoring added to the jungle ambience of the place; it sounded like a rhino on heat.

In the morning we were so excited – Miles was arriving, by helicopter, and England were playing that day. Isabel had two of her staff up at 6am, scything down the long grass in the field next to us, for the helicopter to land. First a crew from ITV arrived and then half an hour later, the helicopter landed. Miles was in the front, dressed as St George. We were also Georged up, of course, ready to welcome our friend. ITV got us all to get into the helicopter and then filmed us getting out, like we'd all just landed. As the three of us stepped down from the copter, drinking bottles of Castle beer (a perfect name for us), we broke out into song for the camera crew. 'We're on the copter and we're having laugh, we're on the copter and we're having laugh!' They showed the footage of us three prior to the match that night and it has also since been used on *Have I Got News For You* on the BBC.

Later, Dex got a call from the *News of the World*. The

journalist we'd met earlier had given them Dex's number and they wanted to do interview and some pictures with us. An hour later they arrived and said they wanted some photos of us, as near to the ground as possible, wielding the swords from the hotel bar for effect. About a mile from the ground there was a large open field, where you could clearly see the stadium. It was a perfect location. While Isabel waited at the security perimeter, we drove across the field to do the shoot, and once we stopped, we opened the boot and took out our swords.

It turned out that the South African police had set up their headquarters for the match in that very field, and although they were over four hundred metres away from us, they were all looking over very curiously at three blokes dressed as knights and waving real swords around. We were just about to start taking pictures when a policeman on a quad bike came flying towards us. He jumped off the bike and said, 'Hello, I am the head of the Rustenburg police force!' Fuck it, we thought – he's going to stop us taking pictures, or worse arrest us for being in possession of lethal weapons. But instead he smiled and said 'Can I please have my photo with you guys?' Breathing a sigh of relief, we finished the photoshoot, and then the three of us walked over to the massive police operation, wielding our swords and singing 'Come and have a go if you think you're hard enough!' All of the police were laughing their heads off and they all wanted photos with us.

We went back to the security perimeter, where Isabel was waiting. There was a bar right by the security perimeter filled with locals, so we went in to get a beer, still carrying our swords, and no one batted an eyelid. If we'd done it at home, we'd have been nicked immediately, if not shot!

By George

Isabel then drove us to a bar in Rustenburg's busy shopping mall. We got out of the car, grabbed our swords and went in for a drink, yet again with no reaction. This one bloke dressed like Zorro came up to us with a flimsy plastic fencing sword and pretended to stab me in the back. I turned round, looked at him, smiled and raised my real sword in the air, then chopped his sword in half. 'You want to be a bit more careful who you pick on, mate!' I said. Zorro smiled and swiftly left.

As we walked back towards Isabel's car we passed a police car and the policeman in the passenger seat said, 'You will not get in the ground tonight with that,' pointing to the huge sword in my hand. 'Oh yes I will, mate!' I answered. 'My best friend is the head of the Rustenburg police force!' In the end we didn't take the swords with us that night to the match against the USA, which ended 1-1.

We woke the next day and were due to fly back to Johannesburg by helicopter. We got our passports stamped by Isabel at 'passport control' (AKA her office) and we were ready to leave, but there was a problem. Isabel's staff had locked the gate to the landing field with a padlock and they couldn't find the key. We couldn't climb over the six-foot fence because it had razor wire at the top, but then David, one of Isabel's workers, appeared with his mate and a hacksaw! After half an hour of cutting, they cut the padlock, and minutes later the helicopter arrived. As we took off, we waved to Isabel; all of her staff and everyone who was staying at the hotel had all come to see us off.

It was a wonderful experience flying back to Johannesburg and when we landed the helicopter boss drove us to Stanton. With six hours to kill before we needed to go to the airport,

212

we found a bar in Nelson Mandela Square. I was approached by a Norwegian guy, who said he was a presenter for of a Norwegian food show that they were filming in Johannesburg and that he wanted me to appear on their programme. I agreed to participate and followed him to where they'd rigged up a mock studio background there in Mandela Square. We were just about to start filming when, without the producers or presenter seeing, I put on my tunic, red cape and headgear so that I was half-Georged up. When they saw me, the presenter who had originally approached me came up and said, 'I don't know where the other guy has gone, but we'd much prefer you to do the show. Is that OK?' He didn't even recognise me! They asked me and two other people to try all the food and give our verdicts. After the food, they produced four different bottles of drink and poured out a small glass for each of us to try. A lady from South Africa sipped the drink while being filmed, and commented that it tasted too strong for her. The second person, a South African man, said that he liked it and thought it had a nice whisky taste. The camera then moved along to film me, only to find that I was necking the booze straight from the bottle. The presenter started laughing, knowing this was making for some good footage. After five or six swigs, I stopped drinking, looked straight into the camera and said, '*Nor way* am I drinking any more of that crap, that's disgusting!' All the crew and the presenter got my pun about Norway and after drinking a couple more drinks they wrapped the show up.

When we got to Johannesburg airport we said goodbye to Miles, who was flying back to England. He was flying in and out for every game – fuck that! With Miles gone, we went to catch

By George

our internal flight down to Cape Town and at the gate we found
Yorkie Dan, Psycho Phil and our favourite Northerner Clubby,
with a bag of sweets.

Chapter 37

Red cape town

I got up the following morning with one aim: to get some tickets for Italy v Paraguay, the match in Cape Town that night. Dex and I left our apartment and flagged down a sort-of taxi. We were told that before the World Cup the authorities would be getting all the shitty taxis off the road, but this one had obviously slipped through the net. One of the back doors was being held shut with cable ties, the passenger window had a screwdriver holding it up, and the seats looked like Freddy Kruger had been the last passenger; they were ripped to shreds. The driver was from Zimbabwe and his name was Edward. We took his number and told him that we'd use him all the time we were there, which delighted him.

We arrived at the V&A Waterfront, went into a bank and bought some match tickets – job done. We then booked a trip to Robben Island and a safari trip for us and Miles when he came back. With tickets and trips sorted, it was time to find a bar and we found a great one called Quay 4, which became our local. We met two guys from Brighton, who were both called Steve, and another guy called Jason, and the five of us became top drinking buddies (well apart from Jason, who wasn't a drinker and stuck to Coke).

That night we Georged up and went to the match and spent most of it in the concourse, fucking around. There was beer sellers driving around the concourse on bikes like those ones you get selling ice cream, with big boxes on the front. I asked two of the sellers if they would let us get on them while they videoed us with my camera and they agreed. They were laughing, but not for long. We'd started off riding around in a clear area near them, but then we rode off. The beer sellers thought we'd stop, as they still had my camera, but my camera was crap and I didn't care. When they realised we weren't stopping, they gave chase – and they didn't have to run too far to catch Dex, who'd crashed into a concrete post!

After the match, we went to Long Street and found a bar called The Dubliner. It was proper rocking in there and rammed to the rafters. We stood right above the bar area on a balcony, where everyone could see us, and spent the rest of the night dancing and entertaining the crowd. We left the bar at 4am and were heading back to our apartment when we were approached by a guy who asked, 'Where are you going?' He looked a right dodgy fucker and I answered, 'None of your fucking business, mate – now piss off'. 'There's no need to be like that, I'll walk you back to your hotel,' he then said. 'Listen, mate, I said "piss off" and I meant it. You see all these blokes in security jackets? Do you want me to get them to nick you?' Surely the threat of being arrested would deter this fellow. 'They won't arrest me,' he replied, showing us an identity badge. He was undercover old bill. 'My friend, I insist that I walk you back for your own safety. You and your friend are very drunk and could easily be robbed'. The security operation in South Africa was fantastic and the cops really did go out of their way to make sure everyone had a good time and was safe during the World Cup.

When we got in, Dex decided he wanted to get a photo of me underneath the tree in our apartment. It was a sort of tree sculpture that stood seven foot tall and had been cut in half and hollowed out with a hole in the front. It weighed a ton, but we managed to lay it on the floor. I then lay next to it and Dex lifted the end with the hole in it. I slid under and Dex lowered it on top of me. I just about fitted in the hollowed part. 'Hurry up and take the fucking photo!' I shouted, but Dex was laughing too much. 'You look like a fucking giant Twiglet, Stan!' Dex took a few photos with my camera and then said, 'Hang on, don't move, I'm just going to get mine from my bedroom'. 'Don't move? I can't fucking move!' I shouted. A few minutes passed and Dex hadn't returned. 'Dex? Dex? Are you going take some more photos and get this off me or what? Dex? Are you still there?' I shouted, but there was no answer. I was about to shout again, when I heard snoring coming from our apartment. The bastard had gone to fucking sleep and when Dex goes to sleep, Dex doesn't wake up, especially when Dex is that pissed. I shouted for about ten minutes, but it was a waste of time, and I tried to lift the tree myself but I couldn't; I was stuck there. I eventually passed out and went to sleep too, the only difference being that Dex was on top of a nice comfortable double bed and I was stuck under a fucking great tree!

I was woken in the morning, not by Dex lifting the tree off me, but by Dex shouting from his bedroom. 'Jeeves, Jeeves?

Where's my tea and toast Jeeves?' The bastard was calling me to make his fucking breakfast. 'Well, Sir, if you'd like to come out of your bedroom and get this FUCKING TREE OFF ME, I'll kindly make your breakfast!' I yelled. Dex came out and carried on where he'd left off, laughing at me under the tree, and then said, 'What are you doing under there? Hang on – I've got to get my camera!' I couldn't believe it. Eventually he lifted the tree enough for me to squeeze out and God knows why but I made him tea and toast.

Over the next couple of days we got into a routine of going out for breakfast to this garden centre place that had a really nice restaurant, before going down to the Quay 4 all day and then ending up back at Long Street. On the Thursday, our driver Edward dropped us off at the garden centre and as always, the staff were pleased to see us, especially the owner Vaughn, who was a lovely lady. We knew most of the staff's first names, but this morning there was a new waiter working. He took our order from Dex, while I was busy chatting with Vaughn. 'Did you order two pots of tea, Dex?' I asked. 'Shit, only one!' he answered. 'That's alright, I'll just shout to the waiter, what was his name?' I asked. 'Hitler,' Dex said. It was early, I was still pissed and wasn't thinking. 'HERE, HITLER!' I shouted across the shopping mall, with my arm raised to attract his attention. Everyone looked round, thinking I'd said 'Heil Hitler', and of course it also looked like I giving a Nazi salute.

After breakfast, we went outside and found Edward having a problem with a traffic cop. 'What's the matter, officer? This is our driver,' I said. The cop looked at us and said, 'You're driving around in this car? Are you mad? This car is not fit for the road.' He then reeled off a list of faults, gave Edward a ticket and left.

'What's the damage then, Edward?' I asked. 'I have one month to get the repairs done,' he explained. 'What that's it? No fine, no points, just get the repairs done? What happens if you don't get the repairs done?' I asked. 'I go to prison for two months'. 'Oh right, well let's not worry about that now. Take us to Table Mountain,' I said. We jumped in and were on our way.

When we got there we jumped in a cable car, Georged up, and I grabbed the microphone and gave everyone my guided tour of the mountain and all the views, making it up as I went. After that we got Edward to take us to a bed shop, as we needed two single mattresses. Miles was returning the next day and would be staying with us, along with his mate Gary. On the way, we got a puncture. 'You're not having a good day, are you Edward?' I said as we got out of the car. 'Is your spare tyre in the boot?' Dex asked. 'I don't have a spare tyre. I will have to call my boss to bring me one,' Edward said. We continued on foot to the bed shop and luckily they had two single mattresses in stock, so we paid for them and asked about delivery. The guy serving told us three days, but we needed them for that night so there was only one thing for it. Every vehicle that passed beeped their horn at the sight of two crusaders carrying mattresses on their backs – well, it's definitely something you don't see every day!

After an hour, we reached our apartment, dumped the mattresses and called Edward to see if our limo was back on the road. It was, his boss had just changed the tyre. Edward drove us to the V&A Waterfront and we gave him a special mission, to pick Miles up from the airport the following morning. Dex told Edward to make up a sign with Miles's name on it and we said he could have the rest of the day off, as he had an early start in the morning. Dex then called Miles. 'Hello Miles, just wanted to let you know that everything's sorted for your arrival tomorrow,' he said. 'Our private car, with our chauffeur Edward, will be there to collect you at the airport. Have a safe journey and we'll see you in the morning!' Dex hung up and burst out laughing.

We went to the Quay 4 and met our old friend Jeff, who as usual had no top on, but he did have a flashing police light on his head. It was packed in there that evening as South Africa were playing. Every time South Africa played, the fucking vuvuzelas blew. I didn't mind them being blown outside or at matches, but there was always one dickhead who'd blow one inside and that wound me and everyone else up. As I sat eating my burger waiting for the match to start, a South African girl blew her vuvuzela right in my ear. I turned around and angrily looked at her and said, 'Are you trying to fucking deafen me or something, you stupid cow?' She started laughing in my face and said, 'It's only a bit of fun'. I turned back to continue with my meal, and then she fucking blew it again! I slowly turned around in my seat and she was standing there alongside her boyfriend, both of looking smug about her horn-blowing skills. 'Could I have a go of your horn, please? I'll show you how it's done,' I calmly asked. She paused for a moment, before handing me her vuvuzela. I put it to my lips, then stopped and said, 'That's not how you do it. THIS is how you do it,' snapping the bastard thing over my knee. The whole pub – or at least everyone who'd seen what had happened – started cheering and clapping and all because I'd snapped a vuvuzela. The girl and her boyfriend were going ballistic, screaming and swearing at me, until the doorman and a load of South Africans in the pub threw them out. As they were being shown to the door the whole pub sang, 'You can stick your vuvuzela up your arse!'

At half time a live band played for fifteen minutes and I asked the bar manager, Darren, if I could sing a song. Darren asked the lead guitarist and he agreed to let me sing. Darren stood in front of the crowd and announced, 'Ladies and gentlemen, for one night and hopefully one song, the Quay 4 is proud to present the vuvuzela killer himself, STAN!' The crowd cheered and clapped and I turned to the lead guitarist, said, 'Do you know this song?' and started humming the Amarillo tune. He nodded and started to play. I then began to sing my World Cup song from 2006, changing a few words to bring it up to date. The crowd loved it, with South African and English fans alike joining in on the chorus.

Me and Dex left about midnight and headed back up to Long Street. Dex was more pissed than I'd ever seen him and I had to help him out of the taxi. We went in the Cuba bar and I sat Dex down and went to the bar. When I came back, I found Dex chatting with a nun! This was no ordinary nun, though, but a drag queen. I was going to intervene and stop my mate making a fool of himself, which he had a 'habit' of doing, but I was laughing too much at the drag queen sitting on Dex's knee telling him what a sweetie he was. I eventually dragged Dex away (pun intended) and we went to the Dubliner. Long Street was heaving with Algerian fans, beating drums and singing loudly. All the English fans were on the balconies of the bars overlooking the street. The English fans saw us approaching the Algerians and thought we were going into battle. I went up to a big Algerian beating his drum. 'Can I have a go?' I asked, and about eight or nine of them were all shouting, 'No, no, no'. 'Let me start one song, then if you don't like it, I will go,' I said. He handed me the drumstick and I asked for silence. The Algerians are very noisy supporters, but amazingly, hush set over Long

By George

Street and all Algerian eyes were on me. I took a deep breath, then beat the drum and sang, 'ONE TWO THREE! VIVA ALGERI!' The Algerian fans went crazy and all joined in with their new conductor. I gave the drumstick back to the big drummer and the Algerian supporters picked both of us up on their shoulders and started parading us up and down Long Street. When they put us down, I noticed the traffic had come to a complete standstill. A taxi driver, who was stuck behind the wall of Algerians, then slammed his foot on the accelerator! I dived out of the way, but Dex and two Algerians weren't so quick and the three of them went up in the air and landed back on the taxi's bonnet. The endless beating of the drums stopped immediately when they realised their friends had been run over. I was helped up and Dex was lifted off the taxi and sat on the path. 'Are you and your friend OK?' asked one of the fans. 'Yes, were both OK,' I answered. 'Good, now you both go and leave this to us. No one runs our friends over!' The Algerians hauled the driver out and gave him a right good hiding.

Once in the Dubliner, we went to our usual spot on the balcony overlooking the main bar and Clubby, Phil and Dan were already there. The Dubliner was busier than ever and getting to the bar was a nightmare, but I had a plan. I leaned over the balcony and the lads grabbed my ankles and lowered me head first towards the bar. Once I was close enough, I tapped the barmaid on the shoulder. She turned round and looked horrified to see me hanging there. 'Could I have five pints of Castle please?' I asked. She gave me the first two pints and the boys pulled me back up and took the beers. They then lowered me back down for two more and after taking them lowered me a final time to get the last pint and I gave the barmaid the money, I didn't wait for the change. We were all dancing on the balcony when the DJ played that Tom Jones song, 'You Can Leave Your Hat On'. It was used in the *Full Monty* film so of course the five of us then started stripping, to the delight of the crowd. By the time the bouncers got to us we were all down to our pants – they were not happy and told us to get dressed. We put our clothes back on, except Clubby who whipped his pants off and started swinging them round his head.

Eventually we made it back to the apartment, and I was fast asleep when I heard Dex's phone ring. It was Miles: he'd arrived and was down in the car park. Dex gingerly walked through the apartment and pressed the entry button. He was holding his back and said, 'Fuck me, Jeeves, my back's killing me'. 'That's probably due to you getting run over last night,' I told him. 'I never got run over, did I?' he asked. I told him about the taxi and he said 'I must have been slaughtered'. 'You were – do you remember being chatted up by a drag queen dressed as a nun?' I asked. 'Fuck off, now I know you're lying!' Dex said.

At that point, Miles walked through the front door with a smile on his face. 'You pair of bastards!' he shouted. 'You fucking pair of bastards!' 'What's the matter, mate, did Edward not pick you up?' I asked. 'Oh yeah, he was waiting in arrivals for me, holding up a sign reading "Mr Floppy Miles"!' he said, trying not to laugh. We were crying. Miles then continued, 'I went with Edward and we walked past all these top motors, until we got to this fucking old banger held together with fucking cable ties'. I was in pain with how hard I was laughing. 'I went to put my bags in the boot and he tells me the boot doesn't open, it's been riveted shut because the hinges snapped. I sort you two out a helicopter and you send me Shitty Shitty Bang Bang!' Miles complained, before bursting out laughing.

By George

We all Georged up and went to The Dubliner's marquee, outside the V&A shopping centre. When we arrived four workers were erecting a fence by the entrance. I watched them slowly working for five minutes, then told them to stand aside. I grabbed the drill and started drilling into the brick floor, then fired the first steel pole in and knocked it down with a sledgehammer. I put in the other four poles, grabbed the three white picket fence panels and attached them with cable ties (everything was held together with cable ties) and the job was done. I got a round of applause from the watching England fans and then posed for their cameras, raising the sledgehammer over my head. The Irish manager came out and said, 'Fucking great job pal, all your beer is free all day.'

Later on Dex came up to me and said, 'Come on, we've got an interview to do!' A TV production company were filming a documentary called *World Cup A&E* and they wanted footage of fans at the matches. Before we started filming, two smartly-dressed men approached me and said they were a producer and correspondent from BBC News. They asked if we would meet them the following morning to do an interview about the England versus Algeria match at their studios, and we agreed.

After we'd done our bit of filming for the *World Cup A&E* programme (which involved me dancing around holding a fake World Cup trophy and singing 'Football's coming home'). The producer told us they would film us again in Port Elizabeth, where England's last group game was, and after drawing 0-0 with Algeria anything less than a win would mean our World Cup was over.

It was 9am the following day when Gary, Miles's mate, turned up. Miles told him that I'd written him a welcome song. I hadn't – I was put right on the spot, but I sang him a song anyway. 'There's only one Fat Gary, there's only one Fat Gary! He's had a KFC and a Pizza Hut, Gary's got a fucking big gut!' Gary burst out laughing – thankfully he had a sense of humour! We Georged up and Edward arrived to take us to meet the BBC producer. Gary got in the front and said, 'Hello mate, you must be Edward.' Edward replied, 'And you must be Fat Gary', which set us all off laughing again.

We met the BBC producer and followed him to the studio as planned. The BBC had built the studio on top of a hospital near to the Green Point Stadium. We got in a lift, where were joined by the BBC correspondent Nicholas Witchell. 'Fuck me, things must be bad for the England team if they've sent in a war correspondent!' I said, and everyone, including Nicholas, started laughing. Once we got to the rooftop we met the correspondent who was interviewing us, and he asked us a few questions about the previous night's game. After that bit of filming was done, we went into the studio itself, where the BBC broadcast its World Cup coverage. I sat in Gary Lineker's chair and Dex and Miles sat in the guest chairs while Gary took our photos.

Filming complete, we then caught the ferry across to Robben Island. The tour guides are all ex-prisoners, so their knowledge is extensive. We were led into a prison dormitory, which still had a couple of bunk beds for show, and I ran and jumped straight onto the top bunk and said, 'I'm not going underneath Fat Gary, this is my bed!' Then we reached the most famous prison cell of all time: Nelson Mandela's. While everyone took pictures of Mandela's cell, I wandered down the corridor trying all the cell doors and eventually found one that was open. I went into the cell and closed the door behind me. A few minutes later the lads walked past and saw me standing behind the bars. The boys cracked up and Dex and Miles joined me in the cell while Gary took photos of us. He then got into the cell and stripped his top off – and he bore an uncanny resemblance to Charles Bronson. I don't mean the actor.

During the tour, we'd heard people remarking about us needing to show some respect, but when the tour was over we showed true respect to the man who had guided us around the prison. All the other people on the tour walked straight past him to get back on the ferry, but not us. We stopped to chat with him and told him was an absolute disgrace the way he and many others had been treated just because of their political views. We thanked him for a very interesting tour and he was so appreciative and told us it was nice to meet people like us and that we'd made him smile throughout the tour. We gave him the equivalent of about £50 as a tip, which brought a tear to his eye, and he thanked us kindly.

The next morning, our mini bus arrived at 7am to take us to Aquila Safari Park, which was four hours away. But we hadn't even got out of Cape Town when we heard this loud knocking sound. The driver stopped the bus, got off and checked the back wheel, only to discover that the wheel nuts had come loose. This wasn't the best start to the day, but he tightened all the nuts and we set off again. We'd been driving for about two hours when we saw some wild baboons by the side of the road, and the driver stopped so we could take pictures. The driver shouted to Miles, 'Don't open the door!' but Miles misheard him and opened the sliding side door. Everyone screamed at Miles to close the door as we watched the baboons getting closer, but the stupid thing had jammed. The driver sped off with the door open and once we were a safe distance from the baboons, he got out and managed to shut the door.

Red cape town

We arrived at Aquila and got into our George suits before climbing into a safari Jeep. We soon found that more people were taking pictures of us than of the wild animals! About halfway around the safari, the Jeep stopped by some emus. We talked Gary into getting out and having his picture taken with them, so he got out and went to stand as close to the birds as he dared. We'd taken a couple of pictures when Dex screamed, 'Run, Gary, they're coming after you!' Gary sprinted back to the Jeep, but the emus hadn't actually moved a muscle! The look on his face was priceless.

After the safari, we went to the lion enclosure. There was a male lion and two females, and obviously it was the perfect photo opportunity. We crouched down in front of the enclosure and had our pictures taken with the 'Three Lions'. Gary then screamed, 'I'd fucking move now boys, one's coming at you!' We didn't move, thinking Gary was just getting his own back, but then we heard loud footsteps getting closer and we did move! Well Miles and Dex did – they used me for leverage, forcing me down onto the ground. I turned around and looked straight into the lioness's eyes – she wasn't happy! I slowly got up and backed away.

After all that excitement, we got back on the mini bus for the drive back to Cape Town. Miles and Gary weren't flying home until 11pm, so we had plenty of time to spare. Or so we thought – when the driver turned the key in the ignition, nothing happened. Miles went mental. 'What sort of fucking operation is this? First the wheel almost fell off on the way down here and now the fucking battery's gone flat! If I miss my fucking plane, your company's paying for another flight mate!' he screamed. Dex and I cracked up, but Miles wasn't happy. We all got out and tried to bump-start the bus, but we couldn't get it to go. Miles was properly losing it at this point, so the driver suggested we push the bus down a steep dirt track. As we pushed the bus, the driver released the clutch and by some miracle the engine started.

Miles was quite subdued on the way back to Cape Town – until the bus started to splutter again. 'What the fuck is the matter with this fucking piece of shit now, you bastard?' he yelled as we came to a shuddering halt. The driver turned around and said, 'We've run out of petrol!' Miles was having a fit, but Dex and I thought it was hilarious. As we stood by the side of the road, the driver told us that he had put £40 in the tank the night before and thought it would be enough. 'You thought £40 would get us there and back? You're not the full fucking ticket, mate!' Miles said. At this point I think he'd given up on the idea of making his flight. The driver called his mate and told us that another bus would be there in two hours' time. Miles flipped.

We'd been on the roadside about half an hour when a traffic cop stopped and agreed to get us some fuel. We gave him three empty two-litre water bottles and 15 minutes later he returned with the bottles full of petrol. But how far was six litres of petrol going to get us? Shortly after setting off again, I said aloud, 'Come on then, boys. Let's have a whip round for the driver.' Everyone burst out laughing, and even Miles raised a smile. But after we'd driven straight past three garages, Miles lost it again. 'If you don't stop at the next garage and put enough fuel on this bus to get me to the airport, I'm going to kill you!' he said. We must have been driving on fumes.

We saw another garage in the distance, but again the driver kept on driving past. 'Right – pull over now!' Miles screamed. By this point I was getting seriously pissed off as well, so I chipped in. 'I'm gonna get you off this bus and fucking batter you!' 'Calm down, man, the other bus is just up the road waiting for you,' the driver said. He was as good as his word — after a couple of miles we reached the other mini bus and dropped Miles and Gary off at the airport with two hours to spare.

Chapter 38

Sun, sea and Georges

After an eight-hour drive from Cape Town, taking the scenic route, we arrived in Port Elizabeth for England's next match. I had no accommodation sorted, so I ended up sleeping in Dex's room. We were joined in Port Elizabeth by Dex's friends, Stu and his son Ali (who looked like Bruno, the Sacha Baron Cohen character).

We Georged up and headed out with Stu and Ali for the night. We went to a few bars and then a nightclub, where the DJ Norman Cook (Fatboy Slim) was doing a set, but they wanted £30 for us to get in. We weren't paying that, but as we went to walk away the owner of the club approached us. 'Hey boys, you've got to come in dressed like that!' he said. 'Not at that price, mate – we normally get in for nothing wherever we go,' I told him. 'Then you can come in as my VIP guests,' he said, and led us through the club to the VIP area where we were given free drinks. I've always said, it's not who you know, but what you're wearing!

Sun, sea and Georges

We'd been in the club for about an hour when Norman came out to do his set. The crowd went mental and as he raised his hands to salute us he then took a double-take at the sight of us two Georges standing at the front of the crowd. We waved back to him and jumped around with the rest of the crowd for about ten minutes before retreating back to the VIP area, where we stayed all night until the club closed.

I woke up in the morning and thought I'd been buried alive, but in fact I was in Dex's wardrobe. I'd gone to sleep at the bottom of the wardrobe, with the sliding mirrored door open. At some point Dex had got up and closed the door, so it was pitch black and I couldn't see a thing. I slid the door open, only to find Dex's bare arse in front of me – not the best sight first thing in the morning! He'd just got out of the shower. 'Ah, morning Jeeves, did we sleep well?' he asked. 'Yes, Sir, it was certainly one of my more comfortable sleeps since I've been on this trip,' I answered. 'No time to waste, Jeeves – we've got to meet that film crew in an hour, so chop chop!' Dex said, trying to talk posh. He liked calling me 'Jeeves' as I was like his butler, making his morning tea and toast, doing his washing and generally looking after him. Well, Dex was nearly fifty – he needed looking after!

We both Georged up and went with Stu and Ali down to a bar that overlooked the seaside to have breakfast. We'd only been eating for a couple of minutes, when the film crew turned up. 'We'll just finish our breakfast and then we'll be with you,' Dex said. 'If you don't mind, we'll start filming now while you're eating?' the producer replied. I couldn't just sit there quietly eating my breakfast while the camera rolled, so I burst into song about Dex having two eggs on his plate.

By George

After we'd finished breakfast, I suggested that they filmed us coming out of the sea like we'd just swum all the way there. We took our black boots and socks off and walked a few feet into the sea, which was freezing. 'OK, action!' said the producer, and me and Dex came walking out of the sea. I started to speak, totally unscripted – 'My loyal subjects! The M.I.G..S have arrived for battle! We have travelled many miles by sea and horse from a place you all know very well!' I then started to sing, 'En-ger-land, En-ger-land, En-ger-land!' Hundreds of England fans on the balconies in the bars behind the cameraman joined in with my song, and he panned round and zoomed in on my loyal subjects. 'That was brilliant, mate – you'd think we'd rehearsed it! You're a natural at this!' the cameraman said. We then sang 'Oh I Do Like To Be Beside the Seaside' and the film crew were cracking up. When we'd finished the producer said, 'I don't know how you think it up'.

We went back to the bar, but Dex was soon back on the phone to the producer. 'Are you still in the area? Because I've got a great idea for you to film...' Dex explained. The crew seemed interested, so we headed off to meet them on a grassy area by the seaside, where there were two policemen on horses. We asked them if we could get on their horses while the crew filmed us, and the police agreed. I was the first to get on the horse and as always I had something to say. 'My kingdom for a horse!' I shouted, and once again it made for a great bit of footage and the crowd that had gathered around us started laughing. With another shoot in the bag, we left the beach to head to the game. I was so nervous before and during the game and was just so thankful when the referee blew his final whistle. England had beaten Slovenia 1-0. We were through, but as runners up, which meant we were off to Bloemfontein to face Germany.

Chapter 39

Bring on
the Germans

The next day, we left Port Elizabeth and drove to a town that was aptly named George. We then flew on a late flight up to Johannesburg where we stayed in a hotel near the airport for the night before driving on to our final destination, Bloemfontein. There was nowhere to stay in Bloemfontein itself, so we found rooms in a very small town about 30 miles outside the city, but it wasn't the sort of town we were used to. When we arrived it quickly dawned on us that it was more or less a shanty town, and as we drove through we soon realised we were of great interest to the locals. This was the part of South Africa we'd heard about but hadn't intended to visit! 'There's no fucking way I'm staying here, no way!' Stu said. 'Come on, Stu, it's getting better. We must be in the posh area now, that bloke there has got some teeth!' I said, jokingly. Stu didn't laugh.

We drove through the town until we came to a residential area. We found the address of our hotel, but it wasn't a hotel, it was someone's house. 'Fuck me, what's Miles going to make of this place?' Dex said. 'I doubt if we'll find out, we'll probably be dead by morning,' Stu said. He was clearly nervous about our surroundings. A lady came out to meet us, introducing herself as Marti and explaining that she was the landlady of the hotel. We followed her through the front door and into a room with three beds. 'Would you like this room? Three of you, ya?' she asked. 'Have you got something a bit further away from the door…?' I asked. 'Yeah, like fucking miles away?' Stu muttered sarcastically. Marti gave Stu a dirty look and said, 'What's wrong, you have a problem?' 'Me? I haven't got any problem. It's the people out there who are going to mug and rape us, that's the problem!' Stu replied, while the rest of us just laughed. 'No one will get in here, you are safe,' Marti said and showed us two other rooms which were a bit further into the building. Dex and I went for the presidential suite (which was actually Marti's bedroom; she'd moved into the lounge) while Stu and Ali had the furthest bedroom away from the street.

Marti then asked if we'd like to see her aviary, which was at the back of the house. She had all sorts of birds. 'Marti, do you like a cockatoo?' I asked, taking the piss. 'Oh, I love a cockatoo!' she replied, and the boys were wetting themselves. She then showed us some chickens. 'Are these are male chickens, Marti?' I asked her. 'No, they are female, you silly boy!' she answered. 'Oh, do you have a cock?' I then asked. 'Ya, I have a cock, would you like to see it?' Marti innocently said. The boys were crying at this point. 'Nah, you're alright love, but we've got a bloke coming tomorrow called Clubby, and he'd love to see your cock,' I said.

Once we'd settled in, we sat around the pool (which was no bigger than a bathtub) having a beer. Marti came out with a girl of about twenty who was very pretty. 'This is my daughter, would you like her to massage you?' she asked, and we all nearly choked on our beers. 'She is a professional masseur and will massage you for £40,' Marti added. We declined the offer and asked Marti how we could get into Bloemfontein. 'Marco will take you,' she replied. 'Marco!' she screamed, and a bloke came out of the back room. 'This is Marco, my son.'

Marco drove us into Bloemfontein and we told him we'd call him when we were ready to be picked up. Switzerland were playing Honduras that night and we all fancied going to the match, so we picked up four tickets for about £10 each. We were having a drink on the waterfront when a load of Honduras fans walked past. One of them stopped and looked at Stu and then started talking to him. 'Sorry, mate, I don't understand. I'm English,' Stu said. The Honduras fan scratched his head and said in English, 'But why are you wearing a Honduras shirt if you are English?' 'It's a Brighton shirt, not fucking Honduras!' Stu answered. Me and Dex Georged up for the match and as we all stood for the national anthem of Honduras, Stu had his hand on his heart for his new adoptive country's anthem. He looked like Fidel Castro.

During the match, I was getting seriously pissed off with the bloody vuvuzelas, so I started going up to the South Africans who were blowing the things and telling them to follow me. I eventually gathered about 70 South Africans, who obviously thought I'd got them together to blow all of their horns at once. Unfortunately that's exactly what they did, almost blowing my head off. I raised my hands to signal for them to stop and shouted, 'My African brothers! You do not need to blow those horns to be heard! You have a voice; you are the voice of Africa! Let the rest of the world hear Africa!'

By George

They all looked very confused, until I screamed, 'BAFANA BAFANA!' Then I clapped my hands and repeated the words and the clapping over and over again. The fans all joined in and the noise grew and grew. Then everyone in front of us started singing and clapping and they just carried on. My work was done.

After the match, we went to a nightclub and after drinking and partying hard, Dex called Marco to pick us up. It was 4am. 'He said he'll be here in half an hour,' Dex slurred, and I couldn't believe the guy was actually coming out to get us at that time of the morning. Marco called Dex to let him know he was outside the club and we left. We got to Marco's car and couldn't believe what we saw – he'd driven to pick us up in his pyjamas! This was one weird family.

The next morning I got up about 8am, still pissed, and went into the dining room. There was Mad Marti. 'Good morning, Stan, did you have a good night last night?' she asked. 'Yeah, it was great! Fair play to Marco for coming to get us!' I answered. 'What time did you come in?' she asked. 'I don't know, about 5am?' 'What? My Marco was out that late? If I'd known I would not have let him go out! That is way past his bedtime!' she said angrily. 'Hang on, Marti, how old is Marco?' I asked. 'He is 23, but he is still a little boy, ya?' she said. What a fruitcake.

About 12pm, we all headed off with a very tired looking Marco, to a nearby safari reserve. It only cost us £30 each and we got more than our money's worth. We Georged up and got into a truck, and off we went. We drove for miles and didn't see a bloody thing – not until the end of the tour, where they had three lions in an enclosure. There was a 20-foot electric fence surrounding a load of undergrowth, bushes and trees. We stood at the fence, but once again saw nothing. I walked with the tour guide until we were about fifty metres away from the others, and she told me to stop and listen. I could clearly hear the sound of a lioness charging through the undergrowth – towards Dex, who was standing near the fence by the truck! At first Dex wasn't bothered, as there was the massive fence separating him from this very angry-looking lion, but that soon changed. Every time Dex moved, the lion would follow him, like she was stalking her prey. It was clearly spooking Dex out, but the rest of us were laughing. We all stopped laughing, though, when the lion suddenly charged at the electrified fence. You could hear the buzzing of the electric but it didn't deter the lion as she tried to rip through the fence. Dex was shitting himself and the tour guide told him to get back into the truck. The lion took no notice of me, so it must have been Dex's aftershave that wound her up! Or so I thought. As I posed for photos in front of the lion enclosure, the lion leapt forward. As she hit the fence, it was my turn to be worried, and the tour guide said that we should all leave before the lioness ripped through the fence, as she had done it before! Twice!

After the Knights' experience with the Lion King (or Queen…) we went back to the hotel, and by the time we arrived Miles was there with Ian, Bruce and Dave. That night the mini bus that had brought them from Johannesburg to Bloemfontein took us into the city and Marco came with us. We went to a restaurant near the waterfront that was rammed with Germans. We had to sit outside on the veranda, which was freezing, and we were joined by Ian's mate from Luton, DD. With a restaurant full of Germans and a veranda full of English fans, it wasn't long before the songs and comments were flying around, along with the blow-up Spitfires that Miles had brought with him. We picked up a Spitfire and entered the restaurant, running around singing the *Dambusters* tune and pretending to machine-gun the German fans at their tables. When we finished our dogfight, the German fans applauded us as we went back out onto the veranda.

When we'd eaten we made our way to the back to the club that we'd been in the night before. We partied hard into the night and the crowd loved seeing not one but four Georges on the dancefloor. One of those Georges had been singled out by a woman, and that George was me. But the woman was Marti! It was about 1am and Marco, who was smashed, had called his mum to come and pick him up. When she arrived, she grabbed me and started wanting to waltz. Being a gentleman, I danced with her, and we looked like Fred Astaire and Ginger Rogers on acid. After we'd danced, Marti got Marco into her car and they drove home. I sat down with the lads to have a drink and they all started throwing money at me, saying I'd clearly won the 'pull a pig' competition that night. Cheeky bastards.

The next day, everyone was upbeat about the match against Germany later that night. As we arrived in Bloemfontein, I was hanging out of the mini bus, Georged up, with an inflatable Spitfire in my hand. The people on the streets seemed to spark into life once they saw me. I was like the catalyst that started the party. We parked up and made our way through the shopping centre, to a bar we'd drank in for the last two days. We walked through the shopping centre, singing and waving our inflatable planes, and the place went wild.

We walked onto the waterfront, with its surrounding bars, and we could hear 200 or so Germans clearly out-singing the thousand or so English fans. We couldn't stand for that. When the English fans saw us four Georges leading a squadron of Spitfires straight through the German supporters, the noise became deafening. We made our way up onto the veranda of the bar we'd be drinking in the night before. Miles had brought four boxes of inflatable Spitfires, with fifty in each box. They went like hotcakes. I climbed up some fence railings and onto a huge canopy. I was easily 20 foot above the crowd in the bars and I began to orchestrate the singing.

The whole afternoon and early evening was one of sheer exhilaration. I'd been to the first three games of the tournament, but all of them put together did not compare to the atmosphere of this one. Unfortunately that atmosphere ended that evening as England lost horribly, 4-1 to Germany, with the added disappointment of a cruelly disallowed goal. As we trudged away from the ground and through the car park under the shopping centre, the taste of defeat and the sight of the Germans celebrating were very hard to take, but we did. What none of us could handle, though, was the sound of those fucking vuvuzelas. Three South Africans wearing Germany shirts were blowing their horns and the noise was echoing around the underground car park. I stopped and turned around to face them. 'You blow that fucking horn again and I'll snap the bastard in two and don't think I won't!' I shouted angrily. I turned back around and one of them blew it again, so I flew at him and tried to grab the vuvuzela. His mate, who was my height but stockier than me, then pushed his face into mine. 'What's your problem, mate?' he said. 'If you don't get out of my face you'll find out what my problem is,' I replied. The next thing I knew, Bruce had hammered a punch into the stocky guy's mate, who was standing alongside him. The guy was well over six foot, but he was certainly brought down a foot or two by Bruce's punch. He struggled to stay on his feet and when he saw Bruce waving him on, he and his two mates legged it, shouting for the police.

By George

Once we got out of the car park, we found a steakhouse and most of us ordered normal-sized steak, apart from Ian, who ordered a 1kg steak with 500 grams of spare ribs on top. He was in his element. While we ate, our travel agent called. He'd got me booked on a flight home the next day, leaving from Jo'burg at 9pm, and after England's defeat I was thankful to be getting home that quick.

The next day me, Dex, Bruce and Miles left Marti's madhouse and headed for Johannesburg. Once we got there, we spent the day back in Nelson Mandela Square, and when it was time for me and Bruce to go to the airport, saying goodbye to Miles was hard but saying goodbye to Dex was nigh on impossible. It was a worse feeling than when Dave and I had parted company after the World Cup in Germany. I gave Dex a big hug and said, 'It's been a pleasure serving you, Sir'. 'The pleasure has all been mine, Jeeves,' he said.

After our 11-hour flight back to Heathrow, I turned to Bruce and said, 'Come on mate, shall we George up one more time to see what reaction we get now we're home?' We got off the tube at King's Cross to get our train back to Luton and when we came out of the Underground, the response was amazing. Cars and taxis were beeping their horns, people on the street were shaking our hands, and a passing police car stopped and the copper said, 'If only the team had done as good a job as you boys, we'd have been champions!'

Chapter 40

Can I kick it?

After our World Cup disappointment I was soon back on the road – or should I say in the air – again with an away trip to Basel in Switzerland with Bruce, Ian, Dex, Miles, Stu and Liam.

When we arrived we headed to a bar called Pickwick's, where we met up with Dale and Alex from Aldershot. The bar shut at about midnight and we all jumped into taxis and headed to a strip club (which was the only place open) opposite our hotel. We walked in and the place was empty, apart from the dwarf woman behind the bar. Me and Dex thought we'd liven things up so we started pole dancing to entertain the lads. We had separate poles to dance around, but we weren't the most graceful dancers the lads had ever seen. Mind you, the barmaid seemed to be enjoying it.

After ten minutes of us gyrating around our poled, five or six scantily-clad girls walked in from the back of the club. We stopped dancing to let them take over, but they didn't. Instead, they gestured for us to carry on while they sat down and watched. The girls were whistling, cheering and clapping wildly and I managed to climb the pole, clamp my legs around it and lean backwards. I looked great, until I smacked my head on the pole and fell into a heap on the floor. I decided it was a good time to stop and told the girls that they could take over, but they declined, saying they'd finished for the night.

We left the club at about 4am and Dex thought it would be a good idea to go into Miles's room and scare him. It was a good starting point, but we needed something extra. So Dex, Bruce and I got white bed sheets, burnt a couple of holes in them and put them over our heads. We slowly opened the door and with Miles fast asleep, we started making wailing noises like ghosts. We expected Miles to wake up and start laughing, but instead he opened his eyes and proper freaked out, screaming like a girl. It was absolutely perfect – he was petrified!

The following day, we all Georged up and congregated outside Pickwick's with the rest of the England fans. Dale and Alex turned up, as did my mate from Gillingham, Jim. While we were drinking on the street outside the bar, a football appeared and everyone wanted to kick it. About half an hour later, I saw the ball dropping from the sky above me, and I caught it. I moved to a more central position in the street to do a drop-kick, looking around for an ideal target to kick at. Then I saw it. There was a fat English fan in a red football shirt about three storeys up, looking over a glass balcony, and on the next balcony along there was a couple having a meal. I gestured up at the balcony and the crowd looked to where I was pointing. One geezer then shouted, 'Yes, mate! Kick it up there at Buster Bloodvessel!' That was a pretty good description of the guy. 'No, you see that couple having dinner? I'm going to stick it right on her dinner plate!' I boldly shouted back. I steadied myself, licked my finger and raised it as if to check the wind movement, and then drop-kicked the ball. As soon as it left my foot, everything went into slow motion. The crowd were shouting, 'Oooooooooooooooh...' as they watched the football get closer and closer, until it went sailing through over the balcony and crashed right onto the couple's table! I couldn't believe it. I'd actually landed it on the woman's plate! Not only did it send the plate flying, it smashed the couple's glasses and the bottle of wine they'd been enjoying together. The woman went flying backwards in her chair and ended up on the floor. The crowd beneath her balcony was cheering 'One-nil to the Eng-er-land' as loud as they could, but the man on the balcony didn't find it so amusing as he picked his partner and what remained of their romantic meal off the floor.

Next door to Pickwick's was a tall building surrounded by scaffolding, which hundreds of England fans decided to climb. Everyone was looking up at these lads on the scaffolding, until someone saw a bloke on the other side of the street looking over his balcony. He was the spitting image of Harry Potter. As the crowd sang 'You can stick your fucking wand up your arse' he was joined on the balcony by his girlfriend, who got an instant chorus of 'Do you take it up the arse?' – she and 'Harry' seemed to love the attention.

Dex then grabbed me and said, 'Come on, I've got an idea'. We went through the front door of a nearby building and walked up the stairs. 'What are we doing, Dex?' I asked. 'Trust me, if we pull this off we'll be legends,' he said. Dex then knocked on a door and when the door opened, there stood Harry Potter. We pushed past Harry, charged through his flat and went out onto the balcony, where his girlfriend was still standing. When the England fans saw five Georges above them, they went mental. We were like the Royal Family on the balcony of Buckingham Palace. Harry wasn't pleased, though, and tried to drag us back indoors and out of his flat. His girlfriend, on the other hand, found it all quite amusing and asked for our picture. While we posed for a photo with her, we heard Harry on his mobile. 'Can you send the police quickly! There are a load of men in my flat and I think they are going to rape my girlfriend!' It was time to go.

At the match there was one of the best England crowds I'd seen for years, and about a hundred young England fans, all pissed up, were trying to pull the fences down at the front. They eventually forced a security gate open and all tried to rush the stewards to get on the pitch. We were cracking up at what was going on and I laughed even more when Miles pointed to someone in the thick of it. It was Gary! He loved it with all his ASBO crew; he was like their general. The stewards managed to force them back and close the gate, but Gary and his barmy army continued to cause mayhem throughout the match, which ended in a fantastic 3-1 win for England.

After the final whistle, we made our way to a nearby bar. It was packed with people, but not normal people. Everyone there looked like a tramp (and smelt like one, too) and they had a live group playing who were like nothing I'd ever seen before. There was a female lead singer, two men on guitars and a drummer, they were all in their fifties, and they were all wearing bullet-proof vests and Mexican sombreros. They'd sung about four songs when the lead singer announced something and the crowd started cheering. The next thing I knew, everyone in the bar produced two plastic shot glasses on a piece of string, which they wore like earmuffs. The singer then burst into song and when she sang the chorus, the crowd spun their glasses above their heads. It was all very weird, but we were enjoying ourselves anyway! When the band finished their set, the barman set up a karaoke screen and what followed certainly wasn't the *X Factor*. With Georges and tramps singing in unison, it was pure comedy and when someone put on 'YMCA', I thought my sides were going to split.

The following morning, Dex suggested we go on a boat trip down the river. We were just about to board the boat, when I alone decided to George up. Our fellow passengers were in a frenzy to get a photo with me – oh yes, and they were all school kids on a trip. I thought their teachers would object and try to stop them, but they were also pushing in to get a photo. Once we boarded the boat, we made our way up to the control room. There was no one there, but the captain had left his jacket and cap, which of course I put on. As I stood there in the control room, with the captain's jacket and cap on over my George suit, I saw a microphone, so I switched it on and spoke. 'Good Morning, this is your captain speaking! I'd like to welcome you all to George Boat Tours. We will be travelling at approximately twenty miles per hour, until I decide to crash this boat into another. Thank you once again for choosing George Boat Tours, sit back and relax and enjoy the trip – until we sink!'

The boys were wetting themselves, but the captain, who'd now arrived, looked furious and ordered me to get out of his control room and give him his uniform back.

Chapter 41

Just one photo

Five months later, we were off to Copenhagen to face Denmark. This time our group was made up of Dex, Miles, Paul, Ian, Stu, Ben, Liam and the Doni boys Flips, Robs, Podge and Brownie. We went out on the town (all Georged up as usual) and found a bar called the Irish Rover. We'd been in the bar a few hours when I needed a shit – I was busting. As I sat down, just about to drop the kids off, the seat slipped from the toilet and I ended up on the floor. I quickly got up before I shit all over myself and plonked my arse on the cold ceramic toilet bowl, and once I'd finished, I stood up and looked at the seat on the floor and thought it would be a good idea to take it with me. I returned to the boys and when Paul saw the toilet seat in my hand, he said, 'What the fuck have you got that for?' 'Dunno, I just fell off the fucking thing and I thought it would look good on your head,' I answered. I put the seat over Paul's head, but he wasn't impressed. Within five minutes, though, all the lads were posing for photos with this toilet seat on their heads.

Just one photo

We left the Irish Rover (still with the toilet seat) and went to find another boozer. We came across a tramp asleep in a wheelchair and we had to get a photo. I gave the camera to Paul, crept towards the sleeping tramp and carefully placed the seat over his head, then turned to face the camera. The tramp woke up and started going mental. 'Alright mate, we're only having a bit of fun!' I said to him, but he didn't speak English and started trying to hit me. 'Catch me if you can!' I yelled and ran away from him. I'd gone about thirty metres, when the Danish police pulled up in a riot van and some coppers jumped out and grabbed me. 'What the fuck's going on, mate? I'm only having a bit of fun!' I said. 'We've been watching you with your toilet. You must not joke with the Danish people, you will now come with us,' the copper told me. It was time to think fast and speak even faster. 'I'm not joking though, mate, I'm working. I work for the English FA…' I didn't have a clue where I was going with this one. 'You work for the FA?' the cop asked curiously. 'Yes, each away game we go on, we take this toilet seat and take pictures of a local person for the FA website. The best picture wins one hundred English pounds!' I convincingly told him. The next thing I knew, I was rammed by the tramp in the wheelchair, who was still swearing at me in Danish. I pointed to the tramp and said to the copper, 'Look, mate, I'm sure he could do with the money and I'll make sure he wins. I can't say no fairer than that.' The copper once again paused to think and then said, 'No, you will delete the photos and then you will go.' He watched Paul delete all the photos.

We were just about to leave, when I spoke to the copper again. 'Thanks for not arresting me, but I still need a photo…if I could get one of you with the seat over your head, I'll take your name and address and I guarantee you'll be the winner.' The young officer briefly stayed silent, pondering my offer, and then said, 'One photo and I get one hundred pounds?' 'The money's as good as yours, mate!' I told him. 'OK, but quickly,' he said. I was just placing the seat over his head when another officer pushed the copper into the van, then turned to me and said very sternly, 'Leave my policemen alone!' He slid the side door shut, got in the front and drove off. Oh well, their loss, I thought.

We got up the following day and got straight back on the beer, and we were joined by Andy and Gillingham Jim. We'd been drinking for about two hours when these two Danish lads, Freddy and Roy the Boy, came into the bar to meet us. We'd met them the night before and Freddy was a student in Copenhagen while Roy the Boy was a drug dealer. Freddy suggested we should all go to his university bar, where it was a lot cheaper. After three hours in the uni bar, Roy the Boy was trying to get us to go to a strip club, but something else had caught my eye. In the bar's lounge, they'd been setting up a load of chairs as there were some esteemed speakers talking to the students that evening. I knew this was an opportunity that I couldn't miss. All the seats in the lounge were taken and there were people having to stand at the sides and back. I approached the guy on the microphone, who was sitting near the front of the stage. He had a list of the people who would be talking that evening, but he had one name missing: mine. 'I have just spoken with the Dean and he's so pleased that I've come all the way from England to speak tonight. Could you put my name on the top of the list, as I have to be somewhere very shortly after?' I told the guy. I was waiting for him to tell me to do one, when he said, 'What is your name?' 'Professor Stan Stanfield!' I proudly answered and he wrote my name down. Ten minutes later, all of the speakers for the evening gathered at the side of the stage, me included. The lads were pissing themselves as I stood in the middle of these people, and properly erupted into hysterics when the first name announced was mine. 'Please give a warm welcome to Professor Stan Stanfield from the English college of Lickem!' I climbed the four steps to the stage, with my hands held aloft, while all the students gave me a round of applause. I was proper milking it, bowing and blowing kisses to the crowd, while to my right all I could hear was the boys laughing.

I was just about to take my seat on the stage, as the guy was announcing the second speaker, when the uni security guards leapt onto the stage to grab me. They'd seen me drinking all afternoon and knew I wasn't meant to be up there. They dragged me from the stage, while the crowd looked bewildered and confused as to what was going on. Once offstage they marched me to the door and threw me out – I'd obviously outstayed my welcome!

We made our way to the ground and on our way passed a load of people on rickshaws. One driver in particular looked like a very famous English footballer, David Beckham. 'Hello, my English friends,' he said, 'I'm sure you will want me to drive you somewhere?' 'Fuck me, mate, you don't half look like a famous English footballer,' I said to him. He pushed his chest out and had a right cocky look on his face. 'Yeah, you think so? And who might that be?' he said. 'Viv Anderson,' I told him. The boys cracked up, but the Beckham lookalike didn't and drove off with the right hump. On the way to the ground, we stopped at every off license and pub and had a drink. I can't remember how many we had had actually I can't remember watching the game.

Chapter 42

Fish fingers

Ian, DD and I travelled to Bulgaria for our next trip and arrived in Sofia at 3.20am. Paul, who'd arrived earlier with Liam, had told us to get the bus from the airport to the city itself, and the bus duly drove around the city centre dropping people off at different hotels. Eventually we were the only ones left on the bus and we seemed to heading out of the city. I shouted the name of our hotel to the driver and he slammed his brakes on, stopped and opened the doors. 'Your hotel, 500 metres that way!' he said, pointing back towards the city. 'Well turn the bus around, we ain't walking! We'll get lynched on these streets!' I told him. 'Your hotel, 500 metres that way. Bus station, 20 kilometres this way!' he then said, sternly. We got off the bus and the bus drove off. The street had no lighting and it was proper eerie. We could see the lights of the city about 400 metres away so we started walking. As we reached a dimly-lit street, we turned the corner and Ian screamed, 'What the fucking hell's that?' and went to hide behind me. I looked to see what had scared him and saw a metal statue of a soldier with a gun! Me and DD were cracking up at the big man's reaction, although Ian made out he'd just been trying to scare us.

We found the hotel and went down to the bar/disco, which was in the basement. We walked in to find the place heaving with prostitutes, but to be honest, you couldn't have paid me to sleep with most of those women. They must have got all the fattest, oldest, ugliest prostitutes and dropped them in our hotel bar! Ian had one drink and then went to bed, but me and DD carried on drinking and taking the piss out of all these old prossies. About 6am, I approached this big fat woman sitting at the bar. She was so big she sat on two bar stools, one for each bum cheek. 'Here love, if I give you £30 will you come up to my room, sit on my mate's face and let me take one picture?' I asked. 'No, I am closed!' she replied. 'You're fucking what? Listen love, you ain't moved off of them two stools all night and you look like you need more than one square meal a day. I'll give you £60 for one photo on my mate's face and then you can get your fat arse down to the kebab shop for breakfast,' I then said to her. She turned around and firmly said, 'I AM CLOSED'.

Me and DD left the bar to go to bed. As I opened the door of my room, which I was sharing with Ian, the telly was on and Ian seemed to be sitting upright. 'Are you still awake?' I slurred. 'Of course I'm still fucking awake! Knowing that you and DD were down in the bar with all them old ropey prostitutes, I was waiting for you send one of the big fat ones up!' Ian replied. 'I wouldn't dream of doing something like that to you,' I innocently answered, then fell on my bed and passed out.

We woke up in the morning and went down to breakfast, where we met Paul and Liam. DD walked in shortly after. 'Fuck me, Stan, have you told them about that big fat cow you tried to get to sit on Ian's face last night?' he said jovially. 'I fucking knew it! I knew you'd do something like that, you fucker!' Ian roared. We all just started laughing, which wound Ian up even more. Once we'd finished breakfast and finished winding Ian up about taking a doggy bag back to his room just in case Jabba the Gut changed her mind, I called Dex. He and Miles were staying in a really posh hotel, and I told Dex we'd come over to them in about half an hour.

Before we left, I Georged up on my own. As we walked out of Paul and Liam's room, the door next to theirs opened. It's hard to describe what we saw, but my best explanation can only be that it looked like the Elephant Man was standing there in front of us. This guy had a hump on his back like a camel, spindly legs and a face like he'd been hit with a frying pan. To top it all, the geezer was standing there with nothing on, baring his knob and bollocks for all to see. I tried to talk to him, but he didn't speak English. He seemed delighted to see me in my George outfit, though. 'You want to try the suit on?' I asked, but he just smiled. I took the cape, headgear and tunic off and then dressed him in it. The boys were pissing themselves, especially when this guy, who hadn't uttered a word, started screaming and shouting and raising his fist to the air, sort of like Superman. I then took the suit off him, leaving him standing in the hallway stark bollock naked again.

When arrived at Dex and Miles's hotel I realised I had a problem: my crotch! I walked up to the reception desk and the staff started smiling and laughing. 'Excuse me, I wonder could you help me?' I asked. A very slender receptionist answered, 'I will try to do my best, my King!' 'Do you have a needle and thread?' I then asked her, showing her the split in my silver trousers. 'I have a sewing kit right here, Sir,' she said. 'Please allow me to repair your trousers, kind Sir.' She walked around the desk to where I stood, then knelt down in front of me and started stitching the hole in the trousers. 'Go on Stan! Knight her with your knob!' shouted DD, to everyone's amusement. Well, everyone except the hotel manager, who came running towards us. 'What on earth is going on?' he screamed. All he could see was one of his staff on her knees with her hands working around my crotch! The relief on his face when he realised that she was in fact just repairing George the First was hilarious.

When the girl had finished stitching me up, we went to meet Dex and Miles in their penthouse suites. We knocked for Dex first, who was already in his George suit, but he didn't let us into the room in case we raided the mini bar (who, us?). He then led us to Miles's room, and when Miles opened the door, we all bundled in. Miles had his own lounge area, a separate bathroom for guests, and a huge bedroom with an en suite. As we left his room, I made sure I was the last to leave and left the door slightly ajar. I then ran past everyone down the corridor and pressed the button for the lift. The door opened and I pressed every button for every floor; we were on the 21st floor. The boys got into the lift and I took my finger off the door hold button and jumped out. As the doors shut I could hear shouts of, 'You bastard!' but I needed a bit of time to do what I had planned. I ran back to Miles's room and noticed that the next door room was open. Perfect, I thought. I went into Miles's room and picked up the large coffee table, the plant pot and the trouser press and put them next door. I was going to leave it at that, but thought 'fuck it' and dragged the armchair and sofa next door as well. I shut both doors and jumped into a lift. The lads had only just got out of their lift when I came out of mine. 'What have you been up to, Stanley?' Dex asked, curiously. 'Nothing…' I said.

I jumped in a taxi with Dex and Miles, and we asked the driver to take us to a toy shop to get some plastic swords. The driver pulled up outside a toy shop, but they didn't have any swords. There was a bank opposite and Miles said he needed to change some money up. I needed some too, so I followed Miles into the bank. We'd never been in a bank dressed as knights before and from the look on everyone's faces, they hadn't had too many knights in the bank before either. A lot of people looked quite worried and the girl at the counter looked very anxious as we stood in front of her. She seemed very relieved when we gave her money to change, rather than asking her to give us all their money! We left the bank only to find our taxi surrounded by four policemen on motorbikes. The driver told us that the police didn't feel it was a safe area for us to be in dressed as we were, and that we should leave immediately. The police then gave us an escort to the town centre, two bikes in front and two behind. Everyone we passed thought we were VIPs, even though minutes before people had thought we were bank robbers. Funny old world!

When we made it back to the centre of town we sat outside a bar and were joined by Jeff (from Loyal London) and five young lads with a football. 'Alright lads? Fancy a five-a-side game in the street?' I asked, and they agreed. The main high street was closed to traffic, as they were digging a massive hole at one end of the street, so we were free to play. Before we kicked off, Jeff put up his Loyal London flag on the side of a parked delivery van and we got some chairs for goalposts. As we lined up to play the five young lads looked very confident facing Dex in goal, me, Paul, Liam and Miles. Ian was in the toilet. We were 3-2 down by the time Ian came back from the toilet and we put him straight on in Miles's place. As soon as Ian walked on, I put the ball through to him, only to see him blaze it over the bar from five yards. That was the last touch of the match, as no sooner had Ian struck the ball than there was a pitch invasion by the police! They'd received a call that some English fans were fighting in the street with priests! Even though our little football match wasn't what they thought it was, they told us to stop playing or we'd be arrested. We went back to the bar, with a large police presence watching us drink. We'd barely sipped our beers when we noticed the delivery van pulling away with Jeff's flag still attached. It was as funny as fuck to see Jeff chasing and screaming after this van, but fortunately for him it only drove 50 metres to the next drop-off.

About an hour later, Barry Fishcake turned up and even though it was only 2pm, he was pissed as a fart. Fishcake had only been with us ten minutes when this girl of about eighteen turned up begging for money. She was a right state, with greasy hair, teeth that looked like tombstones, a huge abscess on the left side of her face (either that or she'd been given a right good smack in the mouth) and she was wearing this tiny little pink miniskirt. She went up to Fishcake with her hand held out, and Fishcake grabbed her hand and said, 'What, you want to feel my piece, love?' placing the girl's hand on his crotch. The girl pulled her hand away and shouted, 'No!' but she still gestured at Fishcake to give her some money. Fishcake then tried several times to hitch up the little miniskirt that she was wearing, only for her to pull it back into place each time. 'Come here, love, I'm only joking with you,' said Fishcake, then he leant forward, grabbed the girl and kissed her on the head and then on the face. 'You fucking animal, Fishcake!' I shouted. 'You don't know

By George

where she's been! Come to mention it she don't know where *you've* been!' I added.

Fishcake then pulled out some money and gave the girl the equivalent of a pound, which she gratefully took – and then proceeded to show how grateful she actually was. She lifted her skirt up, pulled her knickers to the side and gestured for Fishcake to have a feel. We couldn't believe what was going on and certainly couldn't believe what happened next, as Fishcake started fingering the girl in front of everyone! I thought I was going to be sick. The girl then left and everyone was in total disbelief at what they had just witnessed. The best – or worst – was yet to come. Ian had been sitting closest to Fishcake and unfortunately for him being that close to Fishcake had its downsides, as Fishcake wiped his fingers across Ian's face! We were all cracking up but strangely enough Ian didn't see the funny side.

Things settled down until a tramp woman came wandering down the street towards us. 'Oi, Fishcake, here comes another bird for you!' I shouted. He walked towards her – surely he wasn't actually going to try it on with her? We didn't hear what he said to her but we did see him give her some money. 'Fuck me, you can't finger that old tramp as well? You're sick in the head mate!' I said, laughing. Fishcake then lay down in the middle of the street and poked his tongue out. 'No...you can't! That's fucking disgusting!' I shouted, but the tramp stood over Fishcake's face and then sat down! She'd only sat on his face for a few seconds, though, when he pushed her off and threw up immediately. 'You fucking stink, you dirty cunt!' he said in between being sick. The tramp just continued staggering up the road.

Not long after, Preston and his boys turned up and said they had a spare match ticket in the Bulgarian end. 'Are you lot in the Bulgarian end as well?' I asked. 'Yes, Stan, we've all got tickets in the same end. We'll see you in there later,' Preston said and they left.

Before we headed off to the match, I popped back to the hotel with Ian and DD. Ian opened the door to our bedroom and I stumbled in, not noticing the raised step. Of course I tripped over and fell forwards into the large glass-topped table. I had a bottle of beer in my hand and the bottle slammed onto the table top, breaking the glass into several pieces. 'What the fuck are you doing?' Ian screamed; he thought I was trashing the room. 'They're going to charge us for that you twat! Fuck it, you broke it, you can pay for it!' I stood looking at the broken table and then I had an idea. 'Wait here – I'll be back,' I said and headed down the stairs. When I got back, DD was also there. I held up another room key and Ian and DD looked bemused until I said, 'It's Paul and Liam's room key. We take the broken table and swap it with their good table and everyone's a winner!' DD started laughing his head off and said, 'You're fucking mad, Stan, the poor bastards are each going to think the other one broke the table. They'll probably end up fighting with each other.' 'That won't be my problem, DD, now you keep watch while me and Ian change the tables,' I replied. We carried the broken table and all the glass down two flights of stairs, swapped our table for Paul and Liam's, and took the good one back to our room. We gave both key cards in at the reception and then walked to the ground.

Near the ground there was a big park area and it was packed with English and Bulgarian fans. The atmosphere was fantastic, with loud music and lots of beer. As always I was mobbed by the Bulgarian supporters, and as I posed for photos, I heard a voice shout, 'Stan, you fucking legend!' It was my mate from Doncaster, Bisto, with his sidekick Salt. As we stood talking, a Bulgarian girl and her mate came up and asked for a photo with me. One of them stood next to me while the other went to take the picture. 'Hang on, love, do you want to be in the picture as well?' Bisto asked. 'I'll take the picture.' The girls both stood next to me and we all looked towards Bisto 'Right – big smiles!' he shouted, then turned and ran away with the girls' camera. Me and Salt were cracking up, but the girls were horrified and looked so relieved when Bisto stopped running after about twenty metres and came back. It was Bisto's old party trick and it always made me laugh!

I walked with Ian and DD to the England fans' entrance and told them I'd see them after the game. As I walked away, I bumped into Preston and his mate Jimmy. 'You coming in with me, Preston?' I asked. 'Not yet, I'm waiting for a couple of lads to turn up, I've got their tickets,' Preston replied. 'I'll come in with you, Stan – Preston's told me all about you. You're a fucking legend!' Jimmy said and we left to find our seats. I asked a Bulgarian fan where the red section was. 'You are going in the red section? You are going in there dressed like that? You go in the red and you will be dead! Even we do not go in the red. We go in green. Good luck, my friend!' the Bulgarian said in disbelief, and he pointed to show us where to go. 'Fuck it, Jimmy. I've found over the years that dressed like this everyone loves you, so we'll be alright,' I said and we carried on walking. But I soon realised that we probably weren't going to be alright. The party atmosphere in the park had been replaced by menacing hardcore Bulgarian fans.

We walked through endless groups who were shouting abuse at us, pulling on my cape and generally looking for a reaction.

Fish fingers

'Jimmy, whatever you do, show no fear. The gate's just up there, we'll be OK,' I said. You could tell that poor Jimmy wanted to be anywhere except with me. 'Fuck this, Stan, we're gonna die if we go in there! I'm off,' Jimmy said and walked away, leaving me surrounded by all these fucking nutters. I just kept walking towards the gate, with more geezers pulling and yanking at my suit, but they never once hit me. Maybe I was going to be alright after all.

I eventually reached the guy checking the tickets and all the blokes who'd been following me left. I made my way into the stand. Once in, I could see that all the Bulgarian fans were at the back and there were about fifty rows of empty seats at the front. I headed straight down the stairs to the front, hoping the old bill or security would see me and haul me out of there. I was spotted very quickly, but not by the people I was hoping for. One Bulgarian fan walked down the stairs to where I stood. I turned and looked at him. 'You are English?' he asked. I'd had enough at this point, so I looked myself up and down and said, 'What do you fucking think, you prick?' He then turned, looked up at the crowd, and gave them a thumbs-up. The next thing I knew, 20 or 30 Bulgarians came charging down the stairs towards us. I guessed they weren't coming for a photo.

As they swarmed around me (I was now pinned to the fence) like flies round shit, lots of comments were thrown my way and one of them, who looked a right nasty bastard, starting talking. 'You are English hard man, yes? You come in Bulgaria end to fight? You are fucking English hooligan!' 'Not really…' I said, trying to sound cool even though I was proper shitting myself. I just thought, 'When this goes off, grab the nearest bloke to you and use him as a shield'. As I stood there pinned

By George

to the fence by three of these fuckers, the old bill finally saw me and realised what was going on, and they rushed down the steps with their batons raised. The crowd moved back as the police marched me out of the stand, and the abuse level from the crowd went through the roof as I was shepherded away. For once I kept my head down and said nothing.

The police escorted me to the England fans' section and I bumped into Preston. 'Alright Stan, where's Jimmy?' he asked. 'Fucked if I know, I've just been in that end over there,' I said, pointing towards the Bulgarian end which by now had several seats on fire. 'You went in there? Are you fucking mental? None of us went in there, we all got let in the England end for our own safety! You're crazy, Stan, fucking crazy,' Preston said.

After watching England win 3–0, we headed into town and went to an underground nightclub called Jim Beam's. We had to walk down two flights of stairs to the dance floor and when I came into view, the clubbers went mental. The DJ was playing the Prodigy song 'Smack My Bitch Up' and there was only one thing to do: go fucking mental. I started proper 'avin it on the stairs and the crowd responded by going off their heads as well. I hadn't even got a beer when I was grabbed by this stunning looking girl in a basque outfit. 'You come on the stage with me and dance?' she asked and dragged me to a stage in front of the DJ stand. The DJ saw me climbing up onto the stage and screamed, 'St George from England in the house!' I waved at him and then found myself surrounded by this dance troop. All the England fans in Jim Beam's were somehow able to sing 'Keep St George In My Heart, Keep Me English' louder than the heavy bassline that was pumping out of the speakers, as I found myself raving on stage with six Bulgarian dancers dressed in basques.

260

Fish fingers

The following day, I went with Ian and DD to the airport to fly home, where we met Dex and Miles. Dex was laughing his head off, but Miles didn't look happy. 'Oh fuck me Stan, you've got to hear this,' Dex said. 'When we got back to the hotel last night, someone had robbed all Miles's furniture!' We all burst out laughing, except Miles. 'They took the table, the trouser press and the fucking suite, it's all gone! Who'd fucking nick all that from a hotel?' Miles said, disbelievingly. 'They didn't take any of my stuff, just the bloody furniture!' I walked away from the boys to get myself a drink and spoke to the woman at the counter. I asked for a pen and paper and wrote a note, then handed it to her and asked her to give to Miles. I then joined the lads, who were still laughing about the missing furniture, and the woman from behind the counter approached us and handed the note to Miles. He read the note aloud: 'Miles, we have your furniture and if you want to see it again you will transfer £1,000,000 into the Stan's Tours bank account. If not, your furniture will be fire wood.' Miles burst out laughing at the ransom note.

Paul rang shortly after. 'Hello mate, you alright?' I asked. 'No I'm fucking not! He's the biggest cunt I've ever met!' Paul yelled. 'Who?' I asked. 'Fucking Liam! He's smashed the fucking table and he's denying it. He's saying I must have broken it, but I know full fucking well it wasn't me. It had to be him!' I had to hang the phone up, as I was laughing so much, and when I told Ian and DD, it just set them off laughing again.

Chapter 43

Hair today, gone tomorrow

The night before we were due to travel to Montenegro, Dex, Stu and Ali stayed at my house and we drank right up until 4am. My alarm went off at 5am and I was still pissed, but sober compared to Dex. He was hammered.

We somehow got to Luton Airport for 6am, where we met Ian, Miles, DD, Bruce and Liam. They'd arrived a lot earlier than us and were right at the front of the queue to check in, so we jumped the whole queue of around 200 people and stood with them. By all accounts, comments were made by the disgruntled travellers behind us, but I was too pissed to notice. Once checked in, we were stopped by the old bill, doing their passport checks on those going to Montenegro. As I reached the front of the queue, I heard one copper say to an England fan, 'Are you known or wanted by the police?' and I shouted, 'Well I know I'm wanted!' The copper quickly ushered the guy in front of me through in order to question me about my outburst. He took my passport and said, 'OK, mate. What are you wanted for?' You could see the delight in his eyes that the usually pointless exercise of trying to catch banned travelling supporters had paid dividends with someone actually admitting they were wanted. 'Oh yeah, I'm wanted alright. By my wife! I told her I was going to get a paper and she's just worked out that the shop doesn't open until 7.30 am, so she now wants to know where the hell I am!' I cheekily answered. The copper was not impressed.

They finished their checks and I was just about to walk away when I noticed they'd pulled Bisto from Doncaster to one side. 'Don't worry, Bisto, they won't stop you travelling for nicking a train. They let me through and I've got a record for siphoning petrol from an aeroplane!' I said very loudly. Everyone started laughing, except the old bill.

When I got to the airport bar, the lads were already there. 'How did you lot get here before me?' I asked. 'With all the confusion you were causing we slipped past the police along with about 60 other England fans!' Miles said. I looked around to see most of my fellow travelling England fans raising their glasses at me, as if to say thanks.

While at the bar, I went to get something out of my bag, and as I opened it, I found it stuffed with about two hundred tampons. 'You fuckers!' I said, laughing. It was only a small practical joke, but it was to lead to endless stunts over the next few days. I ordered another round of drinks and everyone had pints except Miles and Ali, who had bottles of beer with a tampon stuffed in each of them. 'You fucking cunt, how am I supposed to drink that?' Miles said, trying to pull the tampon back out of the bottle by its string to no avail. I had roughly half a pint of cider left when I went to the toilet, and when I returned I found that my drink had been replaced by six tampons, which between them had soaked up all of the liquid. As I stood there shaking my head in disbelief, the boys were crying with laughter. It was quickly replaced by groans of disgust, though, as I pulled out the tampons and sucked the cider out of them!

I thought after the tampon stunt, the boys would leave me alone, but they seemed insistent on singling me out for all of their jokes. Bruce went to the bar with Dex and when they turned round to give me my drink, they were crying with laughter. The bastards had got my pint and poured it into a condom, then tied the open end and dropped the condom back into my glass. 'There you go, Stan, there's your pint. And we haven't put anything in it!' Dex struggled to say. 'No but you've put it in something, so that's fine?' I said sarcastically.

I needed to get the bastards back, but what could I do? Then it came to me: hair removal cream! I'd been to Benidorm in the summer for Doni Crawf's stag do and I'd taken some hair removal cream with me. I didn't know how good the stuff was until I tried it out on Loon! We were in a nightclub in Benidorm and I rubbed a load of cream into the back of Loon's head. Minutes later his hair was literally falling out, leaving an almighty bald patch. This stuff was unbelievable and I knew it should only be used in emergencies – but this was an emergency. I was under attack from all parties. It was time for me to raise the chaos bar a little higher. We boarded the plane and as I went to put my bag in the overhead locker, I felt liquid seeping down my arm, and when I looked in my bag, I found the bottle I'd given to Miles with the tampon in. I took the bottle out, sat down next to Ian, pulled out the tampon and drank the rest of the beer.

As I settled into my chair, the plane taxied up the runway

and an uncomfortable feeling hit me. I desperately needed a piss. I couldn't use the toilet as we were about to take off, so I'd just have to hold it until the seat belt signs went out. This was easier said than done. After ten minutes, the pain of holding it in became unbearable. 'Ian, keep holding that paper up, I've got to go right now!' I desperately said. 'Go where?' Ian asked. 'For a piss!' I replied. I picked up the empty beer bottle and carefully started to fill it. The instant relief was fantastic, until I realised the bottle was almost full and I couldn't stop. I desperately tried to slam the brakes on, but it was all in vain. My piss sprayed up the window, and worst of all, over my leather seat. I was truly fucked with all this piss everywhere, until I said to Ian, 'Reach up and get my bag, mate!' Ian passed me my bag and I opened it, taking out a handful of tampons which I used to mop up the urine. They did the trick and the only evidence was my bottle of piss. I knew where to get rid of that. I got out of my seat and walked towards the lads, who were about ten rows back from me. They were all laughing at me walking up the aisle with this bottle in my hand. 'You bastards, I went to put my bag up and got covered in beer dripping out. Here you go, Dex, you might as well have it. I don't really like this beer,' I said innocently and placed the bottle on Dex's drop-down tray. 'Don't mind if I do!' Dex said and took a huge swig! He then sprayed the contents of his mouth over at least three rows of seats in front of him. I was crying with laughter, until the air hostess came up and took the bottle from Dex. When she felt the warmth of the bottle she said, 'I don't even want to know what's in that bottle and I can't believe you just drank it,' which set me off crying again.

When we arrived in Montenegro, there were five buses waiting to transport us to our hotel. We jumped on the last bus and I hopped into the driver's seat and tried to drive the bus, as the engine was running. I stalled the bus as I went to pull away, so I settled for grabbing the microphone instead, singing Sid Vicious's version of 'My Way' to the obvious displeasure of some of the miserable bastards on the bus.

We got to the hotel and went out down to the beach for something to eat, and of course to drink. We then headed back to the hotel so that everyone could get showered and ready to go out, well, everyone except Dex and Miles. Miles had gone back down to the beach for a sleep. He'd tried to sleep at the poolside, but the lads had picked him up on his lounger and thrown him in. Dex, on the other hand, had settled on the safety of his room to have a power nap. With the bedroom door locked from the inside, Dex was safe to snooze to his heart's content – or so he thought. All of our rooms were on the second floor – cue Spider Stan. I climbed onto the balcony window of my room and walked across the two-inch beams which connected it all the other balconies, until I reached Dex's room. He'd left the sliding doors open and I went inside. It was dark as he had the curtains pulled, but there was enough light for me to see Dex unconscious on the bed, snoring as usual. I got the hair removal cream and rubbed it into his hair and all over his leg. Once the deed was done I went back to my room, where I found Ian asleep, and I lay down on my bed for a bit of shut-eye too. I wasn't asleep for long, though, when I heard Ian say, 'What the fuck are you doing?' I opened my eyes to see Bruce standing at the end of the bed with a razor in his hand. 'Nothing, I was looking for something…' Bruce said and quickly shot out of our room. I later found out that Bruce was in fact trying to shave the hair on Ian's leg, thinking that Ian would blame me. The plan had backfired in more ways than one!

Hair today, gone tomorrow

No sooner had Bruce left than Dex walked in. 'Have you seen what that bastard Bruce has done to me?' he said and showed me and Ian his now half-hairless leg and a perfect bald patch on top of his head. We both cracked up. 'How do you know it was Bruce?' Ian struggled to say. 'Because I woke up and could feel my head and leg burning and when I opened my eyes there was Bruce crawling around on the floor in my room!' Dex replied. Poor Bruce! This couldn't be any better, for me anyway. 'Yeah – I just caught the bastard in here trying to do my legs!' Ian told Dex. 'Right, we've got to get Bruce back for this,' Dex said, while I just sat there with a smug grin on my face.

The following morning, we got three taxis to drive the nine of us to Podrica. I shared a taxi with DD and Dex and we'd got six bottles of drink each for the journey. Well the driver told us that it would take about an hour, so we just about had enough to cover us. We'd just got into Podrica when we noticed Ian, Bruce and Liam in a taxi in front of us. 'Get alongside that taxi!' Dex screamed. As we pulled alongside them doing about 50mph, Dex launched a full bottle of beer at the lads in the other car, soaking the driver and Liam, who did not look happy as we drove off laughing.

We got out of the taxi and made our way to a bar called Cheers, which was near to the ground. There were still over nine hours to go until kick off and at two Euros a pint, we were guaranteed to be out of our heads by then. We'd only been there a short while when Dex asked me if I had the hair removal cream. I told him I did and his eyes lit up. 'Keep the cream handy, so I can get some when I need it!' Dex Dastardly said. I didn't have to wait long before he requested a handful of cream. Our old mate Clubby from Tamworth turned up and came to say hello. I bet now he wishes he hadn't. 'Clubby, you old bastard! Let's get a photo with you, mate!' Dex shouted. As me and Dex stood either side of Clubby, we started bouncing up and down. Clubby started jumping as well and this gave Dex his chance. He rubbed the whole handful of cream into Clubby's scalp. Clubby had quite short hair anyway and in a matter of minutes it was going to be a lot shorter. Clubby left us to join the other lads he'd travelled with in the bar next door, and twenty minutes later we decided to go and see what his hair looked like. Even from a distance, we could see that the whole of the top of Clubby's hair had gone. We both fell about laughing in the street.

We were laughing our heads off, when I felt a tap on the shoulder. I turned around to see a tramp standing there with his hand held out begging for money. I have a habit of attracting tramps and homeless people, but I don't normally attract tramps with a four-inch-high flat top. I looked at Dex and Dex looked back and said, 'You can't, Stan. You just can't...' Oh yes I could. 'Alright mate?' I said, cuddling the tramp. 'Can I get a photo with you? We'll give you some money, yes?' I asked innocently. The poor old tramp agreed as easily as Clubby had and as he posed next to me for a photo, I proceeded to rub the killer cream into his head. 'That's it, mate – smile, because you won't be smiling in twenty minutes' time!' I shouted, knowing he couldn't understand a word I was saying.

Over the next half hour or so Dex Dastardly was going crazy with the hair removal cream. He got Miles, who was not best pleased, and about six total strangers. Half of them noticed they had something in their hair, but none of them were sure what it was. They would all find out in due course. With Dex doing his utmost to become the new version of Sweeney Todd,

Hair today, gone tomorrow

Preston turned up with a couple of his mates, and while I was talking to Preston, Liam came and spoke to me. 'Stan, give us some of that hair removal cream,' he said excitedly. I was shocked. Liam came on every trip and went home from every trip and that was about all Liam did, but something had obviously stirred him into action, so I gave him some cream. 'Watch this, Preston!' I said and we watched Liam walk towards an England fan who was talking to Dex. Liam then grabbed hold of the bloke and started rubbing his hand through his dark hair. Before the bloke could respond Liam walked away, sat back down and carried on drinking. 'How good is that stuff, Stan?' Preston asked. 'Well mate, here comes one I done earlier!' I said, pointing at the tramp, who was approaching us again. He didn't look happy.

The tramp got to within ten foot of where I stood and glared at me. 'Alright mate, have you spent that Euro already?' I asked, trying to hold in the laughter. The tramp then started shouting at me, but of course I didn't understand. 'HAIR, HAIR!' he shouted and then bent forward to reveal that most of the hair on top of his head had gone. Everyone in the vicinity started crying with laughter and Preston got some lovely close-up photos of the now bald tramp. The tramp then raised two fingers in my direction and fucked off. 'I told you boys, Stan's a fucking legend! A fucking mad legend, but a legend!' Preston claimed.

While we were sitting outside the bar, having now been joined by Kev Lennon, Wilksie, Fred, Alex and my old mate George, the England fan Liam had got returned wearing a cap. He marched up to Miles and said, 'What the fuck's going on?' Miles looked at him and replied, 'What do you mean?' 'I came over earlier to speak to you lot and since then all my hair has fallen out!' 'I don't know what you're talking about, mate?' Miles said, somehow keeping a straight face. The guy eventually left with the right hump, but not a lot of hair.

I went into the bar to tell Dex about Liam's victim, only to find him pulling a mobile phone out of a full pint of beer. 'Fuck me, who's put your phone in the pint?' I asked. 'Oh it's not mine, it's Bruce's. I told you I'd get the bastard back!' Dex said triumphantly. 'Er…I think there's something you should know, Dex. It was me who did your hair, not Bruce,' I reluctantly said. The look of disbelief on Dex's face was a picture as he quickly tried to see if the phone was still working. Of course it was fucked. 'Right, no one say anything to Bruce. He'll just have to think it's packed up or something!' Dex frantically said.

I thought that after seeing Bruce's phone dunked like a biscuit in a cup of tea that the practical jokes would cease, but how wrong I was. Dex was about to take the madness to whole different level. It was about 5pm when from nowhere the old bill turned up opposite the bar we were in and all started getting dressed into their riot gear. They obviously wanted as much protection from the Hair Removal Crew as possible. While twenty or so police were getting kitted up, we started to sing at them, 'Get out your riot gear, the HRC are here!' We soon found out that they were not gearing up for the Hair Removal Crew but were in fact getting ready for hundreds of Ultras (foreign hooligans) to come marching down the main street. It all looked so organised, more like a protest demonstration than a load of nutters marching down the main road. As the march started, so did the noise as all the Montenegro boys were singing and chanting in unison. Most of it was being directed at us, as we were all now standing outside the bar. This was it: it had to go off, and obscenities and gestures were being launched from both groups. Suddenly they stopped and all turned towards us. I was sure the five M.I.G.S and the Luton Town boys with us would be in battle any second.

As we stood there face to face with fuck knows how many Ultras, they broke into song again. We could never out-sing or out-shout them, so instead we listened to what they were singing and we couldn't believe what we heard. It sounded to all of us like they were singing, 'We love the titty bar whores, we love the titty bar whores, we won't fuck just one, we'll fuck them up the bum, the titty bar whores'. What a fucking song! We all joined in, jumping around with all these mad Ultras and singing our version of their song. With the tension gone, we had a right old party with all the Montenegro fans, who were now not interested in fighting but in having pictures with us.

As I stood posing for a photo with about ten geezers, I noticed Dex rubbing yet more hair removal cream into the heads of the two blokes he was standing with. It was obvious that from here on in no man or beast was safe while Dex had the cream. Shortly after Dex had creamed up ten or so Ultras' heads, a very smartly-dressed man and a woman turned up with their dog. The guy told us that he used to live in England and that he was now a multi-millionaire in Montenegro. As he spoke, we all thought, 'What a prick' but we let him waffle on. Dex walked behind the guy as he spoke to us and I thought 'You might have money, but you ain't going to have much hair in a minute'...but I was wrong. Dex started to stroke the dog. He only rubbed the dog's back for a few seconds, when the dog went for him. We weren't sure if was the George suit or the cream, but the dog did not like Dex. The bloke and his missus then shook our hands and said goodbye. We all watched them walk away from us, trying to squeeze through the Ultra-mobbed streets, and also watched the dog going loopy trying to bite anyone and everyone. With the arrogant prick and his dog gone, we continued to party with the Ultras.

Miles, who was steaming at this point, came up and asked for some cream as well. 'Watch this, Stan,' he said. I thought he was going to get Dex back good and proper, but once again I was wrong. He walked up to the police, who were all now in their riot gear, and stroked a police dog on its tail! The copper holding the dog just smiled at Miles and let him carry on. I kept a close eye on the dog Miles had creamed for the next ten minutes or so, but there was no hair loss. Maybe it didn't work on dogs, I thought. Then I realised that part of the dog's tail had fallen off! I couldn't believe my eyes. What had Miles done? If the copper holding the dog realised, we were fucked. Thankfully five minutes later, all the coppers and all their dogs (even the one with half a tail) left and headed towards the ground.

We hadn't even noticed that it had got dark (probably because we were so pissed at this point) but it wasn't dark for long. The Ultras fired up a load of flares and that was the signal for them to go mental. It was brilliant and it felt like we were in the middle of a firework display going wrong. I walked up to a bloke holding two flares and said 'Oi, mate, let me have hold of them!' The bloke passed me the two raging flares and stepped back, and the crowd went mental at the sight of St George jumping around with these flares in his hand. The bloke who'd given me the flares was now screaming, 'Throw! Throw!' but I ignored him and continued to jump about, conducting the mad crowd. He then screamed at me again, 'Throw, throw! Police! Police!' and I took a bit more notice this time as I could see the police moving through the crowd. I threw the flares onto the floor and swiftly mingled into the crowd.

I was then approached by a female TV presenter, who asked, 'Will you and your friends do a live television interview for Montenegro TV?' I was only too willing to oblige and grabbed the other Georges – well, Bruce and Liam anyway. Dex and Miles had both passed out and were fast asleep. The woman led us down the street and made us stand right in the middle of the wildly cheering crowd. She then said we were going live in thirty seconds' time, and asked us to sing an England song. I looked at Bruce and Liam and said, 'Right, boys – "God Save The Queen", OK?' and they agreed.

The cameraman gave the signal that we were live and the interviewer stuck the microphone right in my face. The camera zoomed in on me as I sang and then slowly turned to film Liam and Bruce…but Bruce wasn't there any more. He was on the floor, fighting with a Montenegro fan, who by all accounts had whacked him in the back of the head. The filming was quickly cut short – their intention was to show both sets of fans partying together.

After the shortest interview in history and a few more punches and a bit of finger-pointing from Bruce, we joined the other lads. Ali called me over to him and said, 'Here, Stan – give that to Dex, will ya?' He went to hand me what I thought was a pint of cider. 'Dex is fucked, mate, he don't need no more drink,' I replied. 'It's not drink. I've just filled it with piss!' Ali explained. I carefully grabbed the pint, but all of a sudden some twat jumped on my back and a fair bit of Ali's piss went all over my hand and arm. 'Hey, sorry man, let me get you another,' the lively Montenegro fan said. 'Nah, you're alright mate. I don't want another one of these pints thanks,' I replied and carried on to where Dex was sitting, fast asleep. I placed the pint of piss just in front of him and was just about to walk away when I thought 'what an opportunity'. I squirted a nice blob of hair removal cream into my hand and rubbed it into the sides and back of Dex's head.

After standing there for ten minutes watching Dex's hair fall like leaves from the trees in autumn, he suddenly woke up as his head was starting to burn. He quickly grabbed the bottle of beer in front of him and tipped the contents over his head to cool his scalp. 'What fucker put more of that fucking cream on my head?' Dex screamed, looking angrily at me. 'What cream, Dex? It's all gone,' I replied. 'Yeah – it's all gone on my fucking head, you bastard!' Everyone cracked up. 'Yeah, yeah, that's it – take the piss out of me why don't you,' Dex then said, picking up Ali's piss-pint and taking a big swig. He sprayed it instantly back out and screamed, 'What dirty cunt has pissed in my pint?' Me and Ali were laughing so hard tears were streaming down our faces, while Dex went mad and threw the remainder of the piss into the crowd. 'Dex, I've heard that drinking human urine is supposed to put hairs on chest – you'd better hope it puts them on your head as well!' I quipped.

We left the pub with about half an hour until kick off, but still had enough time to have a singing battle with the opposition. They were chanting, 'Fuck off England! Fuck off England!' and we were singing back, 'We've got hair, we've got hair! You ain't, you ain't!' and 'Where's your hair gone? Where's your hair gone?' which totally bamboozled them.

Once in the ground, I stood about four rows behind the England bench, with DD, Stu and Ali. Unlike the hostile crowd I'd found myself with on the previous trip to Bulgaria, the Montenegro fans were right up for the craic. The match ended

2-2, which meant that we were through automatically and Montenegro had reached the play-offs. Everyone was happy. The stewards opened all the gates in front of us and we all piled onto the pitch in celebration, it was fucking brilliant.

When we got back to Budva, the hotel had laid on a load of food for us. I was busy eating when I saw the England fan Liam had got with the hair removal cream giving us the right eyeball. 'Boys, there's that geezer Liam got earlier,' I announced and everyone looked round to see. The guy had shaved all his hair off, and to be fair he looked better for it! 'Oh well, Liam, you're alright now – he's shaved the evidence off!' I said.

The following day, I went with Dex, Miles and Ian into the town to get something to eat. We found a nice little restaurant and while we were waiting for our food, Dex picked up a local paper. Inside was a picture of us with our blow-up Spitfires in our hands. It's always nice to see our picture in any paper, but we were a bit confused as underneath our picture was another picture of a place that looked like it had been blown up. We asked the waiter to translate for us, and it turned out that the reporter had written a story about Podrica getting bombed by the English in the Second World War, saying that us running around with blow-up Spitfires had brought back memories of that devastating bombing. It was almost like they were trying to blame us for what had happened! Once again we were famous – but for all the wrong reasons.

We finished our meal and decided to have a couple of drinks in a nearby Irish pub. The Luton boys – Kev, Fred, George, Wilksie and Alex, who we'd had a drink with the day before in Podrica – were already in the bar, which was tiny, forcing most of us to drink outside. As we stood drinking, this big woman in a boutique shop opposite kept coming out and sticking her fingers up at us. Dex asked her what the problem was, but she just stood there laughing insanely. She turned away and went back into her shop, so me and Dex followed her. 'Alright my love? What are you selling in here then?' I asked, but she just looked at me and started hysterically laughing again. We usually got this reaction wearing the George suits, but not in our civvies. 'Is it alright if we try a few numbers on, love?' I then asked. She waved her hands for me to carry on. First I put on this white fluffy top, which only seemed to have one arm, and went outside to show the lads. They cracked up and I continued my fashion parade to the delight of the mad shopkeeper, who then started dressing me.

She got me to go out next in a mink coat, a black wig and some weird hat. As I strutted my stuff in the little side streets, the lads loved it, with one screaming, 'Fuck me, Stan, you look like Liam Gallagher!' I went back into the shop one final time; this outfit had to be a showstopper. The woman got me to put on a full-length dress so big you could have got two people in it, the same wig as before, and this floral headscarf. I went back outside and announced to the boys, 'Look lads! I'm fucking Nana Mouskouri now!' By this time everyone was crying with laughter. What had started as a couple of quiet drinks had turned into the catwalk show from hell.

We went back to the airport, but I just didn't feel right for some reason. All day I'd had this strange tingling sensation in my feet. As we sat outside the airport, I told the lads that there was something not right with my feet and took off both my trainers and socks. I lifted my right foot onto my left leg, and the boys started laughing as I realised that the sole of my foot had turned blue. 'What the fuck have you done, you bastards?' I screamed, looking in the direction of Dex, who I knew was behind it. No one answered me as they were laughing hysterically, and it got even worse when I showed them the bottom of my left foot, which was also blue. They'd put something in my trainers and whatever it was had soaked into the soles of my feet. 'Come on, what the fuck is it? It had better not be bleach!' I said. 'It's alright, it's only toothpaste, it won't harm you,' Dex said eventually. 'I had to get you back somehow!' He did have a point. The only thing was Dex's hair grew back within a week, whereas my feet stayed blue for two weeks.

The draw was made for the Euro finals in 2012 and we were to face France, Sweden and one of the hosts, Ukraine, in the group stages. But were they ready to face the **Men In George Suits**?

TO BE CONTINUED...